THE SERPENT'S GIFT

The Serpent's Gift

GNOSTIC REFLECTIONS ON THE STUDY OF RELIGION

Jeffrey J. Kripal

THE UNIVERSITY OF CHICAGO PRESS
Chicago and London

JEFFREY J. KRIPAL is the J. Newton Rayzor Professor and chair
of the Department of Religious Studies at Rice University and
the author of *Kali's Child: The Mystical and the Erotic in the Life and
Teachings of Ramakrishna* and *Roads of Excess, Palaces of Wisdom:
Eroticism and Reflexivity in the Study of Mysticism*, both published by the University of Chicago Press.

The University of Chicago Press, Chicago 60637
The University of Chicago Press, Ltd., London
© 2007 by Jeffrey J. Kripal
All rights reserved. Published 2007
Printed in the United States of America

16 15 14 13 12 11 10 09 08 07   1 2 3 4 5

ISBN-13: 978-0-226-45380-4 (cloth)
ISBN-13: 978-0-226-45381-1 (paper)
ISBN-10: 0-226-45380-4 (cloth)
ISBN-10: 0-226-45381-2 (paper)

Library of Congress Cataloging-in-Publication Data

Kripal, Jeffrey John, 1962–
    The serpent's gift : gnostic reflections on the study of religion / Jeffrey J. Kripal.
        p. cm.
    Includes bibliographical references and index.
    ISBN 0-226-45380-4 (cloth : alk. paper) — ISBN 0-226-45381-2 (pbk. : alk. paper)
    1. Religion—Philosophy.   2. Gnosticism.   I. Title.
    BL51.K675 2006
    299'.932—dc22
                                                                        2006003044

♾ The paper used in this publication meets the minimum
requirements of the American National Standard for
Information Sciences—Permanence of Paper for Printed
Library Materials, ANSI Z39.48-1992.

FOR MEGG AND SERA,
who donned angel wings for a red graduation
and kept a Spidey suit in the closet
just in case

What if you slept, and what if in your sleep you dreamed,
and what if in your dream you went to heaven and there
plucked a strange and beautiful flower, and what if when you
awoke you had the flower in your hand? Ah, what then?
Samuel Taylor Coleridge

What are we to make of those cases in which a child claims
to have a memory of a former life in another family at another
time and many of the details in the child's account of that
family turn out to be accurate? *Richard Shweder, "Post-Nietzschean
Anthropology: The Idea of Multiple Objective Worlds"*

CONTENTS

Digging Up My Library

IN MOMENTS OF TEMPORARY EXHAUSTION or writing block, I often ponder my personal library, tucked carefully and consciously behind the glass doors of some Amish-crafted cherry bookcases (an odd irony bespeaking my thesis already, since Amish discipline would object to or even ban almost all of the books these beautiful bookcases contain). I marvel at the sheer volume of information, the numerous generations of learning, the millions of hours of hard intellectual labor, and the deep wisdom that this small but significant library contains hidden in its pages. Nor am I unmoved by the art that is displayed on its many covers and spines. Modern libraries can be stunningly, eerily beautiful.

I also often wonder what a future archaeologist or historian might make of my collection, or those of any number of other scholars of religion presently working in the field. And then I remember something one of my seminary professors and spiritual directors, who also happens to be a Benedictine monk, once shared with me in a moment of quiet private conversation. He noted calmly that any contemporary scholar with a Ph.D. in religious studies knows immeasurably more about religion than any revered church father or canonized saint. At the time he said this, this struck me as quite incredible, that is, as literally unbelievable, and as just a bit scandalous, perhaps even blasphemous. How could this be? How could the professor at the local liberal arts college know more than St. Augustine or St. Jerome? After twenty-five years of study and thirteen years of active teaching, public speaking, and professional writing, I think I now understand what my monastic mentor meant. And I believe that he was right. The book you are holding in your hands now is one that tries to express something of this same incredible, "unbelievable" truth.

For indeed, to return to the library example again, I do not think it is an exaggeration at all to admit that the personal library of any contemporary scholar of religion (a good measure of the present state of our knowledge) is significantly richer in cross-cultural materials and theoretical originality than any library of the premodern world (and this is before we even set foot in the million-plus-book library of a modern research university, for which there simply is no historical precedent). After over two centuries of collecting artifacts and translating texts, honing methods of study, and publishing hundreds of thousands (millions?) of primary texts, essays, and books within an immense global network of universities and presses, the state of our shared knowledge about religion is immeasurably greater than it has ever been in the past.

But what does this *mean?* And, whatever it might mean, how are we best to use this new knowledge for our own human flourishing and, just as important, for that of future generations? Certainly no single individual can even begin to read it all, much less understand or assimilate it. Still, assuming for a moment that someone could, how might my imagined future archaeologist (or whatever they are calling such people then) describe such a person's specific forms of knowledge, what it is she claims to know, how she knows it, and, perhaps most important, why she wants to know it. Would such an interpreter look on this imagined knower and her knowledges with a bemused smile as fascinating but hopelessly outdated modes of intellect, bizarre psychic relics from a now very dead and happily forgotten past? Or perhaps, adopting the language of her ancient conservative critics, would such an archaeologist see her as a twenty-first-century heretic, atheist, secular humanist, blasphemer, or infidel?

Or rather, should we be more hopeful? Do her uniquely modern forms of knowledge about religion in fact portend something else, and are her ideas and insights a much more intimate part of the future than anyone presently imagines or, indeed, *can* imagine? After all, whereas an astutely rational and self-reflexive writer like the Stoic philosopher and emperor Marcus Aurelius can be read and understood today more or less as he wrote almost two millennia ago now, many of his culture's religious texts must strike the vast majority of modern readers as bizarre. The usual religious claims aside, it is more often clear, rational thought rather than the dogmas of faith and myth that survive the test of time. Fundamentalists of all stripes do not do well with history (perhaps this is why their imagined golden ages of faith essentially deny it), and I suspect that history will not do well with them. Fundamentalists, I suspect, will become precisely what it is so many of them fear: fossils.

So I return to my question: What will this future archaeologist think of my library, of all of these beautiful books? Without quite answering this question, I want to begin by suggesting that the content, rhetorical style, and substantive conclusions of these present personal libraries often bear a strange resemblance to those of another, the gnostic Nag Hammadi library unearthed in December of 1945 near a buried skeleton and amid several years of bird poop stacked below a cliff in upper Egypt. Muhammad Ali was collecting *sabhakh*, that is, nitrate-laced droppings used to fertilize the fields. As he and his friends dug around a boulder that had recently fallen, they came upon the skeleton and a large, lidded jar. Muhammad paused. He wondered if the jar might contain some mischievous jinni. But he also wondered if it might contain gold. Images of dangerous desert spirits and buried treasure, then, filled his mind as he struck the jar hard. As if to confirm his fantasies of both spirit and magic, little golden flakes sparkled where he struck and then disappeared into the desert air as quickly as they had appeared.

The shimmering flakes were tiny papyrus fragments struck first by Muhammad's mattock and then by the dancing sun and wind. Muhammad and his friends had hit upon one of the most important archaeological discoveries of the twentieth century—thirteen codices of ancient religious texts that would revolutionize our understanding of both ancient Judaisms and early Christianities. Discovered below what amounts, quite literally, to fertile shit, the Nag Hammadi library is a remarkably rich collection of texts about which we previously knew only what the heresiologists or heresy hunters—that is, the ancient enemies of the gnostic Christians—had recorded for posterity in their own angry, "fundamentalist" (and quite orthodox) tirades. Written in a hybrid language of Egyptian and Greek origin called Coptic, the texts represent the religious speculations of some of the earliest strands of Christianity, most of which died out, and some quite ancient forms of Judaism, which would later develop into a type of Jewish mystical thought called the Kabbalah.

But the gnostics of these texts lost their own cultural wars and were effectively suppressed by the orthodox churches into near oblivion; hence their two-millennium erasure. This is also, by the way, the most probable reason for the burial of the Nag Hammadi cache in the first place: some local Christian monks, who lived in a monastery nearby, were most likely trying to protect their own precious library from censoring destruction at the hands of the church authorities. Was the skeleton a monk?

And yet the gnostics never quite died out, since gnostic forms of thought and spirituality continued to arise throughout Western history, as Christian heresy, as various forms of esoteric practice and philosophy (Hermeticism, Boehmian spirituality, Jewish and Christian Kabbalah, Swedenborgian mysticism, Theosophy, and, most recently, the New Age), as Romantic poetry (particularly that of William Blake), as German idealism, as existentialism, nihilism, and Jungian psychology, as popular American culture (the comic book or science fiction novel), and, most relevant for us here, as the modern study of religion.

ACKNOWLEDGMENTS

THIS BOOK, LIKE SOME DISEMBODIED SOUL, has floated through the intermediate realm of the not-yet-published longer than I expected or wished. I have been thinking, for example, about the sexuality of Jesus since I was thirteen, and I am now forty-four. That these long-practiced meditations finally found a beautiful textual body through which to speak to the public is due largely to the intellectual support and enthusiasm of one man, T. David Brent, my editor at the University of Chicago Press. David has now published all four of my books (one still on the way), each of them anomalous in some way, each of them striving for a *theoria,* an intellectual vision that may never fully appear but nevertheless always feels "like the next book." There is nothing quite like having such a supportive editor and such a visionary press.

I have also been fortunate enough to be able to work with Anne Borchardt, a skilled literary agent who took me on five years ago. Anne has taught me a great deal about the publishing world, has faithfully lobbied for my interests, and, in the process, has made this little writing career of mine much more pleasurable and fruitful. I am honored to be counted among her authors.

I also want to register here my deep gratitude to the following individuals: Marcia Brennan, an accomplished art historian and angelic colleague who has powerfully supported and encouraged my aesthetic and metaphysical excesses this past year; Nick Gier and Brian Hatcher, who invited me to deliver an early version of chapter 4 as the plenary address to the Pacific Northwest meeting of the American Academy of Religion and at Illinois Wesleyan University, respectively; Jeremy Zwelling, who invited me to Wesleyan University to speak of things methodological and convinced me, against my own self-doubts, that I am working toward a coherent theory; Jeffrey Perl, who asked me to write an earlier version of chapter 3 for *Common Knowledge*; Gabriel Blau, Sean Fitzpatrick, and Jim Hollis, who sponsored various versions of chapter 1 for their conferences "God and Sexuality" (Gabriel) and "The Erotic Imagination: Refractions of the Spirit" (Sean and Jim for the Houston Jung Center); Mark Jordan and Elliot Wolfson, whom I consider my intellectual and spiritual brothers; Bryan Rennie, with whom I worked closely for nine years at Westminster College and who continues to teach me about Mircea Eliade; Carl Caldwell and Philip Wood, two Rice colleagues who helped me with the German and the French, respectively; Jim Faubion, Rice anthropologist of the gnostic who read the entire manuscript for me, challenged me on my unreformed psychologism and halfhearted postmodernism, and insisted that I change nothing; April DeConick, who taught me about the bridal chamber and who helped me with Secret Mark at the last minute; Jane Schaberg, whose books on the two Marys are as beautiful as they are troubling; and Theodore Jennings, who knows the secret and encouraged me to speak it in my own way again.

I also want to thank Dean Gary Wihl of the Humanities School of Rice University. Dean Wihl extended me important financial support in the summer of 2005 so that I could sit down and revise the present manuscript in light of the Press's reader reports. For that, and for all of his consistent support of religious studies and the humanities as socially relevant and eminently translatable into contemporary American culture, I am very grateful.

Finally, this book is dedicated to two of my former Harvard graduate students, Meggan Watterson and Sera Beak. Megg and Sera are quintessentially themselves, but they are also functioning as symbols here, representatives of all those other readers and students (including and especially my present graduate students) who have shared with me something of their own gnostic lives over the past ten years: Andrea, Ann, Charlie, Daniel, Eric, Nate, Nicholas, "Nightcaller," Prem, Seong, and many others. In many ways, my thought is most indebted to these readers, correspondents, and friends. So much of what I have glimpsed I have caught in the mirror of their faces, quest(ion)s, encouragements, and love. May they see themselves now in the mirror of mine—a double mirror of recognition in which we can all find and lose ourselves.

Chapter 3, "Comparative Mystics," originally appeared in a slightly different form as "Comparative Mystics: Scholars as Gnostic Diplomats," in "Talking Peace with Gods: Symposium on the Reconciliation of Worldviews," pt. 1, ed. Jeffrey M. Perl, *Common Knowledge* 10, no. 3 (Fall 2004): 485–517. Everything else appears here more or less for the first time, except of course for the story about the snake. Someone else made that up.

The Serpent's Gift

> And [God] said to [Adam]: "Who is it who has instructed you?"
> And Adam answered, "The woman whom you have given me."
> And the woman said, "The serpent is the one who instructed
> me." And he cursed the serpent, and he called him "devil."
> Then he said, "Let us cast him out of Paradise lest he take from
> the tree of life and eat and live for ever." But what sort is this
> God? First [he] envied Adam that he should eat from the tree of
> knowledge (*gnoseos*). . . . [And] afterwards he said, "Let us cast
> him [out] of this place, lest he eat of the tree of life and live
> for ever." Surely he has shown himself to be a malicious envier.
> *The Testimony of Truth (second to third centuries)*

THE BIBLICAL STORY of Eve, Adam, and the serpent has captured the imagination of billions of human beings for well over two thousand years now. *The Serpent's Gift* is a retelling of sorts, this time from the perspective of the snake, at least as I imagine this wisdom figure to be embodied in the modern study of religion and its erotic, humanistic, comparative, and esoteric forms of gnosis. It is a strange, perhaps even shocking tale, with the usual protagonists and antagonists more or less reversed. Inspired by early gnostic Christians [1] who could not help noticing just who in the story was graciously bestowing knowledge (the serpent) and who was jealously and rather pettily trying to prevent it (God), I take the ancient gnostic myth as a powerful and ultimately positive parable for all of us who would wish to "grow up," leave the garden of our sexual and religious innocences (and the two, I will argue, are almost always connected), and venture forth into larger, if admittedly more ambiguous, visions of the world, ourselves and the divine.

There is no single message of the myth, nor is there one correct reading. As history has shown us, there are in fact as many readings as there have been generations or communities, maybe even readers. [2] Among its many historical uses, the myth has been employed at different times to explain death (it's our fault) and our fear of snakes (it's the snake's fault), legitimate patriarchal social structures that privilege male interests (it's her fault), set the stage for Christian interpretations of Jesus's execution (it's Adam's fault, but Christ's death can redeem him), prop up Mary's virginity (her purity redeems Eve's fault), justify the murder of women as witches (women, being heirs of Eve, are naturally disposed to sensuality and sin), deny women medical means to lessen suffering in childbirth (who are we to deny God's curse of Eve?), and support slavery in antebellum America (domination and labor are inescapable outcomes of God's punishment of our first parents). More recently, the same myth has been invoked to reject modern science (creationism), demean gay men ("It was Adam and Eve, not Adam and Steve," as one bumper-sticker puts it), and deconstruct patriarchy ("Eve was framed," reads another).

The tale appears to be unusually plastic. Historically speaking, however, the story, like the garden itself, does seem to set some basic boundaries around what is possible, and it has definitely evoked some rather consistent patterns of response or interpretation over the centuries. Among these, the sexual has occupied an important, even central, place. No doubt this erotic focus is partly a function of the first creation myth, in Genesis 1:1–2:4, where God creates human beings "in his own image" (Gen. 1:27). In its original Hebrew context, this is almost certainly a reference to their physical likeness to God's body,[3] which the myth suggests is bisexual or, perhaps better, a male androgyne (hence the earth creatures are created as male *and* female "in his own image"). However we choose to read such biblical gender bending, such ideas certainly constitute, in David Carr's words, "an affirmation of male and female sexual bodies as signs of the divine."[4] In other words, "this ancient Israelite text suggests that our flesh, our body is in the divine image, is one of the primary things that is 'very good' about us. *This is how the Bible begins*."[5]

Early rabbinic interpretations certainly understood as much. They suggested variously that Adam was in fact an androgyne before woman was split off to form the couple, that Adam had sex with the animals before God finally figured out what a woman was (Adam, after all, was trying them out as companions),[6] and that Eve had sex with the serpent. Medieval kabbalistic authors could be equally bold and insightful, if not quite so positive. Abraham Abulafia, for example, unabashedly identified the knowledge of the forbidden tree with sex and the couple's sexual shame with our own: "Intercourse is called the Tree of Knowledge of good and evil and is a matter of disgust and one ought to be ashamed at the time of the act."[7]

Early Christian commentators speculated variously and sexually as well. Indeed, the sexual readings of the story were so common that Augustine (354–430) found it necessary to argue against the symbolic equation of "tree" and "sexual intercourse" in his *The Literal Meaning of Genesis*.[8]

Modern American English use has its own similar insights, even if we do not always recognize their connection to these first few chapters of the Bible. English speakers, for example, speak jokingly of how "he knew her" (with a very heavy and winking accent on *knew*), of "carnal knowledge," and of so-and-so being "forbidden fruit"—all transparently sexual innuendos that take us back to the garden story. Whether we admit it or not, we already *know*.

And after Freud, feminism, and two hundred years of biblical scholarship, we can add even more striking accents to our unacknowledged gnosis. We can notice, for example, that knowledge itself is indeed heavily sexualized in ancient Hebrew thought (the first verse of chapter 4 begins "And Adam knew Eve . . . ," with a long line of "begats" following), that the immediate response of the couple after eating the fruit was sexual shame ("they realized that they were naked"), and that, quite faithful to biblical legal thought, their punishments fit the unspoken but nevertheless transparent crime: Eve will suffer in childbirth, which of course is the result of sexual intercourse, and Adam will toil in the fields, agriculture being in the ancient world an expression of male fertility, privilege, and priority; hence the biblical—and fantastically incorrect—metaphor of the male "seed" containing all that is important except the feminine "ground" it needs to germinate and grow. Put baldly for the sake of my argument, the forbidden fruit of the tree of knowledge of good and evil that God forbade the beautiful couple to eat was sex—sweet, delicious sex.[9]

Sort of. Actually, the fruit was clearly not just "sex," as we use that word much too loosely and mundanely today. Rather, the fruit functions as a type of erotic gnosis that was understood to effect, immediately, both moral awareness and the divinization of the human being. The fruit of the knowledge of good and evil that the knowing serpent offers the couple to eat, after all, is understood by the myth to be both a kind of partial divinization and a preparatory stage to the couple awakening more fully to their own immortal natures. Indeed, God states quite clearly that the two have already "become like one of us" through the act of eating the fruit, exactly as the serpent promised, and later points out that, should the couple manage to eat of the second tree of life, they would live forever.

In a rather tragic way for Western religious thought, then, the story seems to suggest that God stands against our own moral maturity, against sexuality, and against the divinization of human nature through the acquisition of knowledge and sensual pleasure. It also insinuates, when it does not actually shout, that we all die because our first parents *knew* each other within the intimate gnosis of sexual intercourse. Because they fucked, we're screwed. Through this troubling logic, the serpent's gift was turned into an ancient curse and the gracious giver into the devil himself, as the Testimony of Truth, quoted in my opening epigraph, caustically observed almost two millennia ago.

Certainly not everyone was duped, though. Some of the early gnostic Christians, for example, recognized that the serpent's presence involved the revelation of sexual desire. The Apocryphon of John, for example, records the following exchange: "'Lord, was it not the serpent that taught them?' He smiled and said, 'The serpent appeared to them for sexual desire.'"[10] And the elaborate sexual mythologies, sperm mysticisms ("the seed of Seth" of the Sethians), and implied sexual rituals of that ancient corpus of texts generally collected under the rubric of Gnosticism more than bears out the Savior's mischievous smile, as we shall see in due time. In any case, for reasons that are still not clear but that certainly involved rumors and reports of these communities' sexual beliefs and practices, the gnostic Christians were viciously attacked by the orthodox leaders and eventually driven underground until their haunting voices were erased from any accurate historical memory, until, that is, they were dug up again in 1945 near Nag Hammadi beneath the bird poop.

Very much like these early gnostic insights that raged and grinned so against the more traditional readings, the modern study of religion can help us to recognize the wise snake, the lovely loving couple, and the angry jealous god among us. The garden of delight, it turns out, much like Jesus's kingdom of heaven, is still with(in) us, if only we can learn to open our eyes and have the courage to act accordingly. The fruit hangs before us (and on and in us), and the serpent still hisses his promised gift. And it is up to us now how we tell the story from here.

Faith, Reason, and Gnosis

But we will need more informed cultural memories and more bold intellectual and imaginative practices to recognize, accept, and then act upon such a gift. Gilles Quispel, the Dutch historian of Gnosticism and friend of C. G. Jung, once noted that there are three major strands of Western culture: *faith*, a way of knowing the world and oneself via religious doctrines, themselves dependent upon divine revelation and the authoritative creeds of the religious communities; *reason*, a form of knowledge deriving, at least in the West, from Greek philosophy and logic that relies on analytic and linear thought, empirical sense data, and doubt to arrive at the objective truth of things (it is this form of knowledge, of course, that culminated in the scientific method); and, finally, *gnosis*, a form of intuitive, visionary, or mystical knowledge that privileges the primacy of personal experience and the depths of the self over the claims of both faith and reason, traditionally in order to acquire some form of liberation or salvation from a world seen as corrupt or fallen.[11]

Historically speaking, the study of religion arose from the experience of faith and the desire to explain and codify its content for different generations.[12] As faith sought understanding as theology, however, it also encountered serious questions that, when honestly pursued to their end, effected permanent revolutions in both thought and belief. Among these problems, four that were encountered in a particularly acute way in the nineteenth century, especially within the European Protestant universities, and further radicalized in the twentieth, this time in the United States, stand out as particularly definitive for us today: (1) the historical construction of all scripture, (2) the radical religious pluralism of humanity, (3) the incompatibility of particular religiosities with modern science, and (4) the role of gender and the place of women within religious traditions. Finally, a fifth has more recently taken center stage: the relationship between religious authority, community, and violence.

Once faith began to question its own foundations and realize how unstable these foundations truly are, it was only a matter of time before reason separated entirely from its religious roots and sought its own integrity and honest conclusions. The philosophers had led the way here. Indeed, the eighteenth and early nineteenth centuries had known a whole series of intellectuals whose thought both witnessed to and helped effect what amounted to a culturally shared altered state of consciousness, or what we today call, quite appropriately I think, the Enlightenment. Within such an altered state, what was once common knowledge or inviolable sacred truth now became deeply questionable, if not actually silly. Hence, the French philosophes, led by Voltaire and Diderot, took great delight in ridiculing religion's absurdities in a very public way. Along different lines, Immanuel Kant effected an immense Copernican shift in Western epistemology by demonstrating that much, perhaps everything, that we think we know about the external world is in fact filtered through a priori categories of the mind, such as space, time, and causality. In short, the human mind does not simply reflect the world like a mirror; it also actively *constructs* it. Significantly, Kant also nicely defined enlightenment as the ability to think for oneself outside of all external authorities, including and especially religious authorities: "Enlightenment is man's release from his self-incurred tutelage. Tutelage is man's inability to make use of his understanding without direction from another. Self-incurred is this tutelage when its cause lies not in lack of reason but in lack of resolution and courage to use it without direction from another. *Sapere aude!* 'Have courage to use your own reason!'—that is the motto of enlightenment."[13] *Sapere Aude!* More literally, "Dare to know!"

But this reason remained a troubled and unstable one. Hence, alongside these developments involving a faith seeking understanding and a daring reason freeing itself from all external authorities, another more intuitive and poetic strand was always present, one with deep roots in ancient Neoplatonism, Gnosticism, and the ebbs and flows of Western esotericism. Such a knowing recognized the limits of any autonomous reason, even as it insisted on its own forms of more immediate knowledge. In the early modern period, this gnosis surfaced dramatically within the Christian theosophy of Jacob Boehme and was later taken up and developed in different directions by the Romantic poets and the German idealist philosophers. Thus began a centuries-long project of self-exploration and of naturalizing the supernatural.[14] The universe was no longer simply a ticking clock, as it was for the Deists and the early scientists. It now became a living poem, a cosmic epiphany, or a grand and gradual manifestation of an evolving *Geist* or Spirit awakening into its own divinity.

Similar, essentially aesthetic and phenomenological, sensibilities were translated into the churches and entered the study of religion primarily through the early figure of Friedrich Schleiermacher, the German theologian who evoked a deeply felt piety, individual experience, and emotion as the truest and most reliable places to locate a legitimate religious life for skeptical moderns in his *On Religion: Speeches to Its Cultured Despisers* (1799). With this turn to the subjective realm (he could even imagine one developing a religion all one's own), Schleiermacher opened up the way for what would later become the heavy psychological accent of the study of religion, developed by such thinkers as Sigmund Freud, William James, and C. G. Jung, each of whom was also deeply interested in psychical or mystical matters.[15]

Faith, reason, and gnosis, then.

The Premodern, the Modern, and the Postmodern

Another useful way to think about the study of religion is through a second triad, that of the premodern, the modern, and the postmodern. All of these terms are in fact hotly contested in the academy and should best be approached as useful fictions. For our purposes here, we might define them as follows.

Premodernity refers to a form of human consciousness that we assume was more or less common before the sixteenth century in the West (that is, before the Protestant Reformation, the Enlightenment, and the Romantic movement) and is still quite common in traditional societies not heavily influenced by Western forms of thought and experience. Such a consciousness relies heavily on faith and belief to organize the world and—from our modern perspective at least—tends to submerge the ego in communal forms of social life that privilege the community over the individual. Such quintessentially modern values as democracy, the freedom of intellectual, artistic, political, and religious expression, and the inviolability of human rights are relatively foreign to these cultures and attending forms of consciousness, as such values, if truly honored and carried through to their logical conclusions, would dissolve many of the communal social forms that lie at the base of these premodern worldviews.

On the positive side, such premodern forms of thought and life offer human beings something more modern forms seldom can, that is, intimate forms of community and relative certainty about how the world works. Some of us may be appalled at the illusory and often dangerous nature of such "certainties," but it is not difficult to see why fundamentalist religious communities—themselves complex and unstable combinations of premodern and modern forms of religiosity—are constantly building larger parking lots, while liberal communities are shrinking: literal beliefs and high walls of ideological intolerance ensure strong community, whereas openness and toleration render specific faith communities more or less irrelevant. If everyone shares in the truth of things, why belong to this community and not some other? Indeed, why belong at all?

Modernity, on the other hand, refers to a form of human consciousness heavily inflected by an autonomous reason and the rational ordering of human life in all its modes. It tends to privilege the individual over the community, rejects religious appeals to transcendence, and looks to science as the standard of all reliable truth and knowledge. Democracy, the nation-state, capitalism, and science have been the dominant expressions of this modernity, although there have certainly been religious modernities as well. The Protestant Reformation, for example, is emblematic here to the extent that it began the slow process of liberating the individual from the authority of faith and privileging the same individual's critical capacities and economic concerns in every area of thought and life. Such Protestant pillars of faith as the priesthood of all believers and the absolute authority of the scriptures interpreted by the individual (*sola scriptura*) were certainly religious ideas, but they also encoded profound transformations of political thought away from religious authority and toward the freedom and independence of individual readers. It is not for nothing that individuals like William Tyndale were actually burned at the stake in the sixteenth century for translating the Bible into vernacular languages (in Tyndale's case, into English), as by this act they were opening the biblical texts up to interpretation well beyond the control of the church authorities. They were, in effect, setting the foundation for the collapse of the medieval premodern worldview and the birth of the modern one. The modern study of religion began at the stake.

Postmodernity, finally, refers most generally to what comes "after modernity" (the lack of a developed definition is intentional here). Although the expression is a very recent one, witnessing to the past fifty years of critical theory, many thinkers would trace the contemporary roots of the postmodern back to Friedrich Nietzsche's prophetic writings on the "death of God," the aesthetic celebration of a Dionysian sexual spirituality "beyond good and evil," and the rejection of all philosophical or religious foundations (what Martin Heidegger would later similarly condemn as "onto-theology"). Significantly, for our purposes anyway, Nietzsche's texts as postmodern origin are often imbued with a very distinct homoerotic passion and a real mystical fury.[16] He was not a self-confessed devotee of Dionysius and the "mysteries of sexuality" for nothing.[17]

Nietzschean origins aside, as a technical term, postmodernity refers to a form of human consciousness that seeks to move beyond the autonomous reason of modernity and its talk of stable "essences," "laws," and "structures" into a different, presumably more hopeful or workable human future. This it attempts through a rejection of any talk of metaphysical essences or ontological foundations, claims of the effective death of the stable subject (the "individual" of modernity), a rejection of all meta-narratives (those big stories or mythologies—such as Christianity, evolutionary science, or history as social progress—that provided the context for legitimate meaning within modern cultures), and a celebration of plurality, alterity ("otherness"), and, above all, *difference*. "Sameness," "form," and "essence" are all forbidden terms here.

Perhaps most important, though, postmodern forms of thought are radically *reflexive*, that is, they are profoundly aware of their own cognitive processes and so often "double back" on themselves through the genres of confession, autobiography, irony, and even parody. Still within this same reflexive move, a recognizable relativism or perspectivalism also pervades postmodern thought, that is, the insistence that what we call truth is really a function of the power and the perspective of the knower and not an accurate reflection of some "objective" external reality independent of the human observer (in this sense, postmodernity can be read as an extension or development of Kantian modernity). In many places, moreover, postmodern thought radicalizes this relativism further into what we might call a complete constructivism, that is, the position that human cultures actually create or construct the worlds human beings live in through elaborate processes involving language use (words, concepts, ideas), religious beliefs, rituals, and social organization.[18]

Toward a Gnostic (Post)Modernity

Given these two fictive triads (faith/reason/gnosis and premodern/modern/postmodern), one might want to say that, as a function of modernity and its cognitive dilemmas, the study of religion shares in both premodern and modern forms of consciousness, even as it continuously strives for something more or "after"—in effect, a kind of gnostic postmodernity. One might want to say that, but I am not yet entirely convinced that I do.

Certainly, much that I will attempt in the following pages can be framed as "postmodern." For example, I see real mystical or gnostic potential in the postmodern turn. I consistently engage in dialectical both/and forms of inclusive thought that many would recognize as postmodern. And I follow certain postmodern conventions, such as a deliberate mixing and merging of premodern and modern or "high" and "low" cultural forms (for example, gnostics and comics, in chap. 4). Other aspects of my thought, however, are distinctly modern. For example, my comparative method insists on both sameness and difference across all human cultures and times, and I am quite comfortable speaking of "comparative forms" and "structures," even of a certain ontology of human being.[19] I hesitate, then, moving back and forth among and within premodern, modern, and postmodern forms of thought. Hence the tentative parentheses of my section subtitle, which is intended to register an ambivalent embrace of the postmodern, "A Gnostic (Post)Modernity." I stumble here in three steps, two back and one forward: on the ethical, the mystical, and the mythical.

Ethically speaking, I cannot quite shake the conviction—and I am hardly alone here—that postmodernism's "death of the subject" and constructivist leanings, which sometimes devolve into a complete relativism, can too easily render any functional ethical position in the modern world intellectually impossible. I recognize that this is not the intent of the more careful authors, but I fear that it is too often the practical result of postmodern thought nonetheless. The human being, the individual, gender equity, and the notion of human rights may all be Western constructions, cosmic illusions with no objective grounding "out there." These same convictions may also be in constant danger of morphing into an unthinking and arrogant cultural imperialism. Still, they are also visions of our own Enlightenment, precious moral values without which billions of individuals (most of them women, children, and minorities) will almost certainly continue to suffer gross injustice, deprivation, disease, and violence.

Mystically speaking, postmodernism is certainly promising, and perhaps it is here as well that an incipient postmodern ethic can best be celebrated. As numerous authors have demonstrated, there are many historical and structural resonances between postmodern forms of deconstruction and traditional forms of religious thought, particularly Neoplatonic philosophy, medieval "negative theology," and certain strands of apophatic mysticism.[20] All of these systems of thought delight in demonstrating the self-contradictions and absurdities of traditional religious claims, and indeed of all linguistic utterances. What postmodernism sometimes lacks, however, is precisely what the premodern practices possessed in rich abundance, that is, an ontological ground or, if you prefer, a nonground into which the linguistic games and surface illusions can be dissolved and, perhaps even more important, a set of psychophysical contemplative techniques to realize this (non)ground. In a Meister Eckhart or a Nagarjuna, for example, truth claims are deconstructed into a Godhead beyond God or into a meditative experience of infinite and brilliant emptiness. In postmodernism, this is not always so apparent, and one sometimes feels lost in a kind of surface superficiality or even vague nihilism (the same, by the way, has

often been said about many forms of Buddhism).[21] If postmodern deconstruction, then, constitutes a contemporary mystical practice, it is a still
young and developing one.

In any case, it bears repeating: postmodern acts of thought and writing
with respect to religion can be powerfully ethical gestures, as they have the
capacity to "melt down" in the here and now the oppressive dualisms of
religious orthodoxy that are set up to interminably delay salvation, liberation, or enlightenment and so keep the authoritarian structures of
mediation and tradition solidly in place.[22] Just as important, they also demonstrate a profound and quite radical respect for otherness and difference
and so easily morph into intellectually grounded forms of social activism
with respect to people of color, women, gays, lesbians, and formerly colo-
nized peoples.

Having acknowledged all of that, I want to register one final doubt, one
more step backward from a standard postmodernism. Mythically speaking, I also cannot help but read postmodernism's challenge to such things
as the comparative method, to grand theorizing in the humanities or social
sciences, and to modern science as the reappearance of the petty god of
Genesis threatening the beautiful couple for their erotic desire to know one
another and to awaken to a morally mature form of consciousness. If Kant's
Enlightenment shouts "Dare to know!" the motto of postmodernism sometimes becomes "How dare you know!" This seems particularly apparent in
certain deformations or abuses of postcolonial theory, where any strong
claim to comparative, psychological, or historical knowledge is too often
facilely framed as a form of "epistemological imperialism" or "neocolo-
nialism."[23] Knowledge has in effect become a form of evil, a sin, and the
petty god of Genesis is now joined by the petty gods of every other religion
and culture in a desperate attempt to keep us all locked within a thousand
premodern gardens of imagined ethnic, religious, and political purity. I
can think of few worlds more dangerous than this one.

Medi(t)ations

What, then, can I finally say about all of these terms and their relationship
to the study of religion? I can say that whereas the public faces of the study
of religion have alternated back and forth between visages of faith and reason, the field in fact encompasses, and has always encompassed, faith,
reason, and gnosis in both its history and philosophical structures, even
as it now attempts to move beyond all three into a uniquely (post)modern
form of consciousness for which there are many precedents—"echoes of
embarrassment," as Ilse Bulhof and Laurens ten Kate so beautifully put it
with respect to the Western history of negative theology[24]—but nothing
quite like this. For my own part, I want to read our present (post)modernity,
and especially this study of religion, as a deeply gnostic phenomenon that

cannot be properly appreciated, much less fully realized, without engaging its deconstructive, apophatic, and implicitly mystical dimensions.

In other words, without in any way denying the relationship of the discipline to the history of faith, or for that matter to a deeply ambiguous history of colonialism, or its central reliance on reason and doubt as methods of inquiry, I wish to emphasize in the following four meditations its positive, transformative, experiential, intuitive, and gnostic powers. I wish to recover, if you will, some of the mystical depths of our modern Enlightenment and its attending humanism, as well as those of our more recent postmodern turn, itself so deeply indebted to that same Enlightenment. Postmodernity here, then, is not so much a denial or rejection of modernity (or sameness, or form) as its own gnostic radicalization and awakening.

What I am not doing is rejecting the reductive methods and social-scientific scholarship of the contemporary academy.[25] Neither am I suggesting a simple resolution of the tension between faith and reason via gnosis. Nor am I seeking to equate ancient Gnosticism and modern religious studies in any facile or nonreflexive way. I am perfectly aware that I am employing the trope of Gnosticism in rhetorical and essentially theological ways to advance my own intellectual agendas.[26] I am also aware that I am writing in the shadow (really in the light) of an impressive corpus of scholarship produced by previous writers, who have isolated and analyzed these gnostic structures of modernity in much greater detail and who have often come to evaluative conclusions different from my own. For example, I am not exactly arguing for what Cyril O'Regan calls a gnostic return in modernity, which is in effect also a kind of haunting.[27] Although I am awed by O'Regan's erudition and share many of his ambivalences about gnosticism, my specific intellectual framing of a gnostic epistemology is generally more positive, more erotic, and is not dependent in any way on the mythological structures of the Valentinian gnosis or the theosophical system of Boehme. It is also much more engaged with Asia.

In my model, at least, the (post)modern gnostic intellectual is the one who privileges knowledge over belief, who knows that she knows, *and* knows that what she knows cannot possibly be reconciled with the claims of any past or present religious tradition, including the ancient gnostic Judaisms and Christianities, whose common radical dualisms and consistent rejections of the body, sexuality, and the physical world render any simplistic mimicking of these elaborate mythological systems quite impossible and hardly desirable.[28] To borrow an expression from Elaine Pagels, such a gnostic epistemology or way of knowing is quite literally "beyond belief."[29]

It is also, however, quite "beyond reason," at least if we restrict reason to the reductive sociopolitical Marxisms of much humanities scholarship, the quantitative models of the social sciences, or the extreme relativisms of some postmodern thought. I would argue that the former rationalisms are simply incapable of dealing adequately with that immense swath of nonrational, altered states of consciousness and energy that constitute so much of the history of religions, and that the latter postmodern relativisms too easily devolve into an effective denial of reason in which truth has collapsed into identity, knowledge has become mere opinion, and all opinions are more or less equal. The result is intellectual chaos, moral relativism, and the resurgence of fundamentalist and fascist forms of religious nationalism from Indiana to India that draw on these very postmodern models to justify their own identity politics and their rejection of both the critical hermeneutics of the humanities and the universality of modern science. In Meera Nanda's telling phrase, postmodern theorists and their fundamentalist fans can easily become "prophets facing backwards."[30]

The form of (post)modern consciousness I am attempting to theorize here is not any of these things. It is not a pure, untroubled reason that refuses to think a thought that cannot be quantified, falsified, and reproduced in a controlled laboratory (there is little controlled or even controllable about religious experience). Neither, however, is it antireason, even if it sees the limitations of any strictly conceived rationality. It is not antimodern, even if it often feels restricted and unnecessarily bound in by modern forms of thought and being and fully recognizes the dark sides of modernity. It is not relativistic, even if it embraces both deconstruction and pluralism as necessary methods and values. It takes moral positions, even if it recognizes its own fallibility and limited sight. It is not antibody or anticosmos, as so many of the ancient gnostic systems were. On the contrary, it turns to the body, and in particular to the erotic body, as a source of wisdom and delight and as the fundamental ground of its comparative theorizing: the human universals of biology, physiology, gender, and sexuality—infinitely permutated through local doctrine, social practice, and language—define the parameters of the *corpus mysticum* here and its constant, universal dialectic of difference *and* sameness. Perhaps most important, however, the form of gnosis I am arguing for here claims to *know* things that other forms of knowledge and experience (like traditional faith or pure reason) do not and probably cannot know, even as it submits its claims to public review, criticism, and renewal, all of which it listens and responds to as some of its most important ethical acts.

Too simply but instructively put, the study of religion has been defined by a kind of Ping-Pong movement between two modes of human functioning, two sides of the brain, as it were, analogous but not identical to those associated with faith and reason.[31] Thus, we are told that the study of religion should be about the faithful description and comparison of worldviews as members of those cultures might recognize them—a kind of cultural cheerleading. Or we are told that the study of religion should be about explaining religious myths, rituals, and beliefs in the nonreligious terms of the natural and social sciences, that is, reduced to the entirely secular processes of the psyche, society, and political control—a kind of heartless deconstruction. Much of the discussion, moreover, has proceeded on the assumptions that what we have here is a zero-sum game, an either-or choice that must conclude either on the side of a faithful description of revealed truths or on the side of a materialistic reductionism.

As I hope is already obvious (if admittedly not yet quite clear), I am proceeding with a different model, one that seeks to honor and respect the truths of both sides of this perennial tension, even as it places them within a larger structural whole that sees these two positions as opposite, but intimately related, poles of a deeper unity (it is, after all, one brain). Structurally speaking, this model recognizes that the reason of the modern study of religion arose historically within the very heart of faith, that both reductionism and deconstructionism often display distinctly mystical qualities, and that we can detect within certain moments of the (post)modern study of religion a certain explosive fusion of faith and reason—a kind of mental matter and antimatter, if you will—that produces a distinctly third realm of knowing that resembles but cannot be reduced to what has traditionally been called gnosis. As I will use the category here, then, gnosis is a triple-edged word, implying at once a privileging of knowing over believing, an affirmation of altered states of consciousness and psychic functioning as valuable and legitimate modes of cognition, and a critical-but-engaged encounter with the faith traditions themselves.

Although drawing profoundly on the symbols, myths, rituals, and revelations of the faith traditions themselves, such a gnosis must often come to conclusions that are at serious odds with the orthodox traditions. This kind of gnosis, moreover, presumes a certain individualism, an inviolable intellectual and moral integrity, and a privileging of individual conviction, dream, conscience, and vision over any and all authorized truths or revelations, even as it recognizes, through reason, that its own individual convictions have been nurtured and formed by community and tradition. It is certainly not independent of the faith traditions; quite the contrary, it relies on them quite intimately and constantly turns to them for inspiration. There would be no study of religion without religion. But neither is it entirely dependent on them. There would be no study of religion if there were only religion.

It bears repeating. I am not arguing for a simple reintroduction of faith back into the discussion, nor am I suggesting a phenomenological bracketing or "description checked with the authorities," as scholars such as W. C. Smith have famously argued for, as if every scholarly work should be vetted with the tradition before it passes muster as a work of critical scholarship. What I *am* arguing for is radical critical thought and normative debate about religious and spiritual matters, linked to a deep appreciation for and dialogue with the experiential resources of the traditions themselves. From the Boston Catholic scandals involving clerical abuse to the contemporary Middle East with its innumerable religious violences, I believe that we must stop operating with the comfortable, if politically correct, illusion that these are not fundamentally religious problems. As numerous scholars have gone to great lengths to demonstrate, Catholic homoeroticism is a structural necessity of Roman Catholicism's insistence on celibacy and condemnation of homosexuality and an intimate dimension of its mystical and theological traditions, not some modern "blip" on the historical screen that can be fixed through something as simple, stupid, and cruel as banning gays from the seminaries (now they really *will* be empty). Moreover, violence, gross intolerance, and social exclusion are all integral to the history and theology of monotheism itself, not some imagined "abuse" of otherwise "peaceful religions." Anyone who thinks the latter has simply not been paying very good attention.

Our religious problems, in other words, are just that—*religious* problems. Until we confront them as such and are willing to criticize their religious bases as religious in radical dialogue with the traditions themselves, we will not resolve these problems in any long-lasting or viable fashion. It is my own conviction that both a faith-based study and a purely secular approach are incapable of doing this effectively. The former is too bound by traditional assumptions and authorities to break free; the latter is too removed and distant from the same to make any real difference or help effect any lasting change. It will no longer do to set up an inviolable structural dichotomy between the insider and the outsider, or between faith and reason, as if there were not insides and outsides within the traditions themselves (esoteric teachings, for example, which explode the naïvetés of literal belief), as if outsiders did not become insiders (and insiders outsiders), as if much of any inside knowledge were not in fact constructed rationally, and as if believers did not routinely use forms of reductive rationalism to deconstruct other religious traditions (atheism, after all, is the usual prescribed position vis-à-vis the gods of *other* people). Mystically speaking, there *is* no final "inside" or "outside," nor can there ever be.

It will not do, then, to set up the scholar of religion as some kind of distant illuminator of the benighted masses, nor can the believer be similarly privileged as somehow closer to the truth of religion.[32] No, something at once more intellectually radical and more religiously engaged is needed, something approaching a kind of modern gnosis that is as grateful for the contemplative, ethical, and artistic gifts of the religious traditions as it is critical of their forms of false consciousness, their lies.

Writing as Hissing

The sensitive reader might hear a distinct hissing passing through my words. This is how the serpent speaks his gift: in whispered secrets that are never quite made explicit but are nevertheless there, hissing their whispers in both the form and content of the text. Obviously, such claims hardly constitute standard academic arguments. And, in truth, I have no desire to engage in anything standard here. These are not traditional academic essays that exhaust the relevant literature, qualify every truth claim out of existence, and advance only rational, linear arguments. No, the essays circle around and around a common set of largely intuitive themes. They employ myth, rhetoric, apologetic, and polemic. And, like the meaning of a poem, their message resides as much in their form as it does in their content.

I am reminded here of Catherine Clément, the French feminist philosopher, who once wrote that, "I do not exclude meeting Freud, even less encountering Lacan, but it is not enough—or rather, it is no longer enough for me."[33] This line occurs in a book largely about India and its Tantric traditions. What Clément meant, I think, is that she was no longer satisfied with purely psychological or philosophical matters. She wanted to move on into the mystical, into what the French feminist tradition calls the *jouissance* of orgasm, rapture, and religious ecstasy. So too here. I no longer want to study mystical literature. I now want to write it. But this, I would suggest, can be done today only in and through our own (post)modern forms of consciousness and criticism. There can be no return to some kind of premodern garden of religious belief and sexual innocence. In truth, there probably never were such simple things. But even if there were, they are no more. Historically and philosophically, as a culture we have long ago eaten the fruit and now live well outside that garden. My hissing writing embraces this fact as a mark of our maturity and wisdom, not as a sign of some imagined "fall" from grace.

I am partly indebted here to R. C. Zaehner, the Oxford don and comparativist from whom I borrowed my own present book title. Zaehner himself, however, borrowed the idea of the "serpent's gift," if not the expression, from the Canadian psychologist and self-confessed mystic Richard M. Bucke, who had understood Adam and Eve's "fall" not as a fall at all, but as a *rise* into self-consciousness, as a psychospiritual development from a primordial union with nature into individuality that could be completed only in the Cosmic Consciousness that Bucke now heralded as the true Christ and which he himself had experienced one winter night in a carriage on his way home from a poetry reading (itself, I suspect, energized by Bucke's own homoerotic fascination with Walt Whitman, whom he knew, loved, and revered).[34]

The expression "the serpent's gift" for Zaehner (and for me), in other words, signals a specific type of modern mystical consciousness that understands itself as deeply rooted in and gratefully indebted to both premodern "mystical" forms of awareness and to more modern forms of rationality and critical reason. "The serpent," Zaehner wrote, "is the spirit of rationality, the immanent will inherent in the evolutionary process, if you like, which urges the human race to grow up."[35] And to grow up is to leave the garden of innocence, of both our childlike union with the mother of the earth and, perhaps a bit later (in our psychological development, if not in actual history), our obedient submission to the father in the sky. It is to accept, as mature adults, our individual existences as both finite and mortal, even as we intuit our deep hidden communion with the universe.

Zaehner was lecturing and writing on such themes in the 1960s and early 1970s. Twenty-five years later, the contemporary historian of Jewish mysticism Elliot Wolfson returned to a similar idea in order to describe autobiographically what it felt like to encounter the "serpent of philosophy" as a young man growing up in a New York Orthodox Jewish household.[36] Psychology and philosophy were tempting him, successfully, from the safe garden of Orthodox ritual and belief. He could never return, although he could give his years to the intricate study of Kabbalah, the Jewish mystical tradition that dwells so long on the complexities of divine bisexuality, the paradoxical unity of good and evil, and the reconstitution of the divine nature through human sexual practice and intentional acts of piety and prayer. Religious studies for Wolfson, then, is a kind of modern religious quest that, paradoxically, often removes one from traditional religious doctrines and communities. It is a knowing that ultimately renders one a permanent outsider, a wanderer on the edges of belief and faith. It is a "being bitten," a "gift," and an "exile" all at once.

Autobiographical and Pedagogical Contexts

Zaehner, Bucke, and Wolfson, then, have given me the phrase *the serpent's gift*, but it is my own life of faith, reason, and gnosis that have filled in the specific meanings of that little three-word poem and provided an authentic voice to utter it. I have already written much—no doubt too much for the tastes of many—about my own mystical and sexual lives (really the same life) and their intimate relationship to my public writing and thought.[37] I will return briefly to that discussion here not to dwell again on the details, but to point out what a thorough mockery these life-experiences make of the traditional distinctions between faith and reason.

To begin with, I was introduced to the historical-critical study of the Bible, Ludwig Feuerbach, and psychoanalysis (all archetypal voices of Enlightenment reason) in a Catholic seminary setting, itself embedded in the rich contemplative life of a Benedictine monastery. Nor was this faith encounter with reason a purely intellectual exercise. It was also a matter of life and death, as I was slowly perishing from anorexia, and what finally healed me was what appeared in my dreams (that is, in an altered state of consciousness) now translated and analyzed through the hermeneutical methods of classical psychoanalysis with a trained analyst who also happened to be a monk. Nocturnal gnosis and diurnal reason, faith and reason, health and interpretation were inseparable here. Saved by Freud, an enlightened Catholicism and the wisdom of my own dreams, I went on to study the history of religions and to write books on the homoerotic structures of male erotic mysticism in an early modern Hindu saint, in Roman Catholic bridal mysticism, in Sufism, in Kabbalah, and in the modern study of religion itself.

It was the reception of these books that finally obliterated for me any hope of separating (or wish to separate) faith, reason, and gnosis. As an author who employed a whole spectrum of psychological and historical methods in *Kali's Child* (1995), I was viciously attacked for eight years in the Indian media, in the Indian Parliament, and on the Internet as an arch-rationalist, as a despised Freudian, and as an embodiment of all that is "neocolonialist" and "hegemonic" about "Western" reason and the Enlightenment tradition (hence my deep reservations about postcolonial theory). In response to a prominent scholar's published criticism that I should have vetted my manuscript with the believing community before publication, I refused to accept the notion that the religions should set the ground rules for the practice of scholarship and warned the field of the specter of ideological censorship, which soon followed and is still with us.[38]

In my next book, *Roads of Excess* (2001), I explored the homoerotic structures of Roman Catholicism and Western male mystical literature in general, arguing in effect that any heteroerotic mysticism will necessarily be framed as heterodox or heretical within a major religious tradition, but particularly within a monotheistic one. The book appeared a few weeks before the Boston clerical scandals broke. Since then, I have corresponded with a representative of the American Catholic bishops who insisted that I retract and apologize for this book. I refused again. To the faith-filled readers of these first two books, I embody reason worshipped to the point of idolatry, sacrilege, and pure blasphemy.

On the other hand, I have written openly and positively about the mystical, I have insisted on putting psychoanalytic and Asian Tantric systems into creative, even metaphysical, dialogue, I have described and analyzed my own ecstatic and visionary experiences in extensive psychosexual detail, and I have suggested that some of the most creative theorizing in the study of religion has been catalyzed and guided by the mystical experiences of scholars of mysticism. To those in the academy who hold up reason and sociopolitical reductionism as the only legitimate modes of discourse in the study of religion, I represent much that is wrong with the discipline—all that fuzzy talk of "mysticism," all that emphasis on "experience," all that insistence that there really is something unique about studying religion, that everything cannot be explained by Karl Marx and Michel Foucault (or Sigmund Freud), that at least some of what we do and who we are is fundamentally and irreducibly anomalous, inexplicable, uncanny.

But it is neither my religious or rationalist critics who have most influenced my gnostic reflections on the modern study of religion. It is my students and readers, and those few hundred correspondents who have written me literally thousands of letters over the past ten years describing in astonishing psychosexual detail their own mystical lives and how my work on Ramakrishna, on Hindu Tantrism, and on Catholicism helped them to understand and accept their own otherwise anomalous, and fundamentally erotic, mystical experiences.[39] Consider, for example, the one class of readers who have most deeply understood and appreciated my work on sexual trauma and mystical states: women and men who have themselves been sexually abused as children or young adults and later found themselves entering, often spontaneously, into extremely positive and healing altered states of consciousness.[40] Such readers do not "accept" or "understand" what I am trying to communicate. They *know*. Their readings are based on excessive life events, on the most troublingly delightful movements of their own minds and bodies. And they are perfectly aware that very few people will ever understand them, that others cannot possibly "get it."

How could they? They have not been through the same life-altering experiences and had their consciousness and energies permanently shifted into other dimensions of knowing and being. One might as well try to explain an orgasm to a five-year-old. Such readers, in other words, know that there is something essentially esoteric or incommunicable about their knowledge, but they also see in certain types of scholarship mirrored glimmers of both their own mystical experiences and their equally powerful ethical questions. They remember.

But the gnostic patterns hardly end with the traumatic as the mystical.

One of my Harvard female graduate students explains to me in a paper how a Hindu goddess came to possess her genitals, initiating her into a life of poetry, creativity, and devotional ecstasy. She does not understand why postcolonial theorists would want to reduce such an event to a "misappropriation" or "hegemonic theft" of another culture. "How can a woman misappropriate her own vagina?" she asks.

A Western Christian living in Calcutta writes to me about my work on the goddess Kali, with whom he originally came to India to do spiritual battle (along the lines of the then-popular Spiritual Warfare Movement in evangelicalism). Things, however, have not been going quite as planned.

For the past five years, he has intermittently experienced terrifying psychological and spiritual crises as this same goddess takes over his consciousness and body, sending him into ecstatic and devotional moods that turn his whole world upside down as he alternates between states of absolute horror and overwhelming bliss. Such horrific ecstasies would tear him away from his earthly and rational moorings; he often felt like a drifting kite with a broken string. Quite accidentally, he discovered a coping mechanism. Complicated academic studies would almost always bring him "down," back to a rational mode, enabling him to function in the world and fulfill his social duties. This led to an irony of sorts: because of his intensive study habits and choice of reading materials, people began to see him as a cold intellectual, a detached brain devoid of human feelings, lacking in religious affections. No one—not even those closest to him— ever guessed the real dynamics at play. The cycle became established, and it continues to this day: periods of intense mystical experience unhinge him from the earthly realm; when things get too intense, academic study serves to moor him again to the rational and physical world; but inevitably this will again give way to the mystical and ecstatic. Mysticism thus begets knowledge, which then begets new forms of mysticism—in a self-perpetuating and seemingly endless cycle.

We corresponded for months, then years, now almost a decade, becoming close friends in the process (but never actually meeting). Years after his first visit to Calcutta, he returned to a major temple of the goddess to ask her forgiveness for his earlier evangelical Christian hubris. An hour later, at another temple in the nearby cremation ground, he experienced an altered state of consciousness and energy that definitively "married" him to the goddess. He felt the venue to be quite apropos in light of an ancient Hebrew text "[L]ove is strong as death, passion fierce as the grave. Its flashes are flashes of fire, a raging flame" (Song of Songs 8:6). This experience radically altered his perceptions of the social world and of all women, whom he now recognizes as forms of the goddess. Much of this, he claims, was made emotionally possible by his reading of my interpretive work on the homoerotic structure of Christian bridal mysticism and the heteroerotic structure of Hindu Tantric culture.

A man from South Korea writes. When he was sixteen, in 1984, to be exact, he spontaneously entered a state of cosmic consciousness while sitting in the back row of a high school classroom. He was looking out the window, mesmerized by some shimmering sunlight reflecting off the side of a bright white building. Caught by the sight, he found this beauty and joy strangely expanding and growing inside him. And then,

> [s]uddenly, something weird happened to my body. I felt like thousands of hot small worms came into existence inside of me. At first, they appeared near my foot and crawled up my body, making my pleasure bigger and

bigger. As if the dead body of an animal was full of tens of thousands of small maggots without leaving any space, my body was being fully occupied by all these hot and small creeping things. They made me feel that my body was boiling like hot water. In that way, my body was getting hotter and more aroused by the upward creeping of innumerable "energy" worms, and my whole body and mind were filled with even greater pleasure! And when those creeping and crawling things inside reached my whole body, **It** happened! Or more exactly, I exploded into **It**.

He now entered a complete "blank" of consciousness and then emerged on the other side, as it were, into a fuller realization of **It**. "I" as an ego expired, and the cosmic "**I**" now became "infinite and eternal" as space and time became utterly meaningless. He writes explicitly and quite literally of "gnosis" here, as he desperately tries (through the convention of the bold letter) to distinguish his little ego or I from the immense divine **I** with which he was now identified:

> **I** am not created and cannot die or expire. **I** completely know that **I** am absolute. Thus **I** have no need at all, and in that sense **I** am totally satisfying. **I** am everything and at the same time, very paradoxically, nothing. **I** am 'No Thing' at all. **I** am just **I** am. At the same time, **I** am a living energy in great bliss. **I** am so full, so full of living energy, but, paradoxically, **I** am also empty. **I** am moving, but not moved as a whole.

It is crucial to point out that this young man did not ask for such an experience, and that he had neither a cultural frame nor a religious language to understand or explain **It**, even to himself. He was particularly troubled by the moral implications of the state—even though such a cosmic consciousness was fantastically pleasurable, it was also completely beyond all moral considerations. He experienced **It** as dwelling at the deepest core of his own subjectivity. **It** was "him." And yet **It** was also obviously "cool" to all of "his" personal concerns and worries. **It** simply did not care.

For the next fourteen years, he struggled to make some sense of the universe and his life in the brilliant memory of these states, but to no avail. Then, in 1998, he discovered a copy of William James's *The Varieties of Religious Experience* and read its account of something called "mysticism." He recognized immediately that this is what he had been through, that he was hardly crazy, and that William James was articulating his own deepest truths. He recognized, in other words, that William James *knew*. **It** now burst out of him again, and he experienced a conversion of sorts. He remained troubled, however, by how to reconcile this state of cosmic consciousness with the mundane needs of the ego or social self. He now writes often of the "trauma" of these initiatory states. He also writes of how the experience of **It** was hardly his, that he does not own or possess **It** in any way; that, rather, **It** possessed and still possesses him and now wants to speak through his own life. He is now studying in a Ph.D. program in religious studies here in the States in an attempt to articulate this gnosis. Someday he hopes to be the first scholar to translate the Neoplatonic philosopher Plotinus (whose mysticism of the One this man recognizes as a mirror of his own) into Korean. Certainly, he *knows* what he is translating.

A Catholic priest writes about his affirming reading of a selection from my *Roads of Excess* he encountered in a periodical. He had been on a month-long summer retreat during which he felt called to espouse himself to God, prayed with the erotic biblical poetry of the Song of Songs at the advice of his spiritual director, and subsequently experienced a series of spontaneous visionary encounters with Jesus and the love of God that were astonishingly beautiful, deeply loving, and powerfully homoerotic. "Let him kiss me with the kisses of his mouth," he prayed, directly from the biblical text (Song of Songs 1:1). "And He did. I was overcome with the erotic passion of my Beloved. [This was] the first of several such experiences during the retreat. And while my spiritual director affirmed and validated my experiences, I had never heard of anyone else having homoerotic experiences in prayer—until after the retreat, when I read *Roads of Excess*." "*Roads*," he wrote, "was an 'ah ha!' articulation of my experience."

I could go on describing such readers and students for dozens, even hundreds, of pages. Indeed, I have. An earlier draft of this book consisted of hundreds of pages of stories about my students and readers and their remarkable gnostic readings and mystical lives. And my encounters are hardly unique. In a recent study, for example, Jordan Paper estimates that approximately 10 percent of the students who have taken his course on mysticism over the years have had mystical experiences; many, moreover, insist on sharing them with him.[41] Jordan's pedagogical experience, I would guess, is the norm for any teacher who employs both rational and gnostic methods. If we really want to understand how the modern study of religion works, can we afford to ignore such a population? And are such individuals manifesting faith? Or reason? Or gnosis? Such human responses, such *human beings*, have completely obliterated, for me anyway, any final hope of completely separating these epistemological domains.

This is not to suggest, however, that they cannot be separated in different social, institutional, and pedagogical contexts. I still believe that they can and should be. To point out the obvious, my students and readers do not share their secrets with me in the public space of the classroom. They share them in research papers that no one else will read, in arranged or spontaneous office visits, and, most often, in private correspondence. It is important to point out that I have never asked anyone, student or reader, to share anything with me. I do not pry. I do not ask. I do not know why complete strangers write me eight-page letters about their personal lives, but I suspect that they choose to initiate these discussions because I have already shared some of my deepest secrets with them, in print. Vulnerability begets vulnerability, secrets begets secrets, and the result is real insight, real gnosis that is very difficult, but not entirely impossible, to communicate outside these esoteric spaces.

Pedagogically, there are also real distinctions to be made here. C. Mackenzie Brown, for example, has spoken eloquently about the difference between the introductory course and the upper-level course as that between "the classroom of sympathy" and "the classroom of doubt."[42] Brown's distinction is based on the earlier philosophical distinction that Paul Ricoeur made in his study of Freud between a hermeneutics of recollection or trust and a hermeneutics of suspicion.[43] Whereas the former model of interpretation takes religious claims seriously and sympathetically, the latter proceeds on the assumption that all religious claims are not what they claim to be and that, consequently, our best method of study is the method of suspicion and doubt. Brown has adopted Ricoeur's distinction and artfully applied it to the college curriculum. According to this distinction, the primary goal of teaching something like the introductory course on world religions should be a sympathetic representation of the faith traditions more or less as the traditions understand themselves (recognizing, of course, that there is never any single tradition or representation). Not so, however, at the upper level. Here, doubt and suspicion must reign supreme, as the professor and the students learn together how to think critically about anything and everything, including and especially religious claims. In the terms of our present discussion, whereas Brown's classroom of sympathy is a space of faith, his classroom of doubt is one of reason, which is not at all to say that doubt should never enter the introductory classroom or that discussions of faith should be banned from the upper-level course.

This same pedagogical model has major implications for how we read both the religious rejection of the critical study of religion as "blasphemous," "sacrilegious," "offensive," and so on, and the common intellectual rejection of any hermeneutics of trust or existential sympathy as academically illegitimate. Essentially, what is happening on the offended side of things is a rather gross misunderstanding of the nature of the study of religion itself. Such voices are conflating religion and the study of religion. They want the latter to be the former. They want the entire discourse to be dominated by faith, and they want reason, at least any reason that conflicts with their faith, to be banished from both the classroom and the published page. Theirs is *only* a classroom of sympathy. They want nothing to do with the classroom of doubt or a vibrant hermeneutics of suspicion. In their ideal world, there should only be introductory courses. They are, if you will, eternal first-year college students, desperately seeking (in vain) an intellectual blessing for their precritical beliefs.

Seeing such reactionary responses and sensing (quite correctly) the specter of censorship and ideological control here, proponents of reason are understandably concerned that the study of religion will be compromised, if not actually eliminated, by the emotionally powerful (and often extremely well-funded) forces of faith and righteous piety. They thus swing to the opposite extreme and attempt to deny the legitimacy of the classroom of sympathy and the hermeneutics of trust. In their ideal world, there can be *only* the classroom of doubt. They are, if you will, eternal graduate students, desperately trying (in vain) to deny the full scope of the religions, including their aesthetic beauty and their power to transform and liberate.

My own positions are probably obvious by now. Not only do I think that there can and should be both classrooms of sympathy and classrooms of doubt, but I would also point out that these classrooms should (and already are) arranged more or less in a kind of hierarchical fashion that honors something of the insights of both the faith-filled believers and the reason-inspired intellectuals. Having said that, it also needs to be said, and said very clearly, that this remains a real hierarchy, and that this academic hierarchy gives ultimate authority and priority to the intellectuals and to the project of open and free inquiry beyond any and all religious control.

Let us never forget, however, that many gifted individuals are quite capable of deriving reason from faith, and of fusing faith and reason into a deeper gnosis that appears to be much more radical and potentially transformative than any social-scientific or purely rational method. Perhaps, then, we should imagine and enact a third type of classroom alongside the classroom of sympathy and the classroom of doubt. Perhaps we should imagine a new classroom of gnostic epiphany.

Such a luminous space is not "the real world," as frustrated or tired students more than ready to graduate and critics of higher education often point out. They are right, of course. In the real world, one can be killed for being a Muslim or Jew or Hindu, or Christian (inevitably by Christians, Jews, Muslims, or Hindus); in the gnostic classroom, religious identity is respected but never made an absolute marker of humanity or a boundary marker for what can or cannot be said. In the real world, many difficult truths cannot be spoken and even more things, particularly in the realm of religion, cannot be questioned without the fear of reprisal from family, state, or religious authority; in the gnostic classroom, anything can be said and everything can and should be questioned. In the real world, people call for your resignation (or your life) and call you a bitch, a blasphemer, or a threat to the public order when you voice difficult ideas; in the gnostic classroom, the college or university not only further protects your legal right to free speech with the serpent's gift of tenure but actually encourages you to say whatever you think, even and especially if it shakes people up. In the real world, minorities of all kinds are routinely marginalized, oppressed, even killed; in the gnostic classroom, the psychological, social, and religious conditions that make such acts both possible and likely are exposed to the light of reason and analysis. In the real world, it is a depressing, if not actually dangerous, thing to be gay, lesbian, or transsexual; in the gnostic classroom, there are entire disciplines that identify such sexual orientations as uniquely clear windows into literature, art, and religion. In the real world, people act on political and religious convictions that end up wreaking havoc on other human beings; in the gnostic classroom, people are rewarded for being uncertain and for asking questions that cannot be answered with any of the categories, beliefs, or ideas that we have inherited from our pasts. In the real world, the goal is to conform and fit in; in the gnostic classroom, the goal is to provoke, to criticize, and to transgress. In the real world, gnostic truths offend, in the transgressive spaces of the classroom, they excite.

No, such a classroom of gnostic epiphanies is not "the real world" at all. It is much more like a meditative ritual space for some still-unnamed mystical practice striving for a still-unnamed, unimagined freedom. It is our place of gnosis.

The Essays

The four chapter essays that follow are gnostic meditations, thought experiments designed to break what William Blake called the "mind forg'd manacles" of the mind, that is, those restricting assumptions and that systemic failure of imagination that defines the thought of those who can only reason or believe. As such, they constitute a different way of speaking straining to realize itself, an intuitive vision in search of a genre, a *mythos* in search of a *logos*. In terms of actual content, the four essays treat the themes of eroticism, humanism, comparative mysticism, and esotericism, respectively.

It is often claimed, as if this somehow settled the matter, that the critical study of religion is a Western project, and that it was inspired largely, if not entirely, by Christian categories and institutional histories. There is certainly a great deal of truth to this observation; indeed, I suspect it is more true than those who advance such a critique might first imagine. Christianity, after all, contains within itself a very radical critique, even rejection, of religion itself, if we define "religion" as that set of beliefs and social, dietary, and ritual customs inherited from one's family, cultural tradition, or ethnic group. Perhaps, then, it is not surprising at all that the critical study of religion arose within European Christianity and was often advanced most dramatically by secularized Jewish intellectuals, those archetypal "outsiders" of Christian Europe: Christianity and Judaism, after all, were *precisely* the traditions that the various hermeneutics of suspicion were created to suspect.[44] My first two essays demonstrate this deep interlinking of Judaism, Christianity, and the critical study of religion through studies of the erotics of the gospels and gnostic literature and of the radical mystical humanism of the nineteenth-century German Lutheran theologian Ludwig Feuerbach.

The volume leads off with "The Apocryphon of the Beloved." In gnostic literature, an *apocryphon* is a "secret book" or secret teaching usually committed to a trusted disciple by Christ after his resurrection but before he ascends into heaven. It constitutes, in other words, a hidden pedagogical moment of revelatory significance. Taking up just such a moment, I demonstrate here how salient the modern categories of gender, sexual orientation, sexual trauma, and the erotics of mysticism are to understanding the contours of different spiritualities. I do this by examining Jesus's sexuality "from the womb to the tomb" through the paradigmatic works of Theodore Jennings and Jane Schaberg. Jennings explores, for example, the beloved disciple theme in the Gospel of John in order to construct a vision of Jesus as a gender-bending homoerotic wisdom teacher. Schaberg, on the other hand, explores the gnostic understandings of Jesus as a heteroerotic wisdom teacher whose primary apostle was Mary Magdalene, his beloved friend, companion, and disciple whom later Christian tradition under the authority of Peter turned into a repentant whore in order to deny her, and with her all women, apostolic authority and the power to teach. Juxtaposing the homoerotic Jesus of Jennings alongside the heteroerotic Jesus of Schaberg, then, leads us to a kind of gnostic riddle or koan—here an *apocryphon*—in which the identity of the beloved disciple (and hence of Jesus's own love) is rendered historically, textually, and sexually ambiguous.

In chapter 2, "Restoring the Adam of Light," I turn to some of the gnostic contours of modern critical thought. It is striking that the gnostic texts claim repeatedly that the original Adam or Human One knew more and more deeply than the creator-god. The goal of much gnostic ritual and speculation, moreover, was to restore humanity to its unitary source in the Pleroma ("the Full") via what the texts call "the bridal chamber," an initiatory or baptismal rite that may have had actual sexual components. Well before Freud or Nietzsche, Ludwig Feuerbach attempted something similar through a radical reversal of the psychological dynamic of projection. For Feuerbach, religious ideas are human projections that alienate and impoverish us by denying what is best in us and projecting it into the sky. In proposing his projectionist method as a means to get at the "essence of Christianity" and help effect the incarnation of God in humanity, Feuerbach, I suggest here, was essentially proposing a kind of mystical humanism. This second essay takes up these ideas as the historical foundations of later critical thought, particularly as it is found in

Marx, Nietzsche, and Freud, those three critical thinkers whom Paul Ricoeur so beautifully called our "masters of suspicion."

This is not to suggest, however, that the modern study of religion and its specific forms of Gnosticism are restricted to Europe, or that they have not enjoyed other streams of influence and transmission. In historical fact, these same gnostic strands were immeasurably enriched and strengthened through what Raymond Schwab called the Oriental Renaissance, that immense efflorescence of cross-cultural contact between Europe, the Middle East, and Asia that occurred in the seventeenth through the nineteenth centuries and thereby set up the cultural conditions, linked to both European Romanticism and colonialism, that made the comparative study of religion possible at all. These historical encounters, as both Romantic enthusiasms and colonial crimes, display both deeply problematic and profoundly positive dimensions. In chapter 3, "Comparative Mystics," I turn to one of these historical moments, the encounter between Shakta Tantric Hinduism and British colonialism in nineteenth-century Calcutta, and attempt to employ both its Romantic and colonial lessons to think anew about the comparative method as a radical mystical practice (*sadhana*) of universalism, assimilation, and cultural transcendence.

These first three essays, then, constitute a triple meditation on eroticism, humanism, and comparativism, respectively. It is at this point in the text that I stop to take stock within an interlude and its three theses (*logoi mystikoi*), before moving on to a different sort of exercise, that is, a playful application of the first three meditations via a conscious allegory.

Here, more specifically, I am finally concerned about how gnostic intellectuals might best communicate what it is they claim to know to the broader American and global public without falling into the ethical trap of an unnecessary elitism or arrogance. This problem is significantly magnified in the present context for the reasons already enunciated above, namely, the essentially esoteric nature of the gnosis involved and the histories of rejection and censorship that have defined both the historical religious traditions themselves and the contemporary fundamentalist or nationalist rejection of religious studies as blasphemous, imperialist, hegemonic, and so on.

As an imaginative way around this basic epistemological problem, I turn in the fourth and final essay, "Mutant Marvels," to popular and material culture, and in particular to the modern American mythologies of the comic book. Taking up Stan Lee's tale of "The X-Men," of Professor X(avier) and his secret band of extraordinary individuals, or "mutants," as a kind of multidimensional allegory, this chapter probes the interfaces between religious studies scholarship, American popular culture, and possible psychical phenomena. In particular, I point out that the double forms of knowledge that scholars of religion often possess (at once intuitive and rational, mystical and reductive) are unknown, even secret, to the vast majority of Americans, and that the often provocative and subversive implications of such knowledges routinely render scholars suspect, if not actually censorable, in the public eye as cultural or religious mutants. More radically, I suggest that the fantastic superpowers of the comic book heroes are relatively "accurate" exaggerations of erotic, traumatic, psychical, and dissociative phenomena well known to the historian of religions. Finally, I ask how scholars of religion can now face the challenge of communicating their own "mutant" forms of knowledge and consciousness, their own rational gnosis, to an American and global public that may well reject them.

〜〜

If my own hissing sense of the serpent's gift expressed in these four essays is gnostic in any sense for its readers, it need not be so because it represents or mimics a set of subjective experiences that some might wish to label "mystical" or "spiritual." Rather, it might be because the writing's explicit intent is to show that those levels of human experience that first seem separate are in fact intimately related, even united, on some deeper level or hyperdimension. The male and the female, the heteroerotic and the homoerotic, Adam and Eve, the sexual and the spiritual, faith and reason, East and West, sameness and difference, the reader and the author, the premodern and the postmodern, "high" and "low" culture—all of these binarisms collapse in the (post)modern gnosis of the serpent's gift offered here.

In the end, I seek not so much to communicate a rational message (reason) or undergird a particular system of belief (faith) as to transmit a sudden shock (gnosis), rather like what happens when you stumble upon a snake . . . talking to you through the hissing whispers of your own secret mind.

The Apocryphon of the Beloved

The Bible must be shaken upside down before it will yield all its
secrets. The priests have censored and clipped and mangled:
they give us a celibate Jesus born of a virgin without the slightest "stain" of sexual contact, which is blasphemous nonsense.
William Blake (1757–1827)

Not all men can receive this saying, but only those to whom it
is given. *Jesus on the eunuch saying in Matthew 19:11*

Invocation

In gnostic literature, an *apocryphon* (literally, a "hiding away" or "concealing") is a secret teaching usually committed to a trusted disciple by Christ
after his resurrection but before he ascends into heaven.[1] It is, in other
words, a hidden pedagogical moment of deep revelatory significance. The
word is also related to what is often called the apocryphal literature, a class
of ancient religious texts that did not always make it into the canons of the
Jewish and Christian scriptures but that are nevertheless considered important for the development of both—a kind of "scriptural shadow," hov-
ering between the two traditions. By calling my reflections here an *apocryphon*, I intend to evoke all of these meanings—hidden, secret, personal,
revelatory, not quite "right" or "straight" (*ortho-dox*), maybe even a bit
queer.[2] I also offer what follows as a distinctly "mystical" text in the ancient hermeneutical sense of that adjective, that is, as a radical technique
of interpretation that reflects the altered states of theory and reveals via
the labor of human learning some of the deepest and most transformative
meanings of the texts, meanings that often go directly against the assumed "obvious," commonsense, or literal readings that have more or less
captured the conservative ideologies of contemporary Christianity.

Let me be very clear, then: the goal of this *apocryphon* is not yet another "historical Jesus" who can ground a public faith or who meets all the requirements of historical reason. Other scholars, far more qualified than this one, have met that task for us. This is different. What I am after here resembles more a kind of historical koan (a nonsensical riddle Zen masters use to cognitively shock—or shut down—their students into sudden bursts of enlightenment), an intentionally paradoxical picture, a free act of imagination, an openly "heretical Jesus" who can provoke new thought, self-reflection, and revelation, not in the first- or second-century Mediterranean world, but here in America *in us*. In the end, what I am after is a kind of sexualized gnosis, *an erotics of the Gospel* that can meet and learn from, on a very deep transgressive level, the erotic mysticisms of other climes and times, particularly the Tantric traditions of South Asia, the Himalayas, and China. I hiss and write, then, through a specific Tantric *imaginaire*, but one that is in the background here, seldom making it onto the page, usually secreted in the endnotes, but nevertheless fundamentally, *gnostically*, informing how I think, read, and write.[3] The Gospel read and revealed through the Tantra, if you will.

But this is not just a (post)modern *apocryphon*. It is also an *apocryphon of the Beloved*. Most simply put, my topic here is love: love expressed and celebrated, love censored and allegorized away by the orthodox, love restored and healed through the serpent's gift of scholarship, love finally transmuted and gnostically realized as divine. And why not? Ideally speaking, Christianity is a religion of love. "God is love," John tells us in one of his famous brief letters preserved for us in the New Testament (1 John 4:16). But what kind of love? And, more to my present interests, how is this love related to human sexuality and, more specifically, to Jesus's sexuality? The Gospel of John speaks rather teasingly of "the beloved disciple whom Jesus loved" (ho mathetes hon egapa ho Iesous) (John 13:23, 19:26, 20:2, 20). But who was this Beloved; that is, what sort of person was the object of Jesus's most intimate and quite public love? The canonical gospels are not at all clear about this; indeed, the Gospel of John, although quite clear that Jesus had a lover, goes out of its way *not* to tell us the identity of the Beloved. This loud silence, as we shall see, is itself highly significant. Bisexual confusion, gender ambiguity, and erotic paradox are themselves a kind of answer to our riddle, to our own Apocryphon of the Beloved.

The Quest for the Heretical Jesus

Biblical critics have often made a distinction between the historical Jesus and the Christ of faith, perhaps a kind of modern secular echo of the ancient gnostic distinction between the true Godhead and the lesser creator-god or demiurge. I invoke this strategy again here, not to arrive at

historical certainty about what Jesus did or did not do (or, even more spec-
ulatively, about what Jesus did or did not feel), but rather to posit a broad
structural theory about the orientations—at once spiritual and sexual—
of early (and contemporary) Christian memory and imagination. Through
such a rhetorical strategy, I seek to isolate a series of tensions or paradoxes and, through them, transmit an erotic energy and effect a shift in
consciousness.

This erotic shift in consciousness, I would suggest, is already implicit,
if seldom made fully conscious, in the collective work of the academy,
which often functions very much like a contentious, riven, but truly
knowing gnostic community. Seen in this imagined light, certain strands
of New Testament scholarship can be read as constituting an esoteric
vision of Jesus that departs so dramatically from that set of public or
exoteric images that have come down to us in the conservative churches
that we might be led to see the present Christian moral debates involving
such topics as homosexuality, gay marriage, and "family values" as terribly cruel and deeply ironic charades that deserve both our wildest tears
and our most mocking, knowing laughter. If ever there was a reason for the
gnostically inclined, for those who prefer personal knowledge over official
belief, to believe that the world is ruled by a stupid and sadistic archon or
ruler, this is it, and if there were ever a case to be made for the radical,
essentially heretical nature of religious studies, it is here. The quest for the
historical Jesus is finally better named the quest for the heretical Jesus, not
because history is false and heresy is true, but because writing history is
always quite literally "heretical," that is, a deeply personal choice (*hairesis*)
or series of choices that one makes out of one's own deepest convictions,
disciplined study, and still-inarticulate intuitions, regardless of whether
these conform to orthodoxy and religious authority. Often, of course, they
do not.

"One Will Know Them by Their Roots"

William E. Phipps, who has done as much as anyone to explore the question at hand,[4] has written that there is much confusion surrounding
Jesus's sexuality "from the womb to the tomb."[5] That is certainly correct,
but it is also something of an understatement. We will address both the
womb and the tomb in due time, but before we do, it is important to point
out that the problem of Jesus's sexuality appears even earlier than the
proverbial and literal womb, that is, in his alleged ancestors who lived
hundreds of years before he was conceived.

The Gospel of Matthew is the first book of the New Testament. The first
chapter (Matt. 1:1–17) of this first book consists of Jesus's "family tree."
This family tree contains four, and only four, women: Tamar, Rahab, Ruth,
and Bathsheba. Provocatively, three of these foremothers possess marginal

or anomalous sexual characteristics that would have been obvious to any educated first-century Jewish reader (and scholars are in broad agreement that Matthew was writing for a Jewish audience). The fourth woman's life, moreover, can be read in an equally provocative fashion with little effort.

Tamar was the daughter-in-law of Judah, one of the early patriarchs of Genesis (Gen. 38:6–30). After her first husband, Er, was killed by God for some unspecified crime and her second husband, Onan (Er's younger brother), was killed by the same God for spilling his semen on the ground in a refusal to honor the Hebrew custom of producing an heir for one's elder dead brother,[6] Tamar found herself denied the third brother in line by her father-in-law. Apparently, Judah was not about to lose a third precious son to this woman and the mysterious happenings that swirled around her. But Judah's bloodline was rightfully and legally Tamar's, Judah was wrong to deny it to her, and Tamar would not be frustrated. She thus resorted to a sexual ruse to acquire the seed that was hers by divine law. Dressed up as a prostitute at the front gate, she seduced the patriarch himself and became pregnant. Once she began to show, however, Judah, still unaware of whose seed she carried, demanded the extraordinary punishment of having her (and of course the unborn baby) burned alive,[7] until he discovered that the seed in her womb was in fact his (that is, until he discovered that the child would not threaten the family inheritance). Tamar carried to term and had twin sons, a double boon in Hebrew culture and clearly a divine reward for her sexual courage and cleverness. Despite the fact that this remarkable story involves deception, prostitution, and incest, the author(s) of Genesis portrays Tamar as a heroine, as a clever, brave woman who kept the line of Judah going through a sexual ruse. Although never made explicit, the moral of the story for Matthew is clear enough: no incest, no line, no Jesus.

As for Rahab, she didn't play the prostitute; she really *was* a prostitute. Rahab was the Canaanite prostitute who saved her family from certain death by helping the Hebrew army conquer Jericho by conspiring with the Hebrew spies (Josh. 2:1–21, 6:22–25).

"The wife of Uriah" (the expression is probably intended to accentuate the scandal of David's sexual intercourse with her) was the beautiful Bathsheba, whose husband (Uriah) king David arranged to have killed in battle so that he could have her for himself. Actually, at the time of the murder, king David had already impregnated Bathseba, whose lovely naked body he had first seen while she bathed on a rooftop unsuspectingly before the horny royal voyeur (2 Sam. 11). What began as a lustful gaze thus led to sexual intercourse, pregnancy, and a premeditated murder, all of which again was quite necessary for this strange sexual line of Jesus the Christ.

Ruth is the only one of the four who is not clearly involved in a sexual scandal. But Ruth was a Moabite, a foreigner, and for Deuteronomy 23:3, all descendants of Moabites are cut off "even to the tenth generation."

This, as Theodore Jennings points out, would include king David, a third-generation descendent of the Moabite Ruth and the Hebrew Boaz. It is also possible, as Jennings points out again, that Matthew may have seen something (homo)sexual in Ruth's relationship to Naomi. Certainly many modern readers have.[8] Then there was Ruth's sexually aggressive style. As William Countryman points out, "she initiated sexual relations with Boaz by uncovering his 'feet' (euphemism for genitals)[9] at the harvest celebration, well before she could be understood properly to belong to him (Ruth 3)."[10] Other scholars have seen here a "midnight striptease," a playful night of "under-cover and cover-over" operations, that is, a night of passionate sex, Hebrew "footsie" and all (which was way more than footsie).[11]

Now what is particularly important for our present purposes is that this sexually anomalous lineage is outlined in the very first chapter of the very first book of the New Testament. Thus, the moment a reader opens the page to this remarkable collection of documents, one is caught immediately in a series of sexual violations and serious moral questions, whether this is recognized or not (and, of course, it is usually not).

Clearly, things are not at all what they seem. Without quite clearly saying so, the author of Matthew is trying his best to prepare his readers for what amounts to a long series of sexual transgressions, often outrageous violations of the Law, offensive, intentionally confusing parables, and some radical teachings about healing, love, and compassion. That is, he is readying his readers for the life and teachings of Jesus.

From the Womb . . .

Nowhere is this general scandal more apparent than in the sexual nature of Jesus's conception and birth, that is, the "from the womb" of Phipps's apt expression. The traditional reading, of course, is that the conception of Jesus was "virginal," that is, without original sin and without sexual mediation (the doctrine implies, without quite stating it, that sin and sex are more or less the same thing). In other words, Mary was a virgin, even a perpetual virgin, if we are to believe the Catholic tradition and its exceptionally dubious reading of those New Testament passages that so clearly state that Jesus had siblings (e.g., Mark 6:3; Luke 8:19–21).[12] But the texts, it turns out, are far more ambiguous and rich than this. For one thing, the story of Jesus's conception and birth, so seemingly well known through the Christmas conflation of Matthew and Luke (the two texts actually contradict each other on a number of important points) and any number of pious additions, is in fact only told in Matthew and Luke. Mark, the earliest gospel, and John, the latest, know absolutely nothing of a virginal conception or a Christmas story of any kind (nor, by the way, does Paul). The stories of Mark and John really begin with Jesus's baptism under John the Baptist, whose community was clearly in competition with that of Jesus;

hence the jockeying for superiority we see in these stories—who baptizes whom and what each says to the other.

Moreover, and most provocatively, Matthew at least is clear that Joseph was not Jesus's biological father (although his genealogy traces Jesus's lineage through Joseph's line, thus effectively separating legal and biological fatherhood). In Matthew, Joseph is about to divorce a very young and pregnant Mary (most commentators put her somewhere between thirteen and sixteen) and thus expose her to a very possible stoning when an angel appears to him in a dream and tells Joseph to keep both her and the child of her womb. Contrary to what is often believed, the famous angelic description of Jesus to Joseph (Matt. 1:20) as conceived "of a spirit that is holy" (ek pneumatos estin hagiou) or "by the Holy Spirit" signals a divine begetting that need not exclude the sexual participation of an actual human father, as some of the older Jewish traditions (such as the one claiming divine and human fatherhood for the Davidic King) also make clear.[13] All that seems to be required by this phrase is that, whoever the actual father is, God also has a hand in this pregnancy—it is thus "of the Holy Spirit," that is, "divine." It is in this same context of biblical biological common sense that the Gospel of Philip will later ridicule the bizarre notion that Jesus had no human father.[14]

Matthew's angel come to speak of sex (and God's intimate role in it) appears differently again when he is properly placed within the erotics of the ancient Near Eastern religious imagination. Such an *imaginaire* is evident early in texts like Genesis 6:1–4, in which the horny "sons of God" seek out and have sex with the "daughters of men" in order to produce the *nephilim*, a hybrid race of divine-human beings. A much richer angelic erotics appears in the later gnostic texts, which developed a whole host of elaborate, gender-bending angelologies in which human sexual intercourse was understood to be guided and even actually *shared* by angelic presences, twins, and powers of various genders and natures. The mystical and the erotic fuse often in the figure of the ancient angel.

So too does violence. From the first chapters of Genesis to the last lines of the Book of Revelation, the figure of the biblical angel is dominated by hypermasculine messengers and warrior figures who come to protect, announce vengeance, or actually wreak death and destruction. Interestingly, Matthew's angel comes rather to console and protect an unmarried pregnant teenager from the violence of orthodoxy and the righteousness of the religious law. She certainly needed him. As Jane Schaberg has convincingly suggested, the early story of Mary's virginity is most likely a later "spin" on what was originally a narrative of dangerous illegitimacy for which the religious law called for her death. It bears repeating. Joseph was not Jesus's father, but someone else was. Whether this was through a consensual and loving union, a seduction, or a rape—all three are quite possible, although Mary's vulnerable age perhaps makes the second two scenarios more likely—we simply do not know. All that we do know, if we are to believe these two gospels, is that the biological father of Jesus was not the man who married Mary and so became her legal protector.

If the scenario of Matthew and Luke translated here out of its mythological frame with the tools of historical criticism is even approximately correct, then Jesus began his life and lived his entire childhood and adolescence under the shadow of a public secret and a well-known scandal, the scandal of his own illegitimate conception and birth.[15] And an angel hovered around and within both the sex and the scandal.

Sexual Healings: Dispelling the Demons of Abuse

Little wonder, then, that later in life Jesus would display such concern and compassion for those whose sexual and familial situations, like his own, rendered them impure, polluted, and well outside the respectability of the Torah or Law, that all-encompassing framework of purity codes and temple rituals that so profoundly shaped the first-century Jewish experience of the world, the body, and the divine.

Perhaps no one has analyzed this feature of Jesus's scandalous compassion more provocatively than the New Testament critic and scholar of gnosticism Stevan Davies. I wish to highlight Davies's academic gnosis here not because I think it is infallible or beyond criticism, but because its bold forms of speculation dramatically display two of the central features of the serpent's gift I am hissing here: that is, it is explicitly *comparative* in its insistence on placing Jesus's healing ministry in the broader context of the anthropology of healing and possession; and it focuses as much on the psychological category of *experience* as it does on the history, philology, and structure of the texts. Davies, in other words, knows that the Christian scriptures, canonical and gnostic alike, record and mythologize a set of real mystical experiences that can be compared to similar altered states recorded and mythologized in other religious systems.

More specifically, Davies has demonstrated that Jesus's healing ministry can be read fruitfully with the insights of anthropological research on possession cults in colonial peasant societies as a ministry of trance that sought to heal the possessed by removing them from the abusive hierarchies of the patriarchal family (with women and children, and especially female children, all understood to be the rightful property of the patriarch or father)[16] and reestablishing them within a new, imagined family of equals with a single Father in heaven. Put simply, "the family" and particularly "the father" function in the possession and healing scenes and in some of Jesus's core teachings as social fictions that are essentially abusive; hence his otherwise inexplicable teaching that his followers should "call no man your father on the earth, for you have one Father, who is in heaven" (Matt. 23:9).

Previous scholars have missed much, Davies argues, because they have tended to reject the healing scenes as pious fantasy instead of reading them as more or less accurate memories of actual historical events. This is not to say that the healing scenes were of supernatural origin. "*A supernatural event can be a historical event with a supernatural explanation attached to it,*"[17] Davies argues. With this simple methodological principle (what we will later invoke as a form of *super naturalism* or *radical empiricism*),[18] a powerfully comparative grasp of the anthropological literature on possession cults and healers from around the world (especially India), and a working knowledge of modern psychiatry and psychoanalytic theory, Davies can advance his central thesis: "The idea that Jesus was the embodiment of the spirit of God arose not from pious belief alone but from a series of historical events: repeated occurrences of alterations in ego identity, to be classified anthropologically as possession-trance. This set of historical events received a supernatural explanation during his lifetime: that Jesus was possessed by the spirit of God."[19]

Jesus, in other words, appears to have experienced altered states of consciousness that we are very familiar with from other cultures and times.[20] His followers naturally interpreted these in their own cultural terms, that is, as evidence that Jesus was possessed by the spirit of God and, later, that he *was* the spirit of God. Within this perspective, then, the theology and mythology that Jesus was the Son of God developed organically out of a series of very real mystical states and their dramatically charismatic effects on those who witnessed and participated in them as those states arose from their own psychological constitutions and tendencies. Davies thus performs the key theoretical move of the kind of rational-gnostic method I am calling for here: he at once *affirms* the psychological reality of altered states of consciousness and energy as a genetic potential of all human beings[21] (thus Jesus is special, but by no means unique) and reduces or, better, *returns* the altered state of possession back to us as something understandable, even predictable. The mystical and the rational thus become two movements within a single gnostic dialectic.

There is also a real social critique here. Possession trances, after all, tend to happen in groups, usually groups structured along rigid hierarchical lines that demand the extensive suppression of sexual and aggressive drives. Seldom do happy, unconflicted individuals go into dramatic possession states in solitude.[22] Rather, they act out their aggressive and sexual frustrations—interpreted as "demonic"—in front of the very family and social actors who have frustrated or abused them so, and this in a symbolic code that the actors and culture will not find directly challenging ("It's a demon speaking, not my pissed-off wife or abused daughter"). Possession, in other words, is a kind of safety-valve mechanism that cultures use to "let off some steam."

It is also a kind of convenient lie. There are in fact no objectively real "demons" here, just abusive men and some fantastically furious women and children with no other culturally available means to express themselves. Wives and children seem to be the most prone to such states, as they are almost always the most disempowered within the social scale of power and authority. Davies's conclusion is both simple and powerful: "Jesus's clientele who came (or were brought) for exorcism were probably, more than anything else, victims of abusive family relationships."[23] This help explains the biblical fact that Jesus counseled his disciples to hate and leave their families. Certainly, it would do no good to be healed from the trauma of physical or sexual abuse by a charismatic healer and then move back in with the violent father or dysfunctional family. Hence the *real* "family values" of Jesus, that fatherless, unmarried man who encouraged his followers to abandon their families for his new, imagined family of equals and, above all, no fathers: "If any one comes to me and does not hate his own father and mother and wife and children and brothers and sisters, yes, and even his own life, he cannot be my disciple" (Luke 14:26; cf. Gospel of Thomas 55). "He who loves father or mother more than me is not worthy of me: and he that loves son or daughter more than me is not worthy of me" (Matt. 10:37).

Also behind such passages is the social reality of the early churches, whose cultish demands on their followers were essentially breaking up families: "Do you think that I have come to give peace on earth? No, I tell you, but rather division; for henceforth in one house there will be five divided, three against two and two against three; they will be divided, father against son and son against father, mother against daughter and daughter against her mother, mother-in-law against her daughter-in-law and daughter-in-law against her mother-in-law" (Luke 12:51–53). Jesus models this rejection of the natural family by ignoring his own: "And he was told, 'Your mother and your brothers are standing outside, desiring to see you.' But he said to them, 'My mother and my brothers are those who hear the word of God and do it'" (Luke 8:19–21; cf. Gospel of Thomas 99; Matt. 12:46–50; Mark 3:31–35).

This same abusive family context explains why many of the possessed individuals Jesus healed suffered from disorders that we now understand to be psychosomatic in nature. As Davies points out, many of the symptoms that Jesus is recorded as healing (loss of voice, deafness, blindness, paralysis, muscle weakness, and excessive menstrual bleeding) are classified as "conversion disorders" in modern psychoanalytic theory; that is, they are symptoms ("conversions," or symbolic signs) of deeper psychological problems often involving guilt that is not accepted and so is interiorized and expressed through symbolic self-punishment. Demonic possession is essentially a radical version of this same conversion process, here to the point at which the symbolic symptom is converted into an alternate personality that literally takes over the functioning of the suffering human being in order to more dramatically punish the person and, no doubt just as important, his or her abusive family members.

Davies notes that it is likely that those who stayed with Jesus were those that came to him to be healed, that is, that demon possession has something important to tell us about Jesus's closest associates as well. It is extremely unlikely, for example, that Jesus could simply "call" a random individual, and that he or she would immediately abandon family and home to follow him—unless, of course, that family and home were the cause of his or her original suffering and this domestic abandonment the necessary condition of being healed. This, it seems, was precisely Jesus's method. He did not work with the families to restructure them as, say, a modern family therapist might. He called the suffering possessed *out of* their families and into a new family with only one perfect father, God himself: "To another he said, 'Follow me.' But he said, 'Lord, let me first go and bury my father' [that is, let me wait until my elderly father dies and I am free to leave]. But he said to him, 'Leave the dead to bury their own dead; but as for you, go and proclaim the kingdom of God.' Another said, 'I will follow you, Lord; but let me first say farewell to those at my home.' Jesus said to him, 'No one who puts his hand to the plow and looks back is fit for the kingdom of God'" (Luke 9:59–62). Jesus's command to "hate" one's family, then, is not so much a general command to hate as an approval and act of affirmation for those who *already* hated their families.[24] The sayings, in other words, were not universal commands, but advice given to specific individuals at very specific times. And they make perfect sense as compassionate responses to radical human suffering caused by the patriarchal family.[25]

The psychological or social reductionist must be very careful here, however. And as a good modern gnostic, Davies is very careful indeed. He does not, for example, argue any simple "nothing but"; that is, he does not argue that the possession states can be exhaustively reduced to the reality dimension of the socialized ego state. What Jesus called "the kingdom of God," for example, Davies, following the gnostic lineage of Freud,[26] interprets as a psychological experience, as a dissociative trance state that has the capacity to heal and reintegrate the individual into a new family and a new sociocosmic existence. "The kingdom of God is within you," Jesus says in the Gospel of Thomas. And indeed it is, or, in modern psychological parlance, we can understand the kingdom "to entail glimpses into or, rather, differential access to, creative powers of an individual's own unconscious functioning."[27]

Davies might seem to be replacing the later theological explanation of who Jesus was and what he taught (the literal Son of God and some sort of postmortem state of salvation) with a psychological explanation (Jesus was possessed by unconscious forces that he and his culture interpreted as coming from God), and in some sense this is perfectly true. Reason and reductionism have indeed overtaken faith and its literalisms here. But gnosis returns in the form of a crucial dialectical observation, namely, that the stable "reality" of the human person, of what we call, again following Freud, the ego, is hardly beyond doubt. In fact, the final reality of the states of consciousness and energy represented by both the possessing spirit and the possessed person is a matter of philosophical preference. Neither can be easily established as permanent or unproblematic entities. Thus, "[t]his whole line of thought leads to a historical Jesus who not only claimed to be the Son of God, but who really was the Son of God (depending on the philosophical perspective one takes toward the reality of an alter-persona)."[28]

Davies, in other words, understands perfectly well that the socially constructed ego—and with it, *all* social and political methods of analysis—need not, and probably does not, encompass the full range of human being and experience. Something more is thus needed to understand the empirical realities of possession, trance, and healing in the history of religions. That something more is gnosis.

Sexual Teachings

Jesus's healing ministry, then, can be read as both a product of and a response to dissociative trance states that were often probably connected to abusive families and gave psychological access to altered states of consciousness and healing energy. Perhaps this is one reason Jesus counseled his closest disciples to "become eunuchs" for the kingdom of heaven, that is, to castrate themselves and so cease to reproduce the abusive patriarchal family: "Not all men can receive this saying, but only those to whom it is given. For there are eunuchs who have been so from birth, and there are eunuchs who have been made eunuchs by men, and there are eunuchs who have made themselves eunuchs for the sake of the kingdom of heaven. He who is able to receive this, let him receive it" (Matt. 19:11–12) This, of course, is the locus classicus for the practice of Christian celibacy. It is not a minor passage; indeed, it is absolutely central to the entire history of Christian celibacy, not to mention the institutional structure and teaching authority of the Roman Catholic Church. Understandably, it has also been the object of intense bowdlerization, allegorization, and simple denial, as if "becoming a eunuch" and "being chaste" were the same thing. They are not, of course. What, then, might have this *logos mystikos*, this mystical saying, meant when it was first uttered by Jesus? The most likely answer to this question, it turns out, throws a rather brilliant, perhaps *too* bright light not only on the transgressive intentions and possible psychosexuality of Jesus, but also on our own modern moral debates surrounding homosexuality and the sexual-religious crises involving clerical celibacy and the "gay priest."

We know, for example, that eunuchs were often central to the administration of ancient kingdoms, and that they were richly rewarded for their services. They certainly made ideal administrators, primarily because they could produce no children to advance their own dynastic ambitions. Hence, Jesus's use of the figure fits in nicely (if quite mischievously) with his central metaphor of "the kingdom of heaven" or "the kingdom of God": kingdoms need eunuchs to run efficiently. We also know that castration was condemned by Jewish law (Deut. 23:1–2; Lev. 21:20, 22:24), and that, although there are a few passages in both the Hebrew scriptures (Isa. 56:4–5) and the New Testament (Acts 8:26–40) that suggest a more positive view, eunuchs were generally despised by pious Jews as deformed, impure, unholy, that is, as not whole.

We also know that young boys were castrated (or had their testicles crushed) to preserve or at least extend their youthful beardless beauty and render them especially apt objects of homosexual or pederastic desire (an accepted and sometimes idealized norm in the Hellenistic and Roman worlds), and that this "feminization" made them, at least in the popular mind, particularly appropriate for "passive" or "feminine" sexual inclinations. *Eunuch* could thus function as a virtual synonym in Greek and Roman culture for any male who preferred passive homosexual sex. Indeed, the conflation of eunuch and passive homosexual goes back at least as far as Assyrian law (1300–1100 BCE), and probably much earlier.[29] Eunuchs, moreover, were also well known as male prostitutes, and their sexual prowess was often legendary. Contrary to popular belief, castration (which removes only the testicles) did not necessarily prevent them from sexual activity. Rather, it rendered them conveniently infertile and so "safe" sexual partners. Thus, as Gary Taylor observes, "[e]unuchs are in fact not impotent, but powerful; they are often sexually active, and capable of erections; castration does not so much suppress eros as redirect and in some ways liberate it."[30]

There are actually three different classes of spiritually potent eunuchs listed in Jesus's saying: those born that way, those made so by men, and those who make themselves so. All three categories, it turns out, find very plausible examples in Jesus's first-century world. Those born so, Jennings speculates, could describe either hermaphrodites (those born with both male and female genitals, almost always partially formed) or men with an exclusive preference for passive same-sex activity. Those made so by other men describe quite well administrative or prostitution professionals. Those who make themselves so aptly describe such religious enthusiasts as the famous *galli*, a troupe of men dedicated to the goddess Cybele who castrated themselves in a kind of ecstatic frenzy and who were know for their sexual passions.[31] In short, in Jennings's words now, this saying of Jesus "is scandalous, linking together hermaphrodites or persons who engaged exclusively in same-sex practices, men castrated for purposes of prostitution, and persons who castrated themselves in religious frenzy."[32]

Beyond the obvious intent to provoke, scandalize, and generally infuriate the pious, Jesus was also most likely hinting at the homoerotic dynamics of "the kingdom of heaven." The figure of the eunuch as model and exemplar of this kingdom certainly suggests as much, as does the historical rarity of a truly heterosexual mysticism.[33] Put simply, the men who could receive such a teaching, who "had ears to hear," were those whom we would today call gay, and those who could not receive such a teaching were those whom we would today call straight. Sexual orientation, in other words, determined the hierarchy of Jesus's kingdom of heaven, and it was the gay man, not the heterosexual married man, who was clearly privileged by Jesus. This is certainly an imperfect and anachronistic way to gloss such a saying, but it is hardly, I think, an inaccurate way.

Other than the homoerotic, Jesus probably also had in mind an ideal of *nonreproduction*.[34] Certainly he called the barren woman "blessed" (Luke 23:29) and insisted that there was no marriage in the resurrection (Matt. 22:30; Mark 12:25; Luke 20:35–36), and we have already noted how he encouraged his listeners to hate their families. It is thus probably no accident that the long ancestral line with which the New Testament begins effectively *ends* with Jesus, who produces no heir, who fathers no children—that is, who dies childless. To preach and live such a rejection of sexual reproduction, however, is by no means to renounce sexuality. Hence Jesus's glorification of the despised eunuch, whose sexual activity, whether with males or females, is entirely nonreproductive. "Not all men can receive this saying, but only those to whom it is given." That is putting it mildly.

Such a reading certainly fits well into other gospel representations of Jesus's person and teachings, particularly those portraying his attitude to the religious laws that regulated acceptable sexual activity, that is, the holiness code of Leviticus and the Torah in general. It is certainly true that the gospels portray Jesus honoring particular traditions and purity codes. The gospel texts are clearly uneasy syntheses of both traditionalist and radical tendencies.[35] Still, it is very difficult to read the gospels as a whole and not come away with a distinct impression that this man tried his best to offend the religious authorities, violate the Law, and scandalize the pious. And it is more than obvious that he did not hesitate to ignore the purity codes that were—and are to this day—used to demean or even condemn everything from menstruation to same-sex activity. William Countryman's conclusion seems inescapable: "the Gospels dismiss purity, not selectively, but across the board. They do not isolate some one aspect of it (food laws) for repudiation while tacitly retaining other aspects (leprosy, say, or circumcision, or sex). It is physical purity as such, in all its ramifications, that they set aside."[36]

Hence, such a setting aside runs right through both Jesus's teaching and his early communities, determining the most basic meanings and central rituals of early Christianity. This was a man, after all, whose first reported miracle in John was turning large vats of water into delicious wine for an already drinking (and probably drunk) wedding party (John 2). This was also a man who was described by his contemporaries as both "a glutton and a drunkard" (Luke 7:34), who violated the Sabbath, and who socialized and ate with sinners, tax collectors, and loose women (Matt. 5:30; Mark 2:16).

And this is only the beginning. Numerous scholars have made similar points, but Jennings's summary of a particularly offending gospel, the Gospel of John (which also happens to be the most mystical and homo-erotic of the gospels), can serve us best here for its eloquence and relative brevity:

> Jesus is portrayed as disregarding the commandment regarding the Sab-bath, the commandment generally viewed as definitive of Judaism (5:9–10, 16; 7:23; 9:14). . . . [The] water he turns to wine in chapter 2 is water that is rit-ually impure since it had been used to wash the hands and feet of the party guests. His discussion with Nicodemus in chapter 3 associates the new life with birth, a process that renders the woman ritually impure. He breaks the taboo on association with the Samaritans in chapter 4. He speaks quite provocatively about eating his flesh—flouting another taboo—(5:51) and compounds this by speaking of not only eating his flesh but also of drinking his blood (5:53–58). The consumption even of animal blood was considered prohibited, and any contact with human blood rendered one ritually im-pure. The author(s) of the Gospel seem to have deliberately sought to select "impure" symbols for the activity of Jesus. . . . None of this should be too sur-prising within a community that asserts that an executed man (the height of impurity) is the Messiah, the Christ, the Son of God.[37]

This is not to suggest that Jesus can be read as a kind of modern liberal intellectual or social prophet of sexual freedom. He cannot be, as other passages, such as the one on cutting off the hand or plucking out the eye that "offends" (almost certainly cultural allusions to manual masturba-tion and the lustful gaze), make quite clear (Matt. 27:30). Still, Jesus's gen-eral attitude toward the Law, its purity codes, its sexual regulations, and piety in general is "one of insistent, persistent subversion. From the very beginning, Jesus's intention seems to be to drive the representatives of conventional piety crazy."[38]

This is a crucial point to keep in mind as we proceed now to the topic of whom Jesus loved, that is, to the Beloved, for we should not expect this love, whatever its direction and nature, to follow the paths of purity and religious appropriateness. After all, little else about the man did. Indeed, I would go so far as to suggest that we might best explain Jesus's systematic subversion of his culture's purity codes as an apt expression and required function of the deepest nature and movements of his desire for the Beloved. The psychological roots of both Jesus's radical subversion and transgression of the Law and his teachings on love, in other words, are fundamentally related to his psychosexuality. The latter psychosexuality helps explain, indeed requires, the former breaking of the religious Law. Put most simply, *love must obviate the Law because Jesus's love could not be fitted into the Law.*

The Man Jesus Loved

Although such a thesis was foreshadowed, sublimated, suggested, historicized, and theologized in authors ranging from the medieval monastic writers Bernard of Clairvaux and Aelred of Rievaulx,[39] the English Renaissance poet and dramatist Christopher Marlowe,[40] the nineteenth-century British philosopher Jeremy Bentham,[41] and the psychoanalyst Georg Walther Groddeck[42] to the biblical critic and "magician" Morton Smith,[43] the historian John Boswell,[44] the British canon Hugh Montefiore,[45] and Catholic theologians Robert Goss[46] and Mark Jordan,[47] it is the contemporary biblical critic Theodore Jennings who has most effectively advanced the idea that the gospels preserve multiple traces of a certain dangerous memory, the memory of Jesus as a lover of other men.

Such a love, for example, is particularly evident in those passages that reveal a Jesus accepting and concerned about same-sex love, if not physically expressing it through subtle looks and body postures. The young rich man whom Jesus gazes at (*emblepein*) lovingly (Mark 10:17–22), the beloved disciple who lies on Jesus's breast, basically sitting in his lap, during the passion narrative in John (John 13:21–26), the healing of the Roman centurion's servant boy and likely lover (male slaves were often used as homosexual lovers) (Matt. 8:5–13),[48] and the idealization of the eunuch as model for the kingdom of heaven all come immediately to mind.[49] Indeed, as Dale Martin points out, there is only *one* place in all four gospels where Jesus is said to "love" a woman (John 11:5), and even there it is a group, not an individual, he is said to love (Martha, her sister, and Lazarus). "Jesus' attraction to specific men, on the other hand, is explicit." There are in fact many of what Martin calls "sites of the sensual" in the gospels, but they *always* involve men, not women (and usually, Martin points out, they occur in that most homoerotic of the gospels, John). So, for example, whereas Thomas is invited, in Martin's gloss now, "to penetrate the holes in Jesus' body (John 20:24ff)," "[i]n contrast, when Mary wants a hug, Jesus won't let her even touch him (John 20:17)." The latter scene, Martin speculates, is "the Gospel version of Paul's homoerotic slogan, 'It is better for a man not to touch a woman' (1 Corinthians 7:1)."[50]

It is in this same homoerotic context that we should perhaps read the Johannine expression "the disciple whom Jesus loved" (ho mathetes hon egapa ho Iesous). The Greek expression, after all, carries with it some rather clear, if also somewhat sublimated, erotic connotations. Foremost

among these are the Greek sexual conventions, based on standard pederastic models, of the active older "lover" (*erastes*) and the younger passive
"beloved" (*eromenos*), who is the feminized recipient of the older male
lover's masculine advances. The Johannine beloved disciple trope, in other
words, recalls the *eromenos*, or "beloved," of Greek sexual conventions and,
in the process, suggests that Jesus was the older *erastes* of the beloved
disciple as younger *eromenos*.

This "open secret" has been muted or missed, if not actually censored,
by a very traditional but fantastically false assumption that the Greek
noun *agape* (the nominal form of the Johannine verb *egapa*) connotes only
a "pure" or "spiritual" love, as opposed to the lustful meanings of the
Greek *eros*.[51] Despite the lush eroticism of the Hebrew Bible, much of it
structured around an all-defining homoeroticism between Yahweh as
kingly *erastes* and Israel as beloved but often whoring *eromenos*,[52] and despite the open sexual discussions of the New Testament texts, neither the
Greek Septuagint (the Greek translation of the Hebrew scriptures) nor the
New Testament ever use the Greek *eros* for "love," even when they are describing clearly sexual acts or illicit erotic desires. Rather, nominal and
verbal forms of *agape* are consistently used *both* for sexual acts (for example, between a husband and a wife or between two lovers, as in the Song
of Songs) *and* for the passions of divine love for individual human beings
or the community of Israel (which, again, is always transgendered and
coded female in relationship to God as male lover; hence the male homoerotic structure of biblical love).[53] To assert, then, that God's *agape* is necessarily nonsexual, or that texts about Jesus's "beloved" could have been
meant only in a "spiritual" sense is patent philological nonsense.

As Jennings points out, however, there *is* one central feature of the biblical *agape* and the Christian experience of being "beloved" of God that sets
the entire biblical frame apart from its Greek erotic contexts. In Greek culture, the perspective of a text treating love inevitably privileges the perspective of the older lover, that is, of the *erastes*. This is because the Greek *eros*
encoded an elaborate hierarchical system of men whose sexual activity
(who penetrated whom) helped define and preserve their hierarchical social
relationships. It was the man "on top" who counted most, not the man on
the bottom. What makes the biblical texts so remarkable is that they effectively reverse this perspective; that is, they represent the interests and ultimate value of the *eromenos*, the beloved, whether this beloved is understood
to be the community of Israel, the early church, a representative of the
Christian initiate, or a specific individual. What makes biblical love "spiritual," then, is *not* its lack of sex (there is plenty of that), but its sublimation
of the erotics of the Beloved into a systematic denial of social hierarchy and
a radical affirmation of the man or woman "on the bottom."

There is, of course, a very thin line between the spiritual sublimation of
sexuality and its bowdlerization; hence, the original erotics of the Beloved

was quickly lost, if not actually suppressed. It can always, however, be easily brought back to mind through a simple reversal meditation. Dale Martin puts it this way: "For those unable to imagine anything erotic going on here [between Jesus and the beloved disciple], just consider what people would think if we took the 'beloved disciple' to be a woman (as has in fact been sometimes imagined, presumably by heterosexuals); in that case, most people wouldn't be able to resist the consequent erotic imaginings." [54] Nor should they. Such implications are patently obvious in both the homoerotic and heteroerotic scenarios once our eyes have been opened with the gnosis of gender theory and an adequate knowledge of Hebrew and Greek sexual conventions. A little simple honesty and emotional openness about all things sexual also help a great deal.

But the best reason to adopt an open-minded orientation toward homoerotic readings of the Beloved is not a bit of Greek philology, which admittedly remains ambiguous, or a specific reading of this or that biblical text, which is always open to other interpretations, or even a contemporary reverse-thought experiment, which may be anachronistic. It is the hermeneutical fact that such a reading is *countercoherent* with so many other gospel passages; that is, it is the striking realization that, once one adopts a homoerotic hermeneutic, *the pieces fit*, even and especially when, taken together, these same refigured pieces now counter the assumed "orthodox" or "straight" meanings of the texts. [55] It is not, then, this or that piece of the hermeneutical puzzle, but rather *the whole picture* the puzzle forms when the pieces are put together with a coherent theory and set of disciplined readings. [56]

Consider, for example, that set of diverse gospel traditions surrounding the passion narrative and the institution of the eucharist. Consider, that is, Jesus's instruction to his disciples to follow a man carrying a water pitcher to find the place of the last supper (Mark 14:13, Luke 22:10). "Carrying water was women's work," Morton Smith comments in one of his many one-liners, "so this was like saying 'Look for a man wearing lipstick.'" [57] In other words, that is, in modern words, to find the gay men, follow the effeminate gay man.

So too with the famous ritual of Jesus washing the feet of his male disciples (John 13:1–11). After taking his clothes off (yes, he strips) and tying a towel around his waist, Jesus does something that only slaves and women did in his culture, something that "real men" never did: he washes other peoples' feet. More provocatively still, it is this unmanly or womanly act, he teaches, that signals both his own divinity and the way he wants his own disciples to live. As Jennings has it, "Jesus's 'divine' identity thus is expressed in his disregard for the most intimately enforced institutions of worldly society: gender role expectations." [58] Not everyone, of course, is pleased with such a queer act: "Jesus stripping naked and washing the feet of his friends," Jennings reminds us, is "something that Peter at least regards as quite unseemly."[59] Dale Martin makes a very similar point: although "Jesus allows a woman to wash his feet (and we biblical scholars—who know our Hebrew—recognize the hint [foot = penis]), when it is his turn, he takes his clothes off, wraps a towel around his waist, and washes the feet of his *male* disciples, again taking time out for a special seduction of Peter."[60] Modern readers, then, may be blind to the gendered and sexual meanings of such acts, but the original participants certainly were not, nor are our contemporary gnostic scholars.

There is also, of course, the last meal itself. The practice of eating human flesh and drinking human blood, however metaphorically or literally intended (and Jesus was being *very* literal in John 6), would have been highly unusual at best—and deeply offensive—in a traditional Jewish context, despite the ritual's apparent connection to the Passover meal (indeed, linking such an offensive act to the Passover would have made it *more*, not less, outrageous). What we seem to have here in the ritual sharing of male flesh and fluids is another tradition from early Christianity that suggests a homoerotic mysticism, that is, a secret tradition through which males mystically united with another divinized male, here through the eating of his body and the drinking of his blood. And, remember, we are still in the realm of *canonical* memories inscribed in the central texts of the New Testament. This is before we even get to the noncanonical sources, for example, an early second-century tradition that Jesus taught his disciples the highest truths "in the third stage, clearly and nakedly, in private."[61]

I recognize that such a reading must sound, at best, outrageous to the orthodox believer. But consider, for a moment, the following thought experiment. Let us begin by imagining that: (1) there were men in first-century Palestine who sexually desired other men; (2) some of these men were Jewish, and (3) a few of these Jewish men were mystically inclined and tried to adapt their Jewish rituals and beliefs to fit their deepest desires. Now how might such a homoerotic Jewish male possibly express himself in a culture, such as first-century Judaism, whose sacred scriptures were filled with sacral forms of homoeroticism (particularly between Yahweh as the *erastes* of Israel as transgendered *eromenos*) but which would have associated actual homosexual acts with pagan Greek culture and denied their expression through an elaborate system of purity codes and a patriarchal ethic that established marriage as a divine commandment and requirement of the revealed Law? How might such a man respond to a simultaneously homoerotic and homophobic religious culture?

He might systematically subvert the homophobic purity codes through his teaching, preach the rejection of the traditional family ties that undergird both the codes and their patriarchal, heterosexual intentions, celebrate the figure of the passive homosexual eunuch, and finally spiritualize his own homoerotic desires by locating them squarely within the central ritual of his faith, that is, the Passover seder meal, employing its sacrificial and liberatory meanings within a new erotic language through which to unite himself symbolically with his beloved male disciples.[62] Since the physically intimate acts of eating and drinking are both technically removed from an explicit sexual register and widely used as a sexual register (I will leave it to the reader's own hissing imagination to suggest any number of examples), such deeply symbolic acts could both avoid the social censor and act as an effective place of male mystical union.

In other words, such a first-century Jewish homoerotic mystic might do *exactly* what the gospels have Jesus doing. It is in this way that the multiple transgressions of Jesus's acts and teachings, even the central ritual of later Christianity, are rooted in and best explained by his psychosexuality, that is, by his love for the Beloved, snuggled up and lying on his breast at that secret supper. In the terms of the serpent's gift of our present meditations, we are, in effect, back to the garden and the erotic act of eating, only here the act of eating, which is also an act of love, is salvific, not shaming. For the male at least, it is the sublimated homoerotic food of the eucharist that saves, and it is the expressed heteroerotic fruit of the garden that exiles.

However condemnable such suggestions must sound to some, it is important to point out that such a eucharistic erotics is in historical fact not entirely unusual. Morton Smith certainly saw the same.[63] Nor would it be difficult to imagine a psychoanalytic reading of the eucharist as a kind of sublimated oral sexual act. One hardly needs psychoanalysis, however. A good history of Western esotericism will do just as well. George Le Clément de Saint-Marcq (1865–1956), for example, penned a pamphlet, *L'Eucharistie*, in 1906 to argue—based, he later suggested, on a spiritualist communication (and, no doubt on his admiring reading of Freud)—that the bread and wine of the Catholic rite is a symbolic representation of what was actually shared at the original meal, namely, the sperm of Jesus. Outrageous? Certainly. But oddly familiar to the historian of early Christianity, who could cite remarkably similar claims going back to the first few centuries of the Christian era, when some of the gnostic communities (of course) were accused of actually using sexual fluids, that is, semen and menstrual blood, in place of the bread and wine.

Such claims are not as unbelievable as they might first sound. They certainly fit into both the symbolism and structural logic of some of the gnostic mythological systems. Symbolically speaking, seed and sperm are everywhere in the Coptic texts. Sperm, of course, is usually coded as symbolic seed (the Coptic Greek borrowings *spora*, or "seed," and *sperma*, which also means "seed," are more or less interchangeable), masturbation appears as seed in the hand, forced fellatio is transformed into the polluting of Eve's voice, and ejaculation is euphemistically expressed as "defilement." Still, the message is clear enough: male sexual fluids flow throughout the Nag Hammadi library along rivulets and in directions that help define the very soteriologies (models of salvation) of the gnostic worldviews. These meanings, of course, are by no means stable or simple. They too flow, if often within a distinctly Neoplatonic structure of descent and ascent, emanation and return. Consider, for example, how the figure of Eve, here the Reflection hidden in the man, assists the Adam of Light in the following passage from that most remarkable of secret books, the Apocryphon of John:

> And she assists the whole creature, by toiling with him, and by restoring him to his perfection and by teaching him about the descent of his seed and by teaching him about the way of ascent, (which) is the way it came down. And the Reflection of light was hidden in Adam, in order that the rulers might not know (her), but that Reflection might be a correction of the deficiency of the Mother.... Thus the seed remained for a while assisting him in order that, when the Spirit comes forth from the holy aeons, he may raise up and heal him from the deficiency, that the whole pleroma may (again) become holy and faultless.[64]

Within such a soteriological system, consuming sexual fluids would make perfect sense: such a ritual act (aided no doubt by Eve) might well be understood as a returning of the seed back to its source, as a "way of ascent, (which) is the way it came down." Also relevant here is the fact that the image of the "seed" (*sperma*) is central to Sethian Gnosticism, of which the Apocryphon of John is an expression. The "seed of Seth" is a kind of mystical substance that carries divinity across the generations, from Adam to Seth to Jesus to the Sethian gnostics themselves (who loved the snake and accepted his gift). What we seem to have here, in other words, is a cult of mystical semen.

A eucharistic erotics, then, is hardly beyond the boundaries of possibility. Indeed, it is almost predictable within some of these ancient gnostic systems. This does not mean, of course, that such meanings can be projected backwards into the intentions of Jesus himself. Still, these texts are much closer to the religious worlds of the gospels than we are, and their manifest myths may still throw some light on the latent meanings of the original events, whatever those were. However unbelievable such claims are as accurate history, then, such early and modern spermatophagic theories and such ancient accusations of blasphemy may witness dramatically to a real symbolic insight, namely, that the origin of the eucharist lies, like the Beloved in Jesus's lap, in the erotic.[65] In this humbler symbolic reading, what is claimed as the manifest historical content of the original ritual (that is, the literal consumption of sexual fluids) is reread as an exaggerated and naive literalization of a nevertheless accurate perception of the ritual's latent meaning (that is, homoerotic comm-union).[66] Even a road of excess can sometimes lead to a palace of wisdom.

Such a homoerotic hermeneutic also throws some possible light on what is an otherwise inexplicable passage in the canonical Gospel of Mark. The passage occurs shortly after the secret supper during the arrest scene in the garden at the foot of the Mount of Olives. Immediately after Jesus is arrested, Mark drops, out of nowhere, the following on his readers: "And a young man followed him, with nothing but a linen cloth about his body; and they seized him, but he left the linen cloth and ran away naked" (Mark 14:51). Jeremy Bentham suggested in the nineteenth century that the youth in the garden was a *cinaedus* (Greek *kinaidos*), or boy prostitute. In his reading, the loose garment or sheet (*sindona*) the boy wore functioned as a kind of sexual tease or partial display, and Jesus was the patron.[67] Morton Smith constructed a similar thesis with a text he appears to have forged, in Stephen Carlson's reading out of his deep sense of injustice and rage over the police harassment of homosexual men in the New York parks of the 1950s.[68]

Bentham and Smith aside, the fleeing male youth in canonical Mark still calls out for some adequate explanation. He still escapes our own grasp. The Greek word used to describe him (which Morton Smith definitely did not make up)—*gymnos*, or "naked"—is at the very least provocative. Jennings has suggested that the adjective *gymnos* would have evoked the Greek gymnasium as a common place of male bonding and pederasty; that is, the term connotes the homoerotic gazes of older men directed at young males. Mark's noun for the youth, *neaniskos*, is also entirely in keeping with such a reading. None of this, Jennings points out, would have been lost on the gospel's Greek readers, and all of it would have thoroughly scandalized any orthodox Jews, for whom the gymnasium was a classical dividing point between Jew and Gentile, since it made obvious and public the physical mark of being a Jew, that is, the circumcised penis. Interestingly, in Mark 16:5–7 the *neaniskos*, or male youth, returns, now "clothed in a white robe" to announce the gospel of Jesus's resurrection from the dead. As such, the figure of the robed male youth or *neaniskos* frames the entire passion narrative in Mark, from the fleeing naked man in the garden to the resurrection itself.[69] The central event of Christianity is thus implicitly eroticized in Mark.

Finally, there are Jesus's very last words on the cross in the Gospel of John: "Woman, behold your son," and then to his male Beloved, "Behold your mother." Jennings, invoking a by-now-familiar reverse hermeneutic, points out that if such words had involved Mary Magadalene, they would be easily interpreted as a kind of "giving away" of his wife to his family before he dies: "Because Mary of Magdala is Jesus's lover, she is *therefore* his mother's daughter (in-law). . . . In such a case for the sake of the dead son, the mother takes as her daughter the one who had been closest to him in life. And the lover takes the husband's mother as her own mother. That is, they adopt one another." Jennings points out that the story of Ruth and

Naomi follows a similar pattern, and that this "story of love and loyalty between two women has even become a staple of marriage ceremony texts (Ruth 1:16–17) in spite of the same-sex love that the story actually depicts." The same, moreover, seems to be true of the present death-and-adoption scene, and this despite the fact that Jesus's Beloved is another man and not Mary Magdalene (even though she too is present at the same Johannine death scene). "So why," Jennings asks us, "should we permit the feature of the disciple's gender to hide the plain sense of the narrative?"[70] That is, why should we read this text against its most obvious, even most literal, meaning that Jesus is giving away his male lover to his family for protection and support before he breathes his last?[71] Why indeed?

The Woman Jesus Loved

But is the tradition right about the Beloved's gender? Was he John son of Zebedee, or Andrew, or Lazarus, or some other unnamed male? Was "he" a man at all? Jennings has provided us with an extensive discussion of all of these possibilities, finally landing in a sane "We don't know," buttressed by a "But isn't this very ambiguity interesting?"

Certainly the gnostic texts only add to this significant ambiguity. Many of these are quite clear that Jesus indeed had an especially beloved disciple whom he loved in a special way, but "he" was not this John or Andrew or Lazarus. *She* was Mary Magdalene. And this confuses, throws into chaos, everything that was said above. Seen in this comparative light, we cannot be very definite or too confident about Jesus's actual sexuality. The historical sources are simply too contradictory and simultaneously too silent on the matter. But, precisely as Jennings intuited, those contradictions and silences are themselves of great significance, for they suggest to us that Jesus's sexuality was not at all clear to even the earliest Christian communities, who imagined Jesus's love in very different, if not actually contradictory, ways. Such an imagined love simply could not be fit into any neat box or category. It was simply too queer. Not that they didn't try. Indeed, the Christian churches fought over Jesus's loves, often quite cruelly. There were real winners here, and there were real losers.

This is what believers so often misunderstand about history and faith: the "Jesus" or "Mary" (or "Moses" or "Muhammad" or "Buddha" or "Krishna") that they know did not come down to them from the sky or even from an accurately recorded history. Rather, such figures and all that they represent come to us from those who won the cultural wars and defined what would become orthodox, that is, "straight" or true. As has often been pointed out, such things as history and religious creeds are written by the winners. Our beliefs, for better or for worse (often for worse, I think), thus follow closely on the heels of those who shouted down, threatened away, or simply destroyed the historical memories, sometimes even the bodies and persons, of the rest of us. Perhaps this is one reason why our faith traditions are essentially oppressive when it comes to gender and sexuality: that is how they won, that is how they got here in the first place, by oppressing and suppressing the alternative voices. This is also, by the way, why doing real history is so often a heretical exercise. Much of it, after all, is essentially about recovering the voices of those who lost.

Nowhere is this more apparent than in the biblical origins and later cultural fate of the figure of Mary Magdalene. According to the gospels, Mary Magdalene was the first to witness Christ's resurrection. The resurrection faith, then, in some real sense was originally hers. More radically still, Mary's intimate experience of the risen (but not yet ascended) Christ as recorded in John 20 was an experience with textual hints of a simultaneously expressed and frustrated eros. Mary's diminutive address to Jesus, "my Rabbouni" ("my little Rabbi"), his address to her as *gune* ("woman" *or* "wife"), and his command to "stop touching me" (*Me mou haptou*) all carry an erotic charge in the Greek. As in the Gospel of Mark, then, so too in the Gospel of John: the literal origin point of the Christian faith is subtly but really eroticized, the mystical is expressed through the erotic.

Mary's central authoritative role and intimate relationship to Jesus, however, were quickly elided by the early churches, determined as they were to establish the primacy of Peter, James, and Paul within a church ruled by men and their values. Still, her early importance is preserved in some of the gnostic texts and carries through in the later artistic and exegetical traditions, even if in the latter she is increasingly seen as a repentant prostitute rather than as the special companion of Jesus. In Jane Schaberg's elegant, serpentlike expression, Mary Magdalene was the woman "who knew (too) much."[72]

She was also the woman "who loved too much." Schaberg, for example, points out that John 20 is a garden resurrection scene that seems to be drawing on multiple allusions to both the Song of Songs (the Hebrew Bible's love poem) and the garden of paradise of Genesis 1–3. Sadly, however, Mary's tenderly expressed love for Jesus is cruelly rebuffed by Jesus himself: "Stop touching me." Later in history, she will pay dearly for her love. She will be sexually humiliated as a repentant whore, and her early central and organizing role will be nearly forgotten by an entirely male-controlled tradition. In effect, she will be kicked out of the garden of love again, and the mystical eroticism of her resurrection encounter will be rebuffed and replaced by the muted homoeroticism of the youth in Mark's passion and resurrection narrative. The homoerotic will overtake and subsume the heteroerotic, and the queer, ironically, will become that which is straight (*ortho*-dox).

Who, then, was Mary Magdalene? For all four canonical gospels, Mary Magdalene was a primary witness to all that took place around Jesus. She is recorded as participating in his Galilean preaching career. We are told that she followed him to Jerusalem, stood by him during his execution (when all the men, except the Beloved, fled), and went to his burial site to care for his corpse. It was Mary, moreover and most important, who first received an explanation of the empty tomb. Two gospel passages mention that seven demons were cast out of her (Luke 8:2; Mark 16:9)—a detail, in light of Davies, that might suggest a personal history of abuse and healing. According to three other texts, she was sent with a commission to deliver the proclamation of the empty tomb to the hiding disciples (Mark 16:7; Matt. 28:7; John 20:17). According to three more, she was the first to experience a vision of the resurrected Jesus (Matt. 28:9-10; John 20:14-18; Mark 16:9).

The gnostic texts are even richer, consistently presenting this Mary as an inspired visionary, as a potent spiritual guide, as Jesus's intimate companion, even as the interpreter of his teaching. Interestingly, she is identified only by the city from which she came, Magdala, not by any association with father, husband, or son, which would have been the usual practice. As Schaberg points out, Migdal was a fishing town known, or so the legend goes, for its perhaps punning connection to hairdressers (medgaddlela) and women of questionable reputation. This is as close as we get to any clear evidence that Mary Magdalene was a prostitute. Nowhere do the scriptural texts say that she was. The identification would come only much later through a conflation of different gospel texts and their many Marys and a bit of imaginative sixth-century reconstruction on the part of Pope Gregory the Great.

What, then, was the Magdalene's precise relationship to Jesus? The canonical gospels are clear enough that she had some special connection to Jesus but tell us little about the nature of that relationship. Interestingly, Jesus was accused by some of his later contemporaries of living off the money of prostitutes with whom he kept company.[73] A sexual relationship between him and Mary Magdalene, moreover, is explicit in some of the later theologies that build on the Magdalene's legends. The medieval Catharists and Albigensians, for example, held that Mary was Jesus's concubine. The great Protestant reformer Martin Luther also assumed a sexual relationship between the two, perhaps to give some historical precedent for his own dramatic rejection of Catholic celibacy. Finally, numerous contemporary scholars (and at least one recent popular novelist)[74] have suggested as much, if for different reasons and in different contexts.

Wishes, fears and imaginings aside, Schaberg quotes Bruce Chilton for the balanced conclusion that there is no solid evidence to determine whether Jesus was sexually active or not. Chilton believes, however, that if Jesus was sexually active, the most likely candidate of his love was certainly Mary Magdalene, since she was the only woman, apart from his mother, with whom Jesus had persistent and recorded contact. Chilton goes on to speculate that although Jesus's wandering lifestyle would have most likely precluded marriage, and although the Torah clearly prohibited adultery, "sexual contact with an unmarried woman who was not a virgin, particularly a sinner or a formerly demon-possessed person, did not fall under the definition of adultery or seduction."[75]

In any case, the gnostic and early polemical sources go much, much further than the canonical gospels. In the Gospel of Philip, for example, Jesus kisses Mary in order to make her capable of conceiving spiritual offspring (63, 34–36) in what we might fruitfully read as a second-century example of Freud's symbolic "upward displacement" of the genitals to the head.[76] Consider also the following tantalizing passage pitted with well-placed gaps in the text, as if to tease us some more: "And the companion (*koinonos*) of the [. . .] Mary Magdalene [. . . loved] her more than [all] the disciples [and used to] kiss her [often] on her [. . .] The rest of [the disciples . . .]. They said to him, 'Why do you love her more than all of us?' The Savior answered and said to them, 'Why do I not love you like her?'"[77]

Schaberg tells us that *koinonos* can mean "marriage partner, participant, coworker in evangelization, companion in faith, business partner, comrade, friend."[78] Significantly, no one else is called *koinonos* in the gnostic literature. Other related words and their Coptic equivalents, however, are used in the Gospel of Philip, and this in three ways: (1) pejoratively, in order to refer to illicit or adulterous sexual intercourse; (2) neutrally, to refer to the literal sexual pairing of a man and a woman within marriage as a symbol for a deeper spiritual partnership; and (3) mystically, to describe the salvific unity of the gnostic Christian, which was "depicted as union with an angelic counterpart in the pleroma or as its ritual anticipation with another Gnostic of opposite sex in the sacrament of the bridal chamber" (the erotic angel again).[79] The above passage is clearly not pejorative, so we should probably read it in the light of the second and third meanings.

Some scholars believe that Mary and Jesus were seen as the prototypical couple whose mystical-sexual union "readers of the Gospel of Philip tried to imitate in the sacramental act of the bridal chamber,"[80] that is, in a manner strikingly similar to the Hindu Tantric rituals that reenact the sexual unions of Shiva and Shakti or Krishna and Radha.[81] Some scholars have argued that the meanings of these mysterious rituals are intentionally enigmatic,[82] that is, that we cannot really know whether or not the gnostic Christians used sexual intercourse in a sacramental fashion. More recent scholarship, however, has suggested strongly that this earlier position is mistaken. April DeConick, for example, has persuasively argued that the Valentinian gnostics represented in the Gospel of Philip were almost certainly involved in "sacral sexual practices as married couples," that these sexual acts were designed to call down a "grace" that was understood to be a kind of empowering mystical or causal energy "descended from above by means of unspeakable and indescribable intercourse,"[83] and that sex was absolutely central to both the mythology and the ritual practices of the Valentinian community. Indeed, the *mysterion*, or mystical "sacrament" of the bridal chamber, constituted one of the highest levels of religious activity for this group. Nor was this necessarily ritual activity. DeConick in fact argues that the bridal chamber referred to "normal" conjugal sexual activity that was understood by the couple to be a real participation in the erotic life of the divine syzygy or couple, constantly taking place behind the veil of the Holy of Holies.[84] Like the later medieval Kabbalists, the gnostic Christians performed their sexual intercourse in order to heal and harmonize both the divine and human worlds. "How important was sex to the Valentinians?" DeConick asks as a way of conclusion: "The coming of the final day and the redemption of God depended on it."[85]

Not surprisingly, however, "[t]he esoteric reality of the sexual encounter is one that only the pious understand and perform. To the impious, the 'holy mysteries' of intercourse are 'laughable and unbelievable.'"[86] Hence the numerous and quite vicious attacks on these groups that we find among the church officials. A heresy hunter, Epiphanius of Salamis (315–403), for example, wrote a book called the *Panarion,* or *The Medicine Chest,* which he no doubt intended as an antidote to the "disease" or "poison" of the local Christian gnostic communities (and the gift of the serpent?), whose literature and company he claimed to know intimately. In particular, Epiphanius claimed that one Phibionite community shared their women ("Perform the *agape* with the brother," the husband said to his wife),[87] consumed semen and menstrual blood as the body and blood of Christ, practiced coitus interruptus and birth control, performed self-abortions when the latter failed, and consumed the remains of the aborted fetus.[88] Epiphanius also relates the following "obscenity": "[T]hey say that he [Jesus] gave her [Mary] a revelation taking her to the mountain and praying, and that he took from his side a woman and began to have intercourse with her, and thus taking his semen showed that 'we need to do the same thing in order to live,' and when Mary, dismayed, fell to the ground, he at once raised her up again and said, 'Why did you doubt, o you of little faith?'"[89] We are back to the seminal erotics of the eucharist—as imagined, as feared, or as symbolically analyzed and polemically exaggerated.

Scholars have debated whether or not such angry texts reflect actual gnostic behaviors or the hateful fantasies of the polemicists themselves. It is certainly true that religions consistently sexualize their heresies as rhetorical ways of stirring up fear and dismissing their religious competitors as perverts: from the early patristic attacks on the gnostic communities to the *Malleus Maleficarum* and its medieval witches (who were said to gain their magical powers from actual intercourse with the devil), the history of Christian heresy is also a coded history of (male) sexual phobias and fears projected onto the religious other, particularly women.

I certainly do not want to deny any of this, but my comparative senses also tell me that we should take these reports about the mystical utility of sexual practices both suspiciously and seriously. Clearly, an author like

Epiphanius or Irenaeus is writing to discredit, humiliate, and, if possible, persecute. When Epiphanius, for example, reported what he claimed to know to the church authorities, eighteen members of the Phibionites were thrown out. Obviously, we are not dealing with neutral reporting here.

But neither, I think, are we dealing with complete ignorance. Epiphanius's knowledge may have been polemical and sensationalistic, but it was also unusually intimate and, more interesting still, strangely familiar to the historian of religions. We know, for example, of other texts, which are definitely not polemical, that discuss or at least imagine the consumption of sexual fluids in both China and India.[90] Interestingly, as already noted, the gnostic reading of Jesus and Mary as a kind of divine couple to emulate fits well into the numerous theologies and sexual practices of both Hindu and Buddhist forms of Tantra, as do the mysterious bridal chamber ritual, the gnostic texts' enigmatic confusion about the precise nature of the sexual practices, and the dual presence of "male" and "female" ritual substances (that is, the male body and the female blood).[91]

Along related lines, it is also worth noting that the gnostic emphasis on salvation by knowledge or mystical insight rather than on faith or obedience to the Law, along with the doctrinal emphasis on transgression, all fit beautifully with the Asian Tantric materials. Both religious complexes, moreover, speak of an inner divinity or mystical form of consciousness that can be accessed only through direct personal experience. Following the British Buddhologist Edward Conze, Elaine Pagels has noted the obvious parallels and possible allusions that exist between some of the gnostic materials and certain Hindu and Buddhist ideas[92] (including the very title of the Gospel of Thomas, Thomas being the disciple, according to Christian tradition, who founded a Christian community in India). I am also reminded here of the remarkable gnostic text *Thunder, Perfect Mind*, a profoundly sexualized, deeply paradoxical poem whose very title echoes, like thunder, the kind of language we might find in a Tantric Buddhist tract.[93] Pagels has also observed that the erotic dimensions of the relationship between Jesus and Mary may point to claims to mystical communion, since sexual metaphors have been used throughout the history of mysticism to express (and, I would add, catalyze) these very types of unitive experience.[94]

I would simply say the same about the alleged sexual practices of groups like the Carpocratians and Phibionites and certain Hindu and Buddhist Tantric texts. Once we have pared away some of the more fantastic and obviously polemical material, what we may be dealing with here is a kind of early Christian Gnostic Tantrism, if I may put it that jarringly. Moreover, and perhaps most important, whether or not *any* of these groups ever ritually consumed sexual fluids, the rumors, accusations and claims of such acts constitute a powerful witness to the latent mystico-erotic meanings of these same traditions. In short, they may be wrong *and* right. The hoax may be true.

Finally, we can also look at these same Gnostic-Tantric echoes structurally. Thanks largely to the work of such scholars as Barbara Holdredge, it is a commonplace among Indologists now to note that there are important structural similarities between Brahmanic Hinduism and Orthodox Judaism.[95] The two religious systems' oral and textual approaches to scripture (Veda and Torah), their profound interest in ritual and sacrifice, and their concern with purity codes have all been noted. This last feature, however, suggests a perhaps hitherto unrecognized structural conclusion: if these two broad religio-social systems display such similar understandings of purity, then we should expect that their "countercultures," which sought to violate or transgress these same purity ethics (in this case, many of the Hindu Tantric traditions, the early Basileia or "kingdom" movement of Jesus, and some of the early gnostic communities), might also display structural and imaginal affinities, particularly in their use of sexual symbolisms (and likely practices) to effect these same structural transgressions.[96] In other words, we might expect early Christian gnostic transgressions and Asian Tantric transgressions to look very similar.

And indeed they do.

The Secret

It is clear that Peter and the Petrine churches that he represented were at serious odds with the likes of Mary Magdalene and all that she meant to many of the early Christians. One version of Acts of Philip, for example, portrays Peter as one who "fled from all places where there was a woman."[97] Moreover, the Act of Peter—probably the most psychologically precise description of sexual trauma we have in the Nag Hammadi texts—has him healing and then reparalyzing his own daughter so that she will not become sexually active and "wound many souls."[98] In the Gospel of Mary, moreover, Peter expresses exasperation that the Savior would favor Mary, a mere woman, over the men. Mary cries at the implied accusation that she is fabricating secrets, but Levi defends her, telling Peter, "Peter, you have always been hot-tempered. Now I see you contending against the woman like the adversaries."[99] Finally—and we could go on for some time here—in Pistis Sophia, Mary says this to Jesus: "My Lord, my mind is understanding at all times that I should come forward and give the interpretation of the words which [Pistis Sophia] spoke, but I am afraid of Peter, for he threatens me and hates our race."[100] In essence, Peter is envious of Jesus's love for her (he is also, by the way, envious of the Beloved in John 21:20–23). Peter, then, was clearly in competition with Mary, not just for the immense authority that would have come with the claim to have seen the risen Jesus first (1 Cor. 15:5 and Luke 24:34 claim Peter did), but for Jesus's love. "Why do you love her more than all of us?" the Gospel of Philip asks, a question, as Schaberg points out, with clear homoerotic implications.

I would go further still, for what I finally see in the elaborate historical silencing of Mary Magdalene, the female Beloved of Jesus, and the eventual victory of Peter, James, Paul, and the (now male) Beloved is a gender pattern that we can detect throughout the history of religions, namely, a move from an expressed heterodox or heretical heterosexuality (Jesus and Mary) to an orthodox sublimated homoeroticism (Jesus and the Beloved), which is in turn often aligned to a frightening misogyny ("he threatens me and hates our race"). In other words, I am perfectly happy reading the *neaniskos* and beloved disciple tropes of Mark and John not necessarily as the objects of the historical Jesus's actual love (although they might very well represent textual memories of those figures too), but along symbolic or corporate lines, that is, as rhetorical tropes for every Christian initiate. However we choose to read them, though, the structural fact remains that, as we have them now, both the naked fleeing youth of Mark and the beloved disciple of John can easily be read as male homoerotic tropes. This hardly closes the matter, of course, but it certainly makes better sense of much of later Christian history. From the beloved disciple trope of the Gospel of John and the male bridal mysticism of the medieval church, through the Vatican art of the seemingly homoerotic Michelangelo, the castrati of the papal choirs, and that flamboyant King James, who loved young men and commissioned a very famous Bible translation,[101] to the most recent American controversies surrounding the gay priest, orthodoxy, it appears, is not "straight" at all.[102]

All of this is especially evident in the traditional Christian allegory that understands the beloved disciple to be a theological figure of the church as bride of Christ. This latter move, which has had a very long run in Christian spirituality through the traditions of bridal mysticism and the "mystical marriage" of Christ and the human soul and is still with us in various ecclesiological symbolisms and papal pronouncements, is a deeply ironic, if also terribly insightful, move. After all, it implicitly carries along with it the "dangerous memory" of Jesus as a homoerotic mystic. Here is how Jennings puts it: "The identification of the disciple Jesus loved with the bride of Christ does bring to expression Jesus's special relation to that disciple but not in such a way as to make the disciple a type of the church. Rather, that identification (inadvertently) suggests that the relationship between Jesus and this disciple had the erotic character of a bride and bridegroom relationship, except that both are male."[103]

Given all of this, can we say anything about the specific loves of the historical Jesus? Perhaps it is more fruitful and honest to admit what we *cannot* say. We cannot say, for example, what the precise nature of Jesus's sexuality was. Perhaps there was not any such precise nature; maybe such "natural" categories are more reflective of our concerns and modern-day pruderies than of his and his culture's intimate experience. Certainly many have seen a "queer Jesus" that cannot be fitted into any neat modern category. I think it is fair to say that, indeed, we cannot say for certain whether he was sexually attracted to men or to women, or to both (probably the most reasonable solution) or, much less likely but far more traditionally, to neither. But, as I have already pointed out, this in itself is especially significant. The confusion and silence are clear and deafening, like the paradoxical Thunder of Perfect Mind.

One thing seems certain and beyond dispute, however: the eroticism of early Christian literature, of which the New Testament writings are only the tip of the proverbial iceberg, is both immensely rich and richly complicated. Clearly, different early, *very* early, Christian communities remembered and/or imagined a Jesus in different erotic ways. Some appear to have advanced a homoerotic Jesus who loved men, others a heteroerotic Jesus who loved and kissed Mary Magdalene in special ways, others an entirely sexless Christ who avoided real sex from the very beginning, that is, from his "virginal" conception and birth. John, Mary Magdalene, Peter, James, Paul—they and their communities all jockeyed for position, authority, and power in those early years. They all fought for Jesus's real and imagined love.

We, of course, know who won, who became orthodox, who got to write the history: Peter did. But despite this, the secret of the Beloved remains teasingly ambiguous and historically uncertain, and this is precisely how Jesus's love, like the wise snake, might still provoke and call us out of the garden of our spiritual innocence and sexual ignorance.

So ends the Apocryphon of the Beloved.

Restoring the Adam of Light   *2*

Let us call him Adam, that his name may become a power
of light for us. *The Apocryphon of John*

God created men. [. . . men] create God. That is the way it
is in the world—men make gods and worship their creation.
It would be fitting for the gods to worship men!
The Gospel of Philip

The eye with which I see God is the same eye with
which God sees me. My eye and God's eye is one eye, one
sight, one knowledge, one love. *Meister Eckhart*

The Adam of Light Awakened by Her

"In Gnostic speculation the mystical name of God is 'Man,' *Anthropos* or
'*Adam(as)*.' . . . ."[1] There are few more significant observations about the
Nag Hammadi library than this one, even if it is tucked away in a com-
mentarial footnote of a critical edition that few individuals beyond the
academy will ever read: a secreted gem, as it were. Effectively hidden or no,
however, giving such a name to God was an act that carried within it profound philosophical implications that it would take centuries to work out
and, indeed, are still with us today in the more popular form of the central
claim of Christianity, namely, that God became a human being in Jesus of
Nazareth.

The gnostic authors inhabited a world where such claims were common but not yet universally restricted to a single historical individual.
They, unlike their orthodox contemporaries, tended to read such a mythology (of which there were many versions) as expressive of spiritual or
psychic potentials present in everyone, not as the literal prerogative of a

single historical Jewish preacher and healer.[2] Through such polemical, psychological, and theological moves, these authors effectively bestowed immense metaphysical privileges on the human spirit. And even when they did not quite identify the human spirit with the highest Godhead, they bestowed on this spirit some quite remarkable names and mythical narratives. Often working out of either the Jewish tradition and the immense importance it gave to human beings understood to be made "in the image of God" or the Neoplatonic tradition that saw the intellect (*nous*) as the reflection of the One, the gnostic authors consistently saw something essentially divine and immortal deep within human nature, a hidden spark or lost pearl, that could manifest its true nature and glory only through a return back into the primordial Pleroma, the Fullness of the Godhead that constituted for so many of these systems the ultimate origin and goal of all creation.

In the Apocryphon of John, for example, the authorities and the Chief Ruler see a reflection of the first man in the water as "the form of the image." This inspires them to create: "Come, let us create a man according to the image of God and according to our likeness, that his image may become a light for us."[3] After each authority supplies a particular characteristic or part of the first "perfect Man," they give him a name: "Let us call him Adam, that his name may become a power of light for us."[4] This same Adam, because he was given the light of Reflection (*epinoia*) from her "who was in him"[5] and the tree of the knowledge of good and evil,[6] was wiser than the Chief Ruler himself and all his authorities.[7] He was the Adam of Light who needed to be awakened by her and finally restored to his true hidden nature in the divine Pleroma. This, as we have already seen, would be accomplished through Eve's erotic gnosis "about the descent of his seed" and "about the ways of ascent, (which) is the way it came down."

The Fiery Brook

In 1841, a book appeared that, much to the surprise and consternation of its author, quickly became a public sensation in the German-speaking world. *The Essence of Christianity* is one of those rare books that, much like some of the more radical gnostic texts, can be accurately described as "apocalyptic" in the sense that it announces, predicts, and in some sense actually effects "the end of the world," at least as its readers knew and understood the world. "A book on a library shelf is like a Last Judgment in cold storage, waiting for a reader to energize it," wrote the recent editors of William Blake's poetry.[8] So too here. This particular apocalypse-on-the-shelf, however, was the work of neither a visionary British poet nor some anonymous, first-century Jewish or Christian author. It was the work of an aspiring young Lutheran professor of theology named Ludwig Feuerbach (1804–1872), who sought to return religious claims back to their true or "essential" base in the senses, the body, and the dynamics of family, sexual, and social relations.

In a moment of youthful (and quite prescient) *hubris*, Feuerbach predicted that his radical thought would one day be the general property of humanity, that it would, in effect, permanently change the way people understood themselves and the natural world in which they lived.[9] In at least one very important sense, Feuerbach was quite right, for much that he had the courage to think and write in 1841 did indeed become the common property of later creators of European and Western culture. Marx and Engels, Nietzsche, and Freud were all deeply indebted to his thought, either directly or indirectly, and contemporary writers have suggested, rightly I think, that Feuerbach's insights into the dynamics of religious projection constitute the core insight of the modern study of religion. Poetically speaking, he thus more than lived up to his name: the Brook of Fire (*Feuer-Bach*). Engels's oft-quoted confession makes the same point in less poetic terms: "Then came Feuerbach's *Essence of Christianity*. . . . One must himself have experienced the liberating effect of this book to get an idea of it. Enthusiasm was general; we all became at once Feuerbachians."[10] Ludwig Feuerbach is thus the Brook of Fire that constitutes one of the key origin points of both modern critical thought and the study of religion, the high mountain spring that would become a whole series of raging rivers as it cascaded down through the past two centuries.

In another, less important sense, however, Feuerbach's prediction would be proved wrong, for, although most everyone has heard of Marx and Freud, almost no one outside a small circle of professional philosophers and theologians is familiar with the name, much less the thought, of Ludwig Feuerbach. If Feuerbach, then, is one of the most important (and gnostic) origin points for the modern critical study of religion, he is a beginning inspiration that has been largely forgotten by the broader culture. Some have suggested that this is because what is most helpful and convincing about Feuerbach's philosophy was transmitted more effectively into Western thought through the systems of Marx and Freud. Van Harvey, however, has convincingly demonstrated that Feuerbach's thought, and particularly his later thought, cannot be conflated with Marxism or psychoanalysis, and that it is this later "existentialist" theorizing about the subject's dialogical encounter with nature, the body, and death that constitutes his most lasting and most prescient contribution to the social-scientific study of religion.[11] In the twentieth century, this existentialist stream would merge with many others to form an entire river of discourse on the processes of Western secularization, itself a proto-gnostic and essentially ethical phenomenon "in so far as it reflects a human consciousness 'come of age,' which is to say, a consciousness that recognizes that we live in a socially constructed world for which we are responsible."[12]

I am extremely sympathetic to Feuerbach's later existentialist turn from philosophical abstractions of all types to what he called *Sinnlichkeit*, or "sensuality," that is, an insistence on the immediate physical, relational, and sensory quality of human experience, on the primacy of a relational eros in the genesis and formation of human consciousness. Indeed, all of my earlier writings have focused on the body, the erotic, and religion's various modalities of repression, censorship, and sublimation. The present essay, however, will return to Feuerbach's earlier Hegelian (really counter-Hegelian) speculations on the dialectical structure of consciousness and the dynamics of religious projection as especially conducive to the kinds of gnostic epistemologies I am trying to develop here. I hardly want to question the fact that Feuerbach (and, as if following him again, the study of religion) abandoned these early fascinations with the nature of consciousness itself for the more reductive and less dialectical methods of the social sciences. But I do want to suggest that something was lost by such a move "downstream," and that we would do well to return, if only for a moment, to the original source waters of this Brook of Fire, with or without the master himself.

In the process, I also want to suggest that there may be understandable reasons why so many later interpreters ignore the later existentialist and reductive Feuerbach for the earlier Hegelian and dialectical one, that is, for the author of *The Essence of Christianity*, as if this were the only book he wrote. In essence, such readers may be intuiting in the Hegelian speculations of the earlier Feuerbach about the structures of consciousness something of what they also intuit about the structures of consciousness that constitute the study of religion. That is, they may be sensing some very deep, very real, and very important gnostic currents of contemporary theory that hardly constitute the entire river of religious studies but nevertheless burn and flash under the moving water as luminous reminders of the discipline's original (if also still potential) inspirations. In the end, though, what I am trying to imagine in the present meditation is certainly not a rejection of the later reductive Feuerbach for what I am calling the earlier gnostic Feuerbach, but rather an affirmation of both the reductionist and the gnostic as integral modes of a single human life and a single dialectical practice. It must be admitted that Feuerbach achieved no such synthesis in his own life. It remains to be seen if any of us will in our own.

The Sacrilegious Secret of Christian Theology

There is little doubt that one reason Feuerbach was so conveniently forgotten is because both his thought and the way he expresses it are so incredibly difficult to accept for the believing Christian, or the believer of any faith for that matter. The rage against the archons and the demiurge or false creator-god that burns so brightly in some of the gnostic authors is equally luminous in Feuerbach, and there is no doubt that his is a profoundly polemical text, a book aimed at the throat of Christian theology or any philosophy that has given too much away to the destructive demands of what Feuerbach believed were the dangerous falsehoods of faith. His was an angry mysticism, an atheistic, embodied affirmation of life in this world, and this without any hope of a personal afterlife.

This is not to say that he hated religion. Paradoxically—and this is precisely what defines his method as more than rational, as gnostic, for me—Feuerbach was deeply engaged with Christian faith as a lived set of pieties and practices, and he consistently manifested a profound and subtle grasp of theological thinkers and the complex phenomenology of religious experience. Moreover, and most important, he clearly believed that religion contained within its symbols and myths some of the most profound truths of the human psyche and body. But—and this is the crucial point—these needed to be properly interpreted and "freed" from the illusions of faith and theology to be properly activated and integrated into a full human life. In a word, Feuerbach's method in *The Essence of Christianity* was *dialectical*, that is, it used reason to reduce the dogmas of faith back to their ontological ground in the human being, but it also fully acknowledged and even celebrated the extraordinary moral and aesthetic heights of this same human ground. The method thus reduced the divine and sublimated ("made sublime") the human in turns, reproducing, exactly as Feuerbach argued, the dialectical secret of the doctrine of the Incarnation (descent and ascent, manifestation and reconciliation). The result was a radically critical method that paradoxically both deconstructed the literal truths of faith, locating them (that is, incarnating them) in the body, in social relationships, and in desire, and affirmed religion as a kind of secret or unconscious intuition of humanity's essential divinity. As Harvey puts it in reference to Karl Löwith's reading, "[R]eligion was the detour (*Umweg*) by means of which humankind comes to self-awareness regarding its true nature."[13]

In the simplest terms, Feuerbach argued that all statements that Christian theologians make about God are in actual fact statements made about human nature as a species.[14] In a word (really two words), they are *psychological projections*. Put in the form of one of his most famous refrains, "the true sense of Theology is Anthropology," that is, once again, all claims made about "God" are in actual fact reflections or projections of "Man." And anything that has been projected can also be eventually withdrawn, in a word (really a single word now), *reduced* back to its original source, in this case the human mind and body. Projection and reduction, or, as I will suggest later, emanation and return, thus constitute the two poles of Feuerbach's gnostic dialectic.

In it simplest form, such a method possesses numerous premodern precedents. The ancient Greek philosopher Xenophanes, for example, had observed that, if oxen, horses, and lions had religion (and hands), they would no doubt paint their gods to look like oxen, horses, and lions; hence, the Ethiopians worship black gods and the Thracians worship gods with blue eyes and red hair. Closer to home, numerous interpreters have pointed out that Feuerbach's dialectical method is basically an inversion of G. W. F. Hegel's earlier theological method. In his massively complex *Phenomenology of Spirit* (*Die Phänomenologie des Geistes*, 1807)—probably the single most important philosophical work of the era—Hegel had envisioned an elaborate metaphysics that was also a philosophy of consciousness. Absolute Spirit, Hegel argued, gradually unfolds itself through the historical and increasingly complex development of cultures and religions, all of which are at once its temporal manifestations and its self-awakenings. In essence, God wakes up and comes to full consciousness in and through the history of religions, with earlier simpler forms (like animism) becoming subsumed, integrated into, and transcended by later forms (such as monotheism). What Feuerbach did was essentially reverse the causal flow of these evolving self-manifestations and turn the method back on itself. In Harvey's always eloquent terms, he stood Hegel on his head: "Instead of saying that the Absolute Spirit (God) achieves self-knowledge by objectifying itself in the finite world, he argued that the finite spirit comes to self-knowledge by externalizing or objectivizing itself in the idea of God. Religion is not, as Hegel thought, the revelation of the Infinite in the finite; rather, it is the self-discovery by the finite of its own infinite nature." [15]

Feuerbach's entire system, in its early and later forms, implies, indeed requires, a basic split in human consciousness, an internal division in which the human mind quite literally experiences itself as an other, as an "I" *and* a "thou," rather like in a dream, Feuerbach pointed out long before Freud, where the dreamer experiences the content of his own mind, his own desires and fears, as "objective" events of a visionary dream. None of this, of course, really exists "out there," but the dreamer thinks it does and so responds accordingly (down to the real adrenaline that is released in a real body) as long as the sleep state continues.

Feuerbach used a number of colorful metaphors to describe the religious statements that this split consciousness produces. Religious language, for example, is variously described as a code to decipher, as a secret to reveal, as a locked door that needs the proper key, as an unconscious understanding that needs to be made conscious, as a literal surface level that hides deeper depths, and—perhaps most pointedly—as a psychological projection that must be withdrawn and reduced back to its human origins in the psyche in order to restore humanity from the pathological and dangerous split or "alienation" that this same projection caused in the first place. With this fundamental move, Feuerbach in effect announced the modern study of religion, which to this day often works in precisely this way.

Such a method is usually (and not incorrectly) seen as a serious challenge to the truth claims of the religions, but, paradoxically—and, again, this is one of my most basic gnostic claims—this same projection dynamic also suggests that religious doctrines, rituals, visions, and ecstatic states of consciousness possess immense potentials for the thinker concerned with studying human nature, since all of these phenomena, as psychic projections, allow the human mind to examine the contents of its own unconscious depths, which would otherwise, presumably, remain unconscious and so unassimilated into conscious social life. Religious phenomena are certainly not literally true, but they are often necessary and effective "detours" through which an individual can pass into fuller consciousness and being. In Hegel-on-his-head terms, religious ideas and symbols are not how God wakes up in history and culture; they are how *we* wake up from the abyss of nature and the dream-illusions of religion. They are the substance of the serpent's gift.

For all his fury, then, Feuerbach approached religion not as silly game to ignore or a set of simple falsehoods that can be immediately rejected, but as a deeply meaningful system of human thought that hid within itself some of the most profound and truest assessments of the human condition, if only we could recognize religious truth claims for what they secretly are (their "essence") instead of what they consciously claim to be (their literal surface truths). In religion, Feuerbach wrote, "man contemplates his own latent nature" (EC 33). To the extent that we value this latent or hidden nature, we must also value religion, but again, only if we can properly read its fundamental insights as symbolic projections rather than as literal or historical truths. And that, of course, is a *very* big if.

But how did Feuerbach bring to light what he so warmly called, in a gospel image, this "treasure hid in man"? (EC xxii) On one level, at least, his method is really quite simple, as it involves an easily understood and applied grammatical rule that Feuerbach called *reversal* or *inversion*: "[T]hat which in religion is the predicate we must make the subject, and that which in religion is a subject we must make a predicate, thus inverting the oracles of religion; and by this means we arrive at the truth" (EC 60). So, for example, if Christian theology states that "God made man in his own image," what this really means is "Man made God in his own image," or if Christianity states that "God is love," what this in essence means is "Love is God."

Thus, Feuerbach can write: "Man—this is the mystery of religion—projects his being into objectivity, and then again makes himself an object to this projected image of himself thus converted into a subject" (EC 30). Or put in more traditional (and heretical) terms this time: "Man first unconsciously and involuntarily creates God in his own image, and after this God consciously and voluntarily creates man in his own image" (EC 118). Eerily, this is a virtual paraphrase of the passage from the Gospel of Philip that forms one of the epigraphs to this chapter, a passage which Feuerbach could not have possibly read—more evidence that Feuerbach's early system is a fundamentally gnostic one.

Most of *The Essence of Christianity* involves a series of applications of this basic inversion rule or "transformative method" to a wide range of religious phenomena: prayer, faith, miracle, providence, and the vision or dream, to name just a few. Prayer, for example, "is the absolute relation of the human heart to itself, to its own nature; in prayer man forgets that there exists a limit to his wishes, and is happy in his forgetfulness. Prayer is the self-division of man into two beings,—a dialogue of man with himself, with his heart" (EC 123). Or again, this time more succinctly, "[I]n prayer, man addresses God as his '*alter ego*'" (EC 122). And the proverbial faith that one can move mountains? "But if thou believest that nothing is or can be against thee, thou believest—what?—nothing less than that thou art God. That God is another being is only illusion, only imagination" (EC 127). So too with the miracle: it is "a supranaturalistic wish realised—nothing more" (EC 128–129).

This, of course, is essentially what Freud would later write about dreams—they are wish fulfillments expressed in the night. Little wonder, then, that Feuerbach reads dreams in a "Freudian" fashion and takes their structure as emblematic of religion in general: "Religion," Feuerbach tells us, "is a dream, in which our own conceptions and emotions appear to us as separate existences, beings out of ourselves" (EC 204). Or more fully: "[W]hat is dreaming? The reversing of the waking consciousness. In dreaming, the active is the passive, the passive the active; in dreaming, I take the spontaneous action of my own mind for an action upon me from without, my emotions for events, my conceptions and sensations for true existences apart from myself. . . . Feeling is a dream with the eyes open; religion the dream of waking consciousness: dreaming is the key to the mysteries of religion" (EC 140–141).

Very much related to this basic insight into the dual nature of the human mind (conscious and unconscious) is the dual structure of *The Essence of Christianity*. The book is divided into two basic parts. The first involves reading religious claims as coded statements about human nature: this is the "essence" of the title and the method that produces the truth of religious claims. By making these unconscious dimensions conscious, Feuerbach renders otherwise absurd religious truths eminently sensible and meaningful. The second part involves the falsehood or contradictions of religious language when they are left to stand as literal truths. The Trinity, for example, is a logical contradiction if taken as an objective reality (three persons that are also one). Taken, however, as an expression of the inner plurality and unity of human consciousness and the deep structuring of mind through family relations (particularly the father-son relation), the doctrine is eminently sensible, even quite profound. It also happens to look forward to what will much later become object-relations psychology, which similarly posits a psyche composed of "objects" it has internalized via family and other significant social relationships.

Two simple rules follow from Feuerbach's gnostic method. When religious language is reduced back to its human referent, it can be treated as a true and insightful account of human nature deserving of considerable philosophical and humane interest. When, however, religious beliefs and practices are approached literally, that is, as something external to human nature, they immediately become "an inexhaustible mine of falsehoods, illusions, contradictions, and sophisms" (EC 214). It is in this double sense that Feuerbach (and, I think, the study of religion in general) can honestly lay claim to both an appreciative and a critical stance vis-à-vis "religion." It is also what makes Feuerbach's foundational method the father of what I have called our gnosis.

Implications of the Method

At least four corollaries follow immediately from such a method: one involving the essentially unconscious nature of the religious state; a second involving the negative, even pathological or violent nature of this same primordial split in human consciousness; a third involving the privilege of what is often called the "outsider" or unbeliever (the figure of pure reason for us here) in deciphering the dynamics and contents of these religious problems; and a fourth involving what we might call the social acceptance (really rejection) of the critical study of religion. A word about each is in order before we proceed any further, since all four structure Feuerbach's thought and, much as he predicted, are still very much with us today.

First, Feuerbach was clear that the religious individual—that is, the epistemology of faith—would not and probably could not understand what he was trying to articulate in his work. Thus, he did not mean for his dual theory of projection and reduction to be understood "as affirming that the religious man is directly aware of this identity [between the divine and human referents of religious language]; for, on the contrary, ignorance of it is fundamental to the peculiar nature of religion" (EC 13). In other words, religion seems to "work"—and it *does* often work—only to the extent that these processes remain unconscious, rather as a good movie works only to the extent that the audience can suspend its natural disbelief and pretend that what is being projected on the screen from behind them is in fact really happening before and even *to* them. Unlike a movie, however, religious projections proceed on the assumption that all of the action on the screen *is* ultimately real and so have real effects on how individuals think about themselves and their world. Religion, in other words, causes people to act on fictions.

Tragically, the projection and inversion dynamics of faith also convince human beings that all of their best qualities exist outside themselves, that is, in God. In a language that Hegel originated and Marx would later transform, faith is said to alienate human beings from their own deepest selves. Feuerbach put it this way: "To enrich God, man must become poor; that God may be all, man must be nothing. . . . What man withdraws from himself, what he renounces in himself, he only enjoys in an incomparably higher and fuller measure in God" (EC 26). Religion is thus "the disuniting of man from himself" (EC 182). In some fundamental way, Feuerbach saw it as his task to reunite this basic split in human nature, to heal, as it were, the wound of religious faith and its alienating projections. He put this quite beautifully in his *Lectures on the Essence of Religion*: "My primary concern is and always has been to illumine the obscure essence of religion with the torch of reason, in order that man may at least cease to be the victim, the plaything, of all those hostile powers which from time immemorial have employed and are still employing the darkness of religion for the oppression of mankind."[16] Certainly, such projections may have been necessary to a certain stage of human development—the metaphor of childhood is evoked often by Feuerbach to express this conviction—but they are no longer necessary. It is time to grow up now, leave the garden of our innocence, and realize that what we once believed we once truly imagined. The movie, it turns out, is not "out there" at all; it is "in here" (and we made it). The movie is *us* temporarily split in two.[17]

But there is more yet to this second corollary, for not only does this split produce sickness. It also inevitably produces violence, for human beings are extraordinarily skilled at projecting their hatreds and fears onto their gods and then using these gods to justify acting on their own aggression and social intolerance. The movies-as-religions we make and live in are thus often horribly violent ones. What is worse, through the mechanism of projection, we cleverly deny responsibility for writing and producing them: "Religion is the relation of man to his own nature,—therein lies its truth and its power of moral amelioration;—but to his nature not recognized as his own, but regarded as another nature, separate, nay, contradistinguished from his own: herein lies its untruth, its limitation, its contradiction to reason and morality; herein lies the noxious source of religious fanaticism, the chief metaphysical principle of human sacrifices, in a word, the *prima materia* of all the atrocities, all the horrible scenes, in the tragedy of religious history" (EC 197). Although Feuerbach himself does not expand on this, such a model implies that any attempt to end or ameliorate religious violence will have to come to terms with these projection mechanisms and stop treating the religions as basically benevolent forces that are somehow being "abused" or misinterpreted in "inappropriate" ways. No, Feuerbach might say (I would say anyway), these are not misinterpretations at all. It is not for nothing that so many religious traditions begin with or focus on the theme of human sacrifice, for this is what religion *is*—the sacrifice of the human, which really does exist, to the divine, which really does not. The tragedy of religion, then, is that *religion sacrifices what is real to what is not.* Put more dramatically (if that is possible), for religious violence to end, religion as we know it will have to end, or at least lose its present divinely demonic hold on human consciousness. At the very least, it must be defanged through a reversal of projection via the method of reduction. To employ another metaphor, we have to *wake up* and end our religious dream, which is really often more of a nightmare.

A third crucial corollary follows directly from these first two, namely, that anyone caught in such an illusion, illness, or dream certainly cannot be expected to critically analyze what is in fact going on. The dreamer caught in the dream is hardly in a position to decipher it. The priest or religious leader will seldom be willing to call into question the institution that he represents and relies on for his very identity, not to mention his salary. The religious believer will seldom challenge a faith that is tied up with the survival of one's ethnicity, culture, or family. Hence, ironically but truly, the privilege of studying religion falls not on the believer, but on the unbeliever, that is, on the person who stands "on the outside." In Feuerbach's terms, "the essence of religion, thus hidden from the religious, is evident to the thinker, by whom religion is viewed objectively, which it cannot be by its votaries" (EC 13).

A fourth corollary follows directly from this third one, namely, that the acceptance of critical theories of religion by the believing faithful or, much worse, their official representatives, is no measure or criterion of truth and certainly no way to determine the legitimacy and importance of the enterprise. Quite the opposite, really. For Feuerbach at least, the critical study of religion could never be fairly judged by those who stood most to lose from its honest conclusions: indeed, they were the last people in the world that could be trusted to come to a relatively objective conclusion about the results of such a study. Faith is not a criterion of truth here. Reason and gnosis are.

Very much related to this fourth corollary is what we might call Feuerbach's esoteric, elitist, or gnostic expectation that his book would not be circulated among the public (EC xxii). They, after all, lacking the proper philosophical and historically training that was carefully woven into almost every sentence, could not possibly understand it. Only the scholar, "who loves truth, who is capable of forming a judgment, who is above the notions and prejudices of the learned and unlearned vulgar," could appreciate and so properly judge such things (EC xxiii). Any reader ignorant of the historical details assumed by his prose and arguments simply would not "get it" and, consequently, could not possibly be convinced of his ideas: "[N]o wonder," Feuerbach writes in a moment of obvious public exasperation, "if my positions often appear to him baseless, however firm the footing on which they stand" (EC xxiii).

Put differently, the critical study of religion is more or less doomed to social and religious rejection for the simple reason that the public lacks the requisite training and education. And this is before we even get to the question of emotional resistance and all that is politically, psychologically, and ethnically at stake in such an assessment—further contextualized in this way, the possibility of a fair public and religious assessment of the critical study of religion approaches nil. Little wonder, then, that, as various historians have suggested, much of Feuerbach's rhetorical style was a response to the real and active presence of censorship and police harassment on the part of the Christian state.[18]

Feuerbach's esoteric convictions and personal desires, of course, were ignored, and the book was widely read by the German-speaking public, some of whom no doubt "got it" and many of whom, exactly as Feuerbach predicted, most certainly did not. In this, Feuerbach lived through a mythological pattern that has been repeated innumerable times over the past two centuries, that is, the broad public rejection and select private acceptance of the serpent's gift.

The Historical and Intellectual Contexts

To understand both Feuerbach's desire for a kind of secrecy and the public's largely sensationalistic response to his work, we must remember that he was writing at the very beginning of the modern critical study of religion. Not that he was the first. He was not. Certainly he worked in a milieu already deeply influenced by the anxiety and excitement of early biblical studies and the birth of historical criticism. "The Bible contradicts morality, contradicts reason, contradicts itself, innumerable times," he could write (EC 211). Moreover, it was precisely these contradictions and this study that created Feuerbach's problem (and promise) in the first place: "But the more man, by the progress of time, becomes estranged from revelation, the more the understanding ripens into independence,—the more glaring, necessarily, appears the contradiction between the understanding and belief in revelation" (EC 212).

Even so, Feuerbach also can be heard complaining in his text how his name and work were consistently linked to the controversies that surrounded such figures as Bruno Bauer and David Friedrich Strauss,[19] two early pioneers in the historical-critical study of the gospels (CE xxii). It was not that he disagreed with such writers, only that he was not particularly interested in the question of historical origins. Ordinary Christians, after all, do not bother themselves with such questions, and so such concerns seemed tangential, at best, to understanding how religion on the

ground really works.[20] Instead, then, Feuerbach was after the central dogmas of Christianity, what ordinary people actually believe (or at least say
they believe) and how we are to understand or decipher these kinds of
claims in order to make sense of them. Accordingly, he had little patience
with "the historical Jesus": "[O]n the contrary, I accept the Christ of religion,
but I show that this superhuman being is nothing else than a product and
reflex of the supernatural human mind" (EC xxi).

He also worked in a German and post-Enlightenment milieu dominated
by such thinkers as Immanuel Kant, G. W. F. Hegel, and Friedrich Schleiermacher. The latter had famously defended the claims of religion against its
"cultured despisers" (of which there were many) by pointing to the subjective experiences of faith as the best locus of their meaning. Religion, in
other words, was primarily about feeling and states of consciousness, not
objective claims about the universe "out there." Feuerbach certainly lis-
tened to Schleiermacher, but he rejected any notion that religious experiences gave us "facts," and he took Schleiermacher's essentially psychological
insight and radicalized it almost beyond recognition. On the supposed
"facts" of religious experience, he thus wrote mockingly:

> [D]o you not see that facts are just as relative, as various, as subjective, as the
> ideas of the different religions? Were not the gods of Olympus also facts,
> self-attesting existences? . . . Was not the story of Balaam's ass just as much
> believed even by enlightened scholars of the last century, as the Incarnation
> or any other miracle? A fact, I repeat, is a conception about the truth of
> which there is no doubt, because it is no object of theory, but of feeling,
> which desires that what it wishes, what it believes, should be true. A fact is
> that, the denial of which is forbidden, if not by an external law, yet by an in-
> ternal one. A fact is . . . every conception which, for the age wherein it is held
> to be a fact, expresses a want, and is for that reason an impassable limit of
> the mind. (EC 205)

The "facts" of religious experience, in other words, prove nothing except
the fact of experience itself. In this, they are rather like the notion of common sense, since they involve not the objective nature of things, but
rather what a particular culture or time will allow human beings to think
and believe, even feel. This is what later sociologists of religion would call
the social construction of knowledge and the phenomenon of plausibility:
human beings are simply deluded if they think they are free to think anything. In truth, they cannot think anything, for their cultures and their
languages determine largely the boundaries of what is permissible, what
is believable, what is plausibly "real." Was it, after all, not common sense
that human beings lived in the center of a universe created by God, and
that the sun rose in the morning and set in the evening, along with all the
stars and the moon? And would it have not been wildly implausible to
think that the earth circles the sun, which itself circles with billions of

other suns the center of some immense black hole at the center of our "galaxy," itself spinning in empty space with billions of other galaxies, all racing away from one another at unimaginable speeds and distances to who knows "where"? Who could have possibly, plausibly, believed *that?*

As for Schleiermacher's famous turn to feeling, Feuerbach pointed out that human beings do not "feel" or experience God; they feel feeling, they experience experience: "How couldst thou perceive the divine by feeling, if feeling were not itself divine in its nature?" he wrote. "The divine assuredly is known only by means of the divine—God is known only by himself. The divine nature which is discerned by feeling is in truth nothing else than feeling enraptured, in ecstasy with itself—feeling intoxicated with joy, blissful in its own plenitude" (EC 9). Put more radically, that is, after the grammatical inversion: "God is pure, unlimited, free Feeling. Every other God, whom thou supposest, is a God thrust upon their feeling from without. Feeling is atheistic in the sense of the orthodox belief, which attaches religion to an external object; it denies an objective God—it is itself God" (EC 10–11). In more modern terms, we might say that what religious experience really points to is not some objective divine but the mysteries of human consciousness, that is, what Feuerbach called "the supernatural mind."

Interestingly, for Feuerbach, such a move renders all questions about the existence of (an objective) God meaningless, even silly. Of course "God" exists, in and as the human being. Feuerbach thus replaces an existential doubt with a mystical atheism of absolute identity: "Fettered by outward considerations, still in bondage to vulgar empiricism, incapable of comprehending the spiritual grandeur of feeling, thou art terrified before the religious atheism of thy heart. By this fear thou destroyest the unity of thy feeling with itself, in imagining to thyself an objective being distinct from thy feeling, and thus necessarily sinking back into the old questions and doubts—is there a God or not?—questions and doubts which vanish, nay, are impossible, where feeling is defined as the essence of religion" (EC 10–11).

If Feuerbach's text is a sacrilegious one, he was fully aware of this, referring at one point to "the 'unholy' spirit of my work" (EC xxi). He certainly relished this fact, even as he rhetorically denied the stunning originality of his thought, ironically locating his atheistic conclusions in the implicit logic of Christian theology itself, that is, in the doctrine of the Incarnation. Here he provided another distinctly mystical frame for his atheism:

> It is not I, but religion that worships man, although religion, or rather theology, denies this; it is not I, an insignificant individual, but religion itself that says: God is man, man is God.... I have only found the key to the cipher of the Christian religion, only extricated its true meaning from the web of contradictions and delusions called theology;—but in doing so I have certainly committed a sacrilege. If therefore my work is negative, irreligious, atheistic,

let it be remembered that atheism—at least in the sense of this work—is the secret of religion; that religion itself, not indeed on the surface, but fundamentally . . . believes in nothing else than the truth and divinity of human nature. (EC xvi)

Feuerbach, then, had a keen sense for the sacrilegious nature of his thought and the general project of the philosophical study of religion. But he also believed that his sacrilege was implied or hidden in the nature of religion itself. "Yes, it contains that principle, but only by *evolving* it out of the very core of religion. . . . [B]eing evolved from the nature of religion, it has in itself the true essence of religion,—is, in its very quality as a philosophy, a religion also" (EC xxiii–xxiv).

In one of his most famous lines (itself echoing the exegetical techniques of the early gnostics), he went so far as to suggest that his philosophy was the correct form of Christian theology, whose traditional orthodoxy, of course, he has just turned upside-down: "I . . . while reducing theology to anthropology, exalt anthropology into theology, very much as Christianity, while lowering God into man, made man into God" (EC xviii). I will return to this same line later in the chapter to mine its gnostic potentials. For now, it is sufficient to point out that, for Feuerbach at least, the study of religion was a project that evolved organically from Christian theology and, in particular, from its doctrinal stress on the radical embodiment of the divine.

Whether or not we wish to follow Feuerbach as far as he went in this claim (I'm willing), it does seem more than reasonable to accept the general claim, namely, that the modern study of religion did indeed largely evolve out of Christian theology. I would only emphasize both segments of that clause, "evolve out of." That is, whereas it is historically (and probably philosophically) true that the study of religion *evolved* out of Christian theology and so depended on the latter's metaphors and structures for its original insights and energy, it is equally true that it evolved *out of* Christian theology and can no longer be equated with or reduced to a Christian project.[21]

"Man Is God to Man": The Virtues of Pluralism and Polytheism

This conclusion is undergirded already in Feuerbach, who advances—despite a depressingly consistent, if hardly unique, nineteenth-century German bigotry against Judaism—a remarkable appreciation of religious pluralism, even polytheism. Often, of course, one suspects that he is adopting pluralism and polytheism more as clubs with which to gleefully pummel his Christianity than as heart-felt convictions. Still, these convictions are there, and in abundance, and they will only grow stronger with time. If the early Feuerbach, for example, still followed his master Hegel in asserting that Christianity is the absolute religion, the later Feuerbach—evident, for example, in *Lectures on the Essence of Religion*— argued rather that the nature religions are superior to the religions of the spirit, like Christianity, since whereas the nature religions embrace the body, nature, and the earth, the religions of the spirit do not.

All religions, Feuerbach wryly points out, think that they are right, that they are the absolute measure of truth (EC 16–17): "the heathen," for example, "did not doubt the existence of Jupiter," he mischievously notes (EC 19). He also has a very keen sense for the structural or innate violence of monotheism. Adopting his usual psychological acumen, Feuerbach defines monotheism as "egoism in the form of religion." The miracles of the Hebrew Bible, for example, are all flat and impossible contradictions of nature that happen in the text "purely at the command of Jehovah, who troubles himself about nothing but Israel, who is nothing but the personified selfishness of the Israelitish people, to the exclusion of all other nations" (EC 113–114). Feuerbach's conclusion? "Absolute intolerance" is "the secret essence of monotheism" (EC 113–114). Certainly, many other scholars, including many Jewish scholars, have since come to very similar convictions.[22] Once again, Feuerbach was well ahead of his time.

One might legitimately question whether Feuerbach was really ahead of his time, in the light of his vehement denial of Judaism and his anti-Semitism. Two things are worth pointing out here, however. First, the ancient gnostic texts, and particularly those that identify the biblical Yahweh with the lower demiurge, have also been taken to task for what some have identified as a kind of metaphysical anti-Semitism.[23] Secondly, the rejection of monotheism that one finds in both the Coptic texts and Feuerbach is hardly restricted to Judaism. The rejection of orthodox forms of Christianity is just as harsh, and, in many cases, harsher and certainly more consistent. Most of Feuerbach's *The Essence of Christianity*, for example, is a passionate reduction of Christianity, not Judaism, to human categories. At the heart of this faith in particular he finds a "malignant principle" (EC 252), the principle of faith itself that must define its own identity and privilege by excluding or subordinating everyone who is different, who is other, who is "non-Christian." Christianity, Feuerbach points out, knows no distinction between the species and the individual; that is, it falsely imagines that all human beings must fit the same universal mold: "It has one and the same means of salvation for all men, it sees one and the same original sin in all" (EC 159). And hence, "Christianity, in contradiction with the genuine universal human heart, recognised man only under the condition, the limitation, of belief in Christ" (EC 120–121). Feuerbach calls this dubious conflation of the Christian with all of humanity Christianity's "fatal limitation" (EC 121).

Polytheistic pluralism, on the other hand, can produce a stunning vision of humanity at its richest. "Each new man is a new predicate, a new phase of humanity," Feuerbach writes. "The mystery of the inexhaustible fullness of the divine predicates is therefore nothing else than the mystery of human nature considered as an infinitely varied, infinitely modifiable, but, consequently, phenomenal being" (EC 23). At points, Feuerbach even adopts a distinctly mystical language (in this case, perhaps borrowed from the great medieval theologian Meister Eckhart, who provided the last of the epigraphs to this chapter) to express the transformations wrought by a profound engagement with other human beings and other cultures: "The other is my *thou* . . . my *alter ego*, man objective to me, the revelation of my own nature, the eye seeing itself" (EC 158). Here, cross-cultural engagement becomes a kind of implicit gnostic practice.

Perhaps even more radically, it is this same plural human community that "saves" us, that is, completes our natural and inevitable individual imperfections and failings. Unlike Christianity, which for Feuerbach focuses entirely too much on individual subjectivity, lacks the idea of "the species" (a difficult and outdated term that might better be framed today as "humanity"), and so must turn to supernatural aids for "salvation," pluralism turns to nature and humanity for fulfillment and completion. In this polytheistic world, each and every human being is a manifest god relating to and revealing another: "Man is God to Man" (*Homo homini Deus est*). This is what Feuerbach calls the "natural reconciliation" of the species: "My fellow-man is *per se* the mediator between me and the sacred idea of the species. *Homo homini Deus est.* My sin is made to shrink within its limits, is thrust back into its nothingness, by the fact that it is only mine, and not that of my fellows" (EC 159). Thus, for Feuerbach, "the truth of the plural, the truth of polytheism is again affirmed, and the truth of monotheism is denied" (EC 235).

Completing the Incarnation of Love (and Sex): Embodiment in Feuerbach's Thought

Perhaps one of the most striking examples of Feuerbach's gnostic inversion method is his interpretation of the Christian doctrine of the Incarnation. Interestingly, as Harvey reminds us, both Hegel and Feuerbach turned to the doctrine of the Incarnation as the theological crystallization of their own philosophies. Hegel, for example, saw Christianity as the "absolute religion," that is, as the furthest-evolved religious system, because its central doctrine of the Incarnation symbolizes the Absolute Spirit objectifying itself in the universe and then reconciling itself to its own alienated manifestation: the Incarnation thus completes the dialectic begun by Creation.

Feuerbach, at least in the *Essence of Christianity*, also argued that Christianity is the absolute religion,[24] but for a very different reason. Christianity was the absolute religion for him because, as Harvey puts it, "in the doctrine of the Incarnation is articulated the atheistic insight that human-ity's well-being is more important than God's."[25] Or, as Feuerbach put it: "As God has renounced himself out of love, so we, out of love, should renounce God" (EC 53). Just as Christ emptied himself and effectively renounced his own divinity to take on flesh and become a human being, so should we now renounce God for the sake of this same humanity.

The secret of Christian theology, in other words, is atheism. Or, more positively, the secret of Christian theology is humanism, the affirmation of the human being as the projecting source of all the gods and as the ulti-mate ground of all human meaning and love: "The contemplation of God as human, is the mystery of the Incarnation. The Incarnation is nothing else than the practical, material manifestation of the human nature of God" (EC 50). Or again: "In the Incarnation religion only confesses, what in reflection on itself, as theology, it will not admit; namely, that God is an altogether human being" (EC 56).

Very much related to this incarnational logic is Feuerbach's insistence on locating the deepest meanings of religion in the human body and, more specifically, in the sexual body. Perhaps not surprisingly, Feuerbach's most extensive discussions of sexuality and religion occur in his chapter on mysticism, that is, in an analysis of that strain of religious thought that seeks to unite the divine and the human in the person and body of an in-dividual human being: the mystical and the erotic morph into one another here, as everywhere else.

What is the final meaning of the Incarnation so understood for Feuer-bach? Love. Love is a mediating force for the thinker, personified in Chris-tian theology as an individual (Christ) and as a single event in history (the Incarnation). It also constitutes the energy or dynamism of Feuerbach's dialectical thinking: "Love makes man God and God man" (EC 48). The meaning of the Incarnation, then, is love, but a love not fully realized in Christianity because it is still bound to the cruel exclusions of faith, which infects love and turns it into hatred of the excluded religious other. Freed from the specifics of this exclusivistic faith and from the single person of Christ through Feuerbach's gnostic method, love can finally reveal its truly divine nature, not as a person or an event, but as a divine substance shared by all of humanity, symbolized here by the Incarnation. Bound to faith, however, love morphs easily into hatred: "So long as love is not exalted into a substance, into an essence, so long there lurks in the background of love a subject who even without love is something by himself, an unloving monster, a diabolical being, whose personality, separable and actually sep-arated from love, delights in the blood of heretics and unbelievers,—the phantom of religious fanaticism. Nevertheless the essential idea of the Incarnation, though enveloped in the night of the religious conscious-ness, is love" (EC 52–53). And now the inversion or reversal and a stunning conclusion: "Who then is our Saviour and Redeemer? God or Love? Love;

for God as God has not saved us, but Love, which transcends the difference between the divine and human personality. As God has renounced himself out of love, so we, out of love, should renounce God; for if we do not sacrifice God to love, we sacrifice love to God, and, in spite of the predicate of love, we have the God—the evil being—of religious fanaticism" (EC 53).

Here again, Feuerbach seems to be drawing on a creative (mis)reading of the Christian mystics for his inspiration, particularly Meister Eckhart, who once urged his readers to "pray to God that you might be free of God." "The "old mystics" thus had it right when they said of God "that he is the highest and yet the commonest being," for this too "applies in truth to love," but—and now Feuerbach's correction—"not a visionary, imaginary love—no! a real love, a love which has flesh and blood, which vibrates as an almighty force through all living" (EC 48).

Enter the sexual, or what is more traditionally called simply "the *flesh*," for which, Feuerbach complains, the religions prudishly substitute the safer and equivocal terms "*nature* and *ground*" (EC 90; italics his). Feuerbach will have none of this nonsense: "And the strongest of the impulses of Nature, is it not the sexual feeling? Who does not remember the old proverb: '*Amare et sapere vix Deo competit*' [It scarcely suffices for a god to love and to show good sense]? So that if we would posit in God a nature, an existence opposed to the light of intelligence,—can we think of a more living, a more real antithesis, than that of *amare* [to love] and *sapere* [to know], of spirit and flesh, of freedom and the sexual impulse?" (EC 91). "Nature," Feuerbach points out (now returning that abstraction back to real *flesh* again), "as has been shown and is obvious, is nothing without corporeality. . . . The body is the basis, the subject of personality" (EC 91). Nor can such a sexual flesh be safely localized, denied, or completely controlled, for it lies at the very center of reality itself. It *is* human reality in all its physical, social, and ethical complexity. As he slips into his rhetorical "thous," Feuerbach quickly becomes a kind of protofeminist Freudian prophet, affirming the ethical and biological priority of sexual difference and proclaiming that God and sexuality share the same secret nature:

> [F]lesh and blood is nothing without the oxygen of sexual distinction. The distinction of sex is not superficial, or limited to certain parts of the body; it is an essential one; it penetrates bones and marrows. The substance of man is manhood; that of woman, womanhood. . . . Where there is no thou, there is no I; but the distinction between I and thou, the fundamental condition of all personality, of all consciousness, is only real, living, ardent, when felt as the distinction between man and woman. . . . But what is more feeble, what more insupportable, what more contrary to Nature, than a person without sex, or a person who in character, manners, or feelings denies sex? . . . Repudiate then, before all, thy own horror for the distinction of sex. If God is not polluted by Nature, neither is he polluted by being associated with the idea

of sex. In renouncing sex, thou renouncest thy whole principle. A moral God apart from Nature is without basis; but the basis of morality is the distinction of sex. . . . All the glory of Nature, all its power, all its wisdom and profundity, concentrates and individualises itself in distinction of sex. Why then dost thou shrink from naming the nature of God by its true name? (EC 92)

Not only does this basic denial of sex in the Godhead make no sense. It also leads to a denial of death and a false hope for personal immortality. The biological purpose of sex, after all, is intimately linked to death: biological organisms reproduce because they die, that is, because they are not immortal. Sex and death are thus two sides of the same biological coin. Thus, both are an offensive affront to the Christian doctrine of immortality (not to mention the virgin birth):

The belief in personal immortality has at its foundation the belief that difference of sex is only an external adjunct of individuality, that in himself the individual is a sexless, independently complete, absolute being. But he who belongs to no sex belongs to no species; sex is the cord which connects the individuality with the species. . . . He who lives in the consciousness of the species, and consequently of its reality, lives also in the consciousness of the reality of sex. He does not regard it as a mechanically inserted, adventitious stone of stumbling, but as an inherent quality, a chemical constituent of his being. . . . [H]e is at the same time conscious of being rigorously determined by the sexual distinction, which penetrates not only bones and marrow, but also his inmost self, the essential mode of his thought, will, and sensation. (EC 170)

It is worth noting here that Feuerbach's insistence on the sexuality of all of life and his rage against the pathologies of religious prudery is likely rooted in his own life and experience. He belonged for a time, for example, to a group called the Young Germans, who openly embraced the concept of free love. Moreover, he left his first wife for a very young woman, Johanna Kapp, with whom he seems to have fallen deeply in love. Passages such as the above suggest that he experienced something "divine" in his sexual life, even and especially if this sexual life violated the norms of Christian society.

The Sexuality of Numbers

Such a love makes the Two One . . . and then Three. Biologically speaking, the uniting of a man and a woman creates a third human being, a child. But this is also a classically mystical structure of thought, a dialectic so common in the history of religions that scholars have given it a Latin name: the *coincidentia oppositorum*, the "coincidence of opposites," the uniting of Two into a Third (more on this below, in "Interlude"). There are many ways to approach such a religious structure, but Feuerbach will approach it, long before Freud, as something rooted deeply in ordinary human experience, that is, in the human family and the latter's sexual dynamics. And here we come to the traditional problem of the Trinity and its strange desexualization in Christian doctrine.

Feuerbach analyzes the Trinity (that Father and Son whose love is personified as the Spirit) as a theological expression of the human family (or at least one mode of it—the father-son relationship), in essence arguing that Christianity's constant talk of "the Father," "the Son," "brothers and sisters in Christ," and so on is an ideal projection of mundane human relationships into the divinity itself. The implications of this reading, however, force another that is really more of a question: If the Christian Trinity is a human family projected into the sky, then where is the Mother? If God is a Father and has a Son, why does the Trinity lack a consort, partner, or Mother? In actual biological experience, of course, a son has never come straight from a Father (Spirit or no), as the male theological fantasies of the Trinity and the virgin birth imagine it. Feuerbach thus arrives at a gendered conclusion that C. G. Jung and, in a very different mode, feminist theology will return to in the next century, namely, that the Trinity rather desperately needs a Mother—for Jung a fourth member—to complete itself.[26]

The Spirit, often feminized in Christian thought, approaches a solution but never quite gets there, since Latin Christianity at least conceived of the Spirit as more of a relationship between the Father and the Son than as a "separate" individual identity. Hence the Catholic virtual deification of the Virgin Mary: "It was therefore quite in order that, to complete the divine family, the bond of love between Father and Son, a third, and that a feminine person, was received into heaven; for the personality of the Holy Spirit is a too vague and precarious" (EC 70). Feuerbach can thus take his own Protestantism to task (exactly as Jung would do again) for ignoring the divine feminine: "Protestantism has set aside the Mother of God; but this deposition of woman has been severely avenged" (EC 72). In another passage, Feuerbach insightfully links this Protestant-Catholic difference to their social practices and approaches to celibacy: "It is true that Protestantism had no need of the heavenly bride [the Virgin], because it received with open arms the earthly bride [that is, it rejected celibacy]. . . . Only he who has no earthly parents needs heavenly ones. . . . The impoverishing of the real world and the enriching of God is one act. Only the poor man has a rich God. God springs out of the feeling of a want" (EC 73).[27] Feuerbach thus sees what innumerable scholars will later see, namely, that Catholic theology's privileging of the Virgin Mary and the practice of celibacy are very much linked, and that religious sexual language flourishes best in a context of sexual repression or denial.

But, Virgin Mary or no, this is a very strange family indeed, and this for one simple reason: there is no sex in it: "[T]he Virgin Mary fits in perfectly with the relations of the Trinity, since she conceives without man the Son whom the Father begets without woman; so that thus the Holy Virgin is a necessary, inherently requisite antithesis to the Father in the bosom of the Trinity" (EC 70–71). Theologically consistent perhaps, but no less sexually and biologically bizarre.

Finally, Feuerbach's psychological insight into the son's early "feminine" identification with his mother, the tensions he feels between this identification and his later necessary "masculine" independence from his father, and his basic androgynous or bisexual nature all eerily foreshadow what Freud will later call the "family romance" and the "Oedipus complex." Feuerbach even locates the psychosexual source of the man's sexual attraction to a woman in his earlier "truly religious" love for his mother, thereby sexualizing it all, more or less exactly as Freud would later do in a much more systematic fashion:

> The son—I mean the natural, human son—considered as such, is an intermediate being between the masculine nature of the father and the feminine nature of the mother; he is, as it were, still half a man, half a woman, inasmuch as he has not the full, rigorous consciousness of independence which characterizes the man, and feels himself drawn rather to the mother than to the father. The love of the son to the mother is the first love of the masculine being for the feminine. The love of man to woman, the love of the youth for the maiden, receives its religious—its sole truly religious consecration in the love of the son to the mother; the son's love for his mother is the first yearning of man towards woman—his first humbling of himself before her. (EC 71)

It seems important to point out in this context that Feuerbach's thought on such subjects reflects, recalls, or actually recreates the ancient gnostic structures, particularly as set out in such texts as the Apocryphon of John. "There was not a plurality before me," John tells his readers at the very beginning of this secret text as he sets out to describe his vision after the heavens have opened before him, "but there was a likeness with multiple forms in the light, and the semblances appeared through each other, and the likeness had three forms." A few lines down, this trinity speaks directly to the visionary: "I am the one who is with you always. I am the Father, I am the Mother, I am the Son."[28] Feuerbach would have approved of such a vision.

The Cancer and the Cure

Toward the very end of *The Essence of Christianity*, Feuerbach turns to faith and love, a deceptively traditional move that he employs for his own deeply subversive ends. Feuerbach is quite happy with "love," which, as we have already seen, he insists on sexualizing. "Faith" is another matter altogether, again as we have already seen. For Feuerbach, whereas love unites and expresses the actual identity of the divine and the human, faith separates both the divine and the human and, more important, individual human communities. With respect to the human-divine relation, Feuerbach can thus write: "The essence of religion, its latent nature, is the *identity* of the divine being with the human; but the form of religion, or its apparent, conscious nature, is the *distinction* between them" (EC 247). With respect to religion's deleterious effects on a plural society, he observes:

> Now, that which reveals the basis, the hidden essence of religion, is Love; that which constitutes its conscious form is Faith. Love identifies man with God and God with man, consequently it identifies man with man; faith separates God from man, consequently it separates man from man, for God is nothing else than the idea of the species invested with a mystical form,— the separation of God from man is therefore the separation of man from man, the unloosening of the social bond. By faith religion places itself in contradiction with morality, with reason . . . by love, it opposes itself again to this contradiction. (EC 247)

Faith, Feuerbach tells us, "is in its nature exclusive" (EC 248). It is also arrogant, but in a very clever and devious way, since "it clothes its feeling of superiority, its pride, in the idea of another person," that is, in God (EC 250). This "God," then, "is this distinction and pre-eminence of believers above unbelievers, personified" (EC 249–50). Consequently, any social ethic or morality based on this God, or any other deity for that matter, is a dangerous one indeed, since with this single move "the most immoral, unjust, infamous things can be justified and established" (EC 274). In short, "*In faith there lies a malignant principle*" (EC 252; italics in original).

Perhaps the best religious example of this danger is the concept of hell. Elaine Pagels has recently demonstrated that the figure of Satan in Christian thought arose as a mythological embodiment of the bitter hatreds of early Christian-Jewish conflict. "Satan," to put it far too simply, arose as an expression of the early Jewish Christians' hatred for "the Jews," whom the Gospel of John so angrily calls "the children of Satan."[29] The devil, in other words, is a mythical projection of interreligious conflict and hatred (hence, the West becomes "the great Satan" in contemporary radical Islamist rhetoric). Feuerbach possessed none of Pagels's historical-critical acumen, but he nevertheless came to what is essentially an identical, and equally dramatic, conclusion, which I hear expressed in the form of a series of powerful Feuerbachian sayings, a true Brook of Fire . . .

> The flames of hell are only the flashings of the exterminating, vindictive glance which faith casts on unbelievers. (EC 255)

It was faith, not love, not reason, which invented Hell. To love, Hell is a horror; to reason, an absurdity. (EC 257)

All the horrors of Christian religious history, which our believers aver not to be due to Christianity, have truly arisen out of Christianity, because they have arisen out of faith. (EC 258)

Faith necessarily passes into hatred, hatred into persecution . . . where it does not find itself in collision with a power foreign to faith, the power of love, of humanity, of the sense of justice. (EC 260)

Thus does man sacrifice man to God! The blood human sacrifice is in fact only a rude, material expression of the inmost secret of religion. (EC 272)

So what is the cure to this common cancer? Love, but a love disentangled from the malignancy of faith: "God is love. This is the sublimest dictum of Christianity. But the contradiction of faith and love is contained in the very proposition" (EC 263). Or again: "Love is God, love is the absolute being" (EC 264). The ethical and cultural implications of such a metaphysics are profound, for "the very office of love is to abolish the distinction between Christianity and so-called heathenism" (EC 266). In short, no more hell, no more exclusivism, no more religious violence, no more arrogant egoism hidden in religious clothes and "sacred" beliefs. Once again, we finally return to the truth of human pluralism, here imagined as a logical conclusion of a universal mystical eros lifted "above the peculiar stand-point of all religion" (EC 270), in effect a religion of no religion.

Toward a Mystical Humanism: A Gnostic Rereading

At the very end of part 1 of *The Essence of Christianity*, Feuerbach writes this: "Our most essential task is now fulfilled. We have reduced the supermundane, supernatural, and superhuman nature of God to the elements of human nature as its fundamental elements. Our process of analysis has brought us again to the position with which we set out. The beginning, middle and end of religion is MAN" (EC 184).

Historically, Feuerbach's claim here has traditionally been read as a kind of absolute reduction of the divine to the human, as an atheistic humanism that wants nothing to do with religion. I do not want to deny in any way this traditional reading of the book, nor do I want to overlook the biographical and philosophical fact that Feuerbach became more, not less, critical of religion as he matured in age. Still, what strikes me most about this same Brook of Fire, at least as it is expressed in this first book, is how easily it can be read as flowing in a different direction (or at least as possessing many currents) and, moreover, how often its author's language and metaphors draw on Neoplatonic, Jewish, and Christian mystical traditions to make some of their most powerful points. These two observations, I think, are very much related, for, with the slightest "spin" or creative (mis)reading, Feuerbach's *The Essence of Christianity* could quite easily take an honorable, if always controversial, place in the history of Christian mystical literature. Its central teaching, after all, is that God is Man and Man is God, that is, that the divine and the human are identical. Is not this the essential structure of much, if not all, of what we have chosen to call mystical literature?

Certainly I am not the first to see this. Feuerbach himself more than hints at it in the opening pages. Again: "While reducing theology to anthropology," he wrote, "I exalt anthropology into theology, very much as Christianity, while lowering God into man, made man into God" (EC xviii). "Thus," now in the words of the contemporary historian of Christianity Amy Hollywood, Feuerbach's *"The Essence of Christianity* can be read as a call for a new form of religion in which human beings reappropriate divinity and thus make themselves divine." [30] Peter Berger, the sociologist of religion whose deeply influential theory of social construction owes much to Feuerbach, saw the same again. Indeed, in many ways the present essay is an example of Berger's "interesting ploy," which wants to suggest that "man projects ultimate meanings into reality because that reality is, indeed, ultimately meaningful, and because his own being (the empirical ground of these projections) contains and intends these same ultimate meanings. Such a theological procedure, if feasible, would be an interesting play on Feuerbach—the reduction of theology to anthropology would end in the reconstruction of anthropology in a theological mode." [31] Finally, Cyril O'Regan has written exquisitely about the gnostic architectonics of Feuerbach's looming philosophical predecessor, G. W. F. Hegel, and the different ways Hegel's thought, and indeed modernity itself, is informed or "haunted" by the gnostic theosophy of Jacob Boehme, perhaps *the* central figure in the history of Western esotericism. [32] In some ways, my own gnostic reading of Feuerbach and of the modern study of religion follows upon O'Regan's astonishing project, if in a much less learned key. [33] What is gnostic about the early Feuerbach, in other words, is almost certainly connected to his Hegelianism, which in turn is informed by the Boehmian esoteric traditions, which are themselves structurally gnostic.

There are four points to make here, involving four different aspects of my reading of Feuerbach's text: (1) his method's implicit Neoplatonic structure; (2) his vaguely gnostic epistemology; (3) his explicit invocation of traditional mystical anthropologies; and (4) his related rhetorical categories of secrecy, mystery, and mysticism. A word about each is in order before I conclude this second meditation.

NEOPLATONIC STRUCTURE. Consider for a moment Feuerbach's twin poles of projection and reduction. Can these not be read as secularized versions of a much older Neoplatonic cosmology, in which the creation of the world and its reabsorption back into the One are figured in the two cycles of emanation and return? Feuerbach writes: "In the religious systole man propels his own nature from himself, he throws himself outward; in the religious diastole he receives the rejected nature into his heart again" (EC 31). Replace the word "man" with "the One," and you have the basic structure of Neoplatonic mysticism. So too with the dialectical process of revelation and scripture. Feuerbach again: "And so in revelation man goes out of himself, in order, by a circuitous path, to return to himself! Here we have a striking confirmation of the position that the secret of theology is nothing else than anthropology—the knowledge of God nothing else than a knowledge of man!" (EC 207).

I realize, of course, that in Feuerbach's understanding, the accent is to be placed squarely and definitively on "MAN," and the grammatical movement is from the projection ("God") to the reduction ("man"). But must we follow him here? If Feuerbach can "invert" or "reverse" all of Christian theology, why can we not invert the inversion and reverse the reversal, not to make an impossible return to the precritical domain of faith, but rather to produce our own (post)modern gnosis? In other words, if the projection can be withdrawn, why can the withdrawal not be reprojected in a different mode, rather in the manner of Ricoeur's famous second naïveté, that return to the promised land of religion in a new form after a passing through the desert of critical theory? Or, to invoke Feuerbach's invocation of Adam Kadmon, the cosmic Human Form of the Godhead in medieval Jewish mysticism, why can we not see in the double mirror of Elliot Wolfson's kabbalistic hermeneutics and poetics that "envisioning the divine as human mirrors envisioning the human as divine"?[34] First faith, then reason, then gnosis.

GNOSTIC EPISTEMOLOGY. It is also worth noting in this context that Feuerbach appears to understand the intellectual life in distinctly mystical terms. Hence, he can write of the "supernatural mind," describe philosophy, mathematics, physics, and science as "the product of this truly infinite and divine activity," and explicitly evoke the "negative way" (via negationis) of Christian mysticism to describe the inner nature of thinking itself: "[God] is known, i.e., becomes an object only by abstraction and negation (via negationis). Why? Because he is nothing but the objective nature of the thinking power" (EC 35). Or again: "Only when thy thought is God dost thou truly think, rigorously speaking; for only God is the realised, consummate, exhausted thinking power" (EC 36–37). And finally: "To think is to be God. The act of thought, as such, is the freedom of the immortal gods from all external limitations and necessities of life" (EC 41). Thought itself has become a gnostic act.

Once again, Feuerbach is clearly indebted to what O'Regan calls the heterodox Hegel here, and this heterodox Hegel is also clearly a gnostic one. Hegel, after all, insisted that philosophy is superior to religion, since knowing (reason) is superior to believing (faith). For Hegel at least, whereas philosophical cognition actually possesses, actually *knows* its object, religious belief only approximates, approaches, or symbolizes its object. With claims such as "To think is to be God," Feuerbach appears to have inherited something of this same, basically gnostic, conviction. Hence his repeated attacks on the literalisms of theology as grossly inferior to his own rational interpretations of theology's signs and symbols. Once again, philosophy surpasses, even as it subsumes and includes, religion.

How does Feuerbach understand his own speculations in relationship to those of his former teacher? According to Feuerbach, the Hegelian speculative doctrine states that *"man's* consciousness of God is the *self-*consciousness of God. God is thought, cognized by us. According to speculation, God, in being thought by us, thinks himself or is conscious of himself."* Such speculation, Feuerbach argues, "identifies the two sides which religion separates. In this it is far deeper than religion" (EC 226). Put in the terms of my rereading: Feuerbach's method is not "religious," for religion, like faith, separates; it is "mystical," for mysticism, like love and sex, unites.

MYSTICAL ANTHROPOLOGIES. At first sight, Feuerbach seems to understand "man" in some rather positivistic or materialistic ways, which is to say rather superficially. But with a second look, things appear very different indeed, and one begins to suspect that we are much closer here to the gnostic Adam of Light or what Christian theology, following Paul, will later call "the mystical body of Christ" than a simple Humean positivism, Marxist materialism, or Freudian scientism. In a later preface, for example, Feuerbach is quite clear that when he reduces theology to anthropology, he understands the latter "in an infinitely higher and more general sense" than the Hegelian (EC xix). Given that Hegelian understandings of the human being place such a strong emphasis on idealism and the Spirit, Feuerbach's claim to understand the human in an infinitely higher sense is a remarkable statement, and one that should warn us against drawing any hasty conclusions about Feuerbach's reductionism.

In support of this same reading, consider Feuerbach's invocation of explicitly mystical language to describe Man, or what he often describes as the "perfect man" (this same expression, by the way, occurs throughout the Apocryphon of John as the Coptic *teleios* or "perfect man")[35] or even the Adam Kadmon of Jewish mystical thought (EC 154). And indeed, like the cosmic Adam Kadmon of Kabbalah (or the plural bisexual "male and female" God of Genesis 1, for that matter), this "perfect man" is in fact androgynous or bisexual: "Love especially works wonders," Feuerbach writes, "and the love of the sexes most of all. Man and woman are the complement of each other, and thus united they first present the species, the perfect man" (EC 156).

Such language takes us immediately back to early rabbinic and gnostic understandings of the Adam and Eve myth, many of which understood the first Adam to be an androgyne before Eve was split off and sexual distinction as gender was born. Along similar mystico-erotic lines, in a fascinating footnote Feuerbach affirms both "Hindoo" and Old Testament visions of Adam (as sexual) and attacks the Christian Adam, who "has no longer any sexual impulses or functions" (EC 156).

But Feuerbach's cosmic Adam is more than simply bisexual. s/HE is also radically plural, historical, and always developing into something more. "God" for Feuerbach is nothing more and nothing less than the human species, "humanity" imagined as a single individual:

> All divine attributes, all the attributes which make God God, are attributes of the species—attributes which in the individual are limited, but the limits of which are abolished in the essence of the species.... My knowledge, my will, is limited; but my limit is not the limit of another man, to say nothing of mankind; what is difficult to me is easy to another; what is impossible, inconceivable, to one age, is to the coming age conceivable and possible. My life is bound to a limited time; not so the life of humanity. The history of mankind consists of nothing else than a continuous and progressive conquest of limits, which at a given time pass for the limits of humanity, and therefore for absolute insurmountable limits. But the future always unveils the fact that the alleged limits of the species were only limits of individuals. (EC 152–53)

Such a vision in effect "saves" every individual to the extent that all his or her imperfections or faults—"sins," to use traditional language—can be filled up by the corporate "perfect man." "Hence the lamentation over sin is found only where the human individual regards himself in his individuality as a perfect, complete being, not needing others for the realization of the species, of the perfect man" (EC 157). It is thus hardly surprising that Feuerbach, like the ancient gnostics but for different reasons, rejected readings of the Genesis myth that saw it as a "fall" or, much worse, as an "original sin." Original Sin, for Feuerbach, is a perceptual error produced by individuals who expect their own individualities to live up to the total Man. They do not see that they are parts of a greater Whole, and so they feel "sin." There is no "original sin," then, only a false sense of separation from humanity as a whole.

As a side note, it is perhaps worth mentioning that Hegel had also rejected the traditional reading of original sin (*Erbsünde*) in his *Lectures on the Philosophy of Religion*, where he read the Genesis myth as expressive of the necessary development of consciousness into Spirit and freedom. Much as we saw earlier with Zaehner and Bucke, the primordial state here is a state of stupor and pure nature out of which the light of consciousness evolves through the forbidden fruit. For Hegel, such an original "cleavage" of consciousness within moral awareness is necessary as an early step toward reconciliation and the sublation of an undeveloped consciousness into the fuller form of Spirit. Hence, Hegel quotes God in the myth toward his own (gnostic) ends: " 'Behold, Adam has become like one of us, knowing good and evil.' So what the serpent said was no lie; on the contrary, even God himself corroborated it." And he then slyly adds, "But this verse is usually overlooked, or else nothing is said about it." [36]

SECRECY, MYSTERY, AND MYSTICISM. Fourth and finally, it is important to point out that Feuerbach consistently describes religious matters as "the mysteries of human nature" (e.g., EC xviii). Indeed, the word *mystery* (as *Mysterium*), which of course is related to both *mysticism* and *mystical*, appears throughout Feuerbach's text, particularly in the chapter headings (as *das Mysterium*). Certainly, Feuerbach wanted to expose or explain these mysteries, but he used the language nonetheless as both meaningful and important.

Now it is certainly true that Feuerbach would have rejected the designation of "mysticism" or "mystical" for his thought. [37] Indeed, he titles an entire chapter "The Secret of Mysticism or of Nature in God" (Das Geheimnis des Mystizismus oder der Natur in Gott), primarily to deconstruct it and reject this "deceptive twilight of mysticism" (EC 88). There are other places in his text, however, where he speaks quite warmly of both mysticism and "the mystics." More important, he warmly and enthusiastically evokes another common trope of mystical literature, the rhetoric of secrecy or what he calls "the secret" (*das Geheimnis*). The phrase, for example, occurs in his central thesis that "the secret of theology is anthropology." [38]

~~~

How might we, then, understand all of this for our own present purposes? My own rereading of Feuerbach's *The Essence of Christianity* leads me to the following conclusion, which is also the most basic move of the gnostic methodology I am proposing in these four essays. With Feuerbach (and Marx and Freud and Nietzsche), I too want to reduce all religious language to human language. Do we know of *any* religious expression that is expressed by someone other than a human being? And are not *all* religious experiences also human experiences? Even Mircea Eliade, who has generally been misconstrued as some sort of simplistic transcendentalist, insisted that the sacred is an element in the structure of human consciousness, a moment within an always relational dynamic with the natural and social environments, not some easily objective Out There. [39] The question becomes, then: What do we mean by *human being* or *human consciousness*? What is the nature of this referent and producer of all religious experience and expression? In essence, the question becomes a matter of philosophical anthropology, that is, how precisely one understands the metaphysical range of human being to which all religious phenomena are "reduced."

This is precisely where I part company with many proponents of reductionism and rationalism. In my thought, at least—and, I would argue, in the early Feuerbach's as well—this human referent is quite literally ineffable; that is to say, human nature constitutes a secret that is immeasurably deeper and more complex than any strictly rational method or language can possibly grasp and that requires for its fuller (never full) explication hermeneutical methods that are best represented in those forms of religious thinking and practice we have come to call, for our own purposes and in our own poetic terms, "mystical" or "gnostic." Such a (non) ground in turn requires for its appearance the intellectual courage of a truly open-ended anthropology. That anthropology, which is also a general methodological principle, inevitably tends toward what I would call a *mystical humanism*.

Through the specifics of any number of rational-critical methods (historical criticism, anthropology, psychoanalysis, sociology, economics, philosophy, evolutionary psychology, neuroscience, etc.), such a mystical humanism enthusiastically and efficiently reduces all religious language to the human being, but to human being now conceived as an unfathomable biological, chemical, and quantum depth, an immeasurable, unquantifiable potential, an anciently evolved cosmic body literally composed of exploded stars,[40] an instinctually undetermined, ever-receding horizon, and a radical, irreducible plurality expressed and explored in countless cultural forms and practices.[41]

Obviously, within such a transfigured anthropology, mythopoetic language cannot be literalized, but neither can it be bracketed out or denied, as if the poem, the myth, even the religious doctrine did not carry their own truths. Feuerbach, then, has it exactly right when he moves from a literal, faith-defined understanding of the Christian myth to the gnosis of a mystical or symbolic reading of the same: "To believe," he writes in *The Essence of Faith according to Luther*, "is but to change the 'There is a God and a Christ' into the 'I am a God and a Christ.'"[42] This, in turn, gnostically echoes the Gospel of Philip: "For this person is no longer a Christian but a Christ."[43] Feuerbach also recognizes that it is human intention, will and imagination that constitute the power of "faith," and that the power of this human form of consciousness can take on an infinite number of forms, shapes, and languages: "Here we have the meaning of the thoughts so often expressed by Luther: 'As you believe, so it occurs for you'; 'If you believe it, you have it, and if you do not believe it, you do not have it'; 'If you believe it, it is, and if you do not believe it, it is not.' . . . God is a blank tablet on which there is nothing written but what you yourself have written."[44]

Certainly this is no precritical faith, no return to belief in an objective God "out there." Neither, however, is this a pure and sufficient reason, strangely satisfied with some surface view of human nature. This, rather, is a type of erotic (post)modern gnosis whose final goal "is to make God a man and man a God."[45] This is the bisexual Adam of Light restored to consciousness, being, and bliss through an awakened sensuality (*Sinnlichkeit*) and a real and mutual sexual Love. This is the forbidden fruit that delights, awakens, arouses, and exiles all at once. This is the serpent's gift.

Comparative Mystics 3

[O]ften the experience of mystery cannot be confined to the
conceptual categories in which theology barters meaning.
In this sense, every mystical act is itself a shift in paradigms
and the stuff of "heresy." . . . Those who have been guided
into the annihilatory experience know that new theology con-
tinually unfolds both within a tradition and as the break-
through of tradition. The mystical pioneers who have risked
their visions of truth in often hostile climates, and who have
offered us rare glimpses of a God who not only celebrates
new ideas and new revelations, but who births them as well,
provide hope for interreligious cooperation.
Beverly J. Lanzetta, The Other Side of Nothingness

The Rebuke of the Gnostic and the Oriental Renaissance

In a world of singular claims to absolute truth and fundamentalist intolerance, religious bigotry, and violent terrorism, there are few more important questions to ask than those pertaining to the social and ethical
ramifications of monotheism, that is, the idea of a single God (or religion
or nation) whose will and authority should somehow ground human well-
being and global flourishing. The gnostic texts, although often operating
with a transcendent monotheism of their own (which is really often more
of a monism), were also radically critical of popular conceptions of God as
creator, judge, lord, and king, which they tended to see as both literally
ridiculous and as frankly dangerous.

The Apocryphon of John, for example, answers the blind creator-god's
arrogant claim that he is the only God with the stinging rebukes that Man
in fact surpasses him in thinking, and that he is a violent rapist and
illegitimate son of Barbelo the Divine Mother of Light, herself an erotic

emanation of the Father, that invisible Spirit or Pleroma beyond all the gods.[1] The same text teasingly points out that a biblical claim like "I am a jealous God and there is no other God beside me" is self-contradictory, "[f]or if there were no other one, of whom would he be jealous?"[2] And text after text understands the biblical god of creation (Yahweh) as an ignorant fool whose claims to superiority must be rejected within any mature gnosis. Indeed, one of the Aramaic names consistently bestowed on this god by the Coptic texts, Saklas, actually means "fool."

Very much related to this gnostic rejection of popular monotheism was the common gnostic rejection of scriptural literalism. The caustic phrase "not as Moses said," for example, occurs throughout the Apocryphon of John as an angry critique of ancient biblical literalism and its divinization of a violent and cruel creator-god.[3] As with their refusal to submit to Yahweh, many of the gnostic authors thought such literal readings were ridiculous and capable of producing only absurd, morally reprehensible visions of God. They understood, as the Gospel of Philip puts it so beautifully, that "[t]ruth did not come into the world naked, but it came in types and images," and that "[t]he world will not receive truth in any other way."[4]

Such gnostic sensibilities, such rage against the evil literalisms of religion, strike me as oddly modern, even and especially if the archons of our present moment strongly resemble the figures of Saklas or Samael and not those of the dissenting Valentinian Christian or serpent-loving Sethian. We live under the sign of the threatening god of death and his apocalypse, not that of the life-giving snake and his garden. We live in a time of warring Samaels, each of whom mistakenly thinks he is the only God, a time of scriptural literalism, fundamentalist politics, and the crude worship of the nation-state and the ethnic identity.

It is thus all too easy to forget that, not so long ago, intelligent and pragmatic people could hope for a global worldview and even a global spirituality to emerge. It is worth remembering. It is worthwhile resisting the cynicism that comes from knowing that cosmopolitan hopes were at their highest during the colonial era. But however unwelcome the contact (unwelcome, often, on both sides), colonialism brought divergent cultures into intimate relationships whose results were not wholly or finally negative.[5] One result was that brave souls around the planet came to believe that the conflicts among cultures, religions, and "final vocabularies" could eventually be transcended.[6]

The positive results tended to be scholarly and to center on religion, not surprisingly of a distinctly mystical or heretical sort. In 1950, the postcolonial turning point, Raymond Schwab argued that the human venture had been ennobled and transformed during an Oriental Renaissance (1680–1880) when scholars labored diligently, if imperfectly, at the project of translation and religious interpretation. "Few people today," Schwab wrote, "seem to have heard of Anquetil-Duperron or Sir William Jones or what they set out to accomplish in India in the eighteenth century, but they have drastically altered our ways of thinking nonetheless. Why, then, is the fact generally unknown? The truth is that, in seizing upon the treasures of the poor Orient, critics have grasped only superficial influences that conceal the real issues, which concern the destinies of the intellect and the soul."[7] Schwab was most likely thinking of the effects that Asian and Middle Eastern cultures had had on the European mind, but, as we well know, the effects of Orientalism were no less profound in Asia and the Middle East. Indeed, Asian and Middle Eastern actors often did more than anyone to advance the cultural exchange. As participants in cultures that had neither created nor fully participated in the astonishing scientific, political, and cultural achievements of the Enlightenment, these individuals were keenly aware of what might be gained from cross-cultural encounter, even if they usually described their activity in terms of redressing imbalances and injustices. Many, on all sides, saw cross-cultural transformation as the secret to a better, more balanced world, and they often turned to religion as the place to signify or effect these new "destinies of the intellect and the soul."

Schwab locates the beginnings of this "conversion" in the mid-eighteenth century and observes how its rise and development coincided not just with colonialism but also Romanticism:

> The ability to decipher unknown alphabets, acquired in Europe after 1750, had one incalculable effect: the discovery that there had been other Europes. Thus, in that progressive era, the West perceived that it was not the sole possessor of an admirable intellectual past. This singular event occurred during a period when everything else was likewise new, unprecedented, extraordinary. The advent of oriental studies during a Romantic period abounding in geniuses and accomplishments, in great appetites and abundant nourishment, is one of history's most astonishing coincidences.[8]

Shwab, moreover, saw, in the synergies of European Romanticism and the cultural riches of the Orient a hopeful answer to the violence, bigotry, and mass death of the Second World War: "So many prophets of doom cry out to our age of a world near its end that it feels itself susceptible to what has never moved it before. Now is the time to present to our age . . . the birth of an integral humanism, a crucial, unprecedented chapter in the history of civilizations."[9]

I begin with Shwab's postwar "integral humanism" because, first, I recognize myself to be an heir, and a grateful one, of Schwab's Oriental Renaissance.[10] But my reasons for beginning with Shwab go far beyond the personal. The global meeting of Eastern and Western religions has dramatically changed the theologies of Western Christianity, in particular that of the Roman Catholic Church.[11] The Oriental Renaissance has been definitive as well for modern Hinduism—definitive in its pluralistic expressions (Aurobindo's evolutionary metaphysics, for example, or Gandhi's theology of nonviolence) but also in the violent fundamentalism or essentialist politics of Hindutva ("Hinduness"), which, in resisting cross-cultural exchange, models itself on Western fascism, Christian and Jewish fundamentalism, and Muslim exclusivism.[12] It is by now a truism among Indologists that the colonial encounter between East and West crystallized the present semiotic field: Hinduism is a modern idea—indeed, a word that did not exist until fairly recently (the abstract noun did not appear in *Webster's Dictionary* until 1849).[13]

To invoke the Oriental Renaissance, then, is not simply to recall a distant memory; it is also to observe how, in the modern context, the development of a world religion began. Some readers will take "world religion" as a threat. I take it as a hope, though also a warning: we must finally assume responsibility for our social constructions and ask hard practical questions about their ability to produce a world at relative peace. "Solidarity is not," as Richard Rorty puts it, "discovered by reflection but created."[14] Or in Bruno Latour's words, "[t]he common world . . . must be progressively composed . . . an immense task which we will need to accomplish one step at a time."[15]

Comparative Mystics

The construction that Latour and Rorty have in mind will not become possible until we are ready—as Eduardo Viveiros de Castro appears to suggest—to take the risk of mutual contamination and transformation across worldviews.[16] Here I want to make explicit what Viveiros de Castro seems to intimate: the value of the outsider in bringing seemingly incompatible cultural forms together. There are those—in Viveiros de Castro's ethnography, they are shamans—with a scandalous ability to think beyond borders drawn literally on a map or cognitively in the recesses of cultural, religious, and even sexual identity. Given the efforts and successes of such (admittedly rare) people, we need to rethink the ontological status of difference itself, particularly within those literatures and practices that we have come to call "mystical."

My adjective is chosen carefully here as a term of art possessing long lineages in (but irreducible to) Christian spirituality, American psychology, the modern study of religion, and French poststructuralism, all of which I will get to in due time. For now, it is necessary only to explicate my title, "Comparative Mystics," as an intentional double entendre rooted in French psychoanalytic and poststructuralist studies of mystical literature, particularly as performed by the anthropologist Michel de Certeau, whose unique adjectival noun *la mystique* I have employed for eleven years now as "the mystical." Michael B. Smith, de Certeau's translator, explicates his use of the French term this way:

> The theme of Michel de Certeau's *Mystic Fable* is *la mystique*. This term cannot be rendered accurately by the English word "mysticism," which would correspond rather to the French *le mysticisme*, and be far too generic and essentialist a term to convey the historical specificity of the subject of this study. There is no need here to retrace the steps by which *la mystique*, the noun, emerged from the prior adjective, *mystique*. . . . But it may be of some interest to note that this grammatical promotion has its parallel in English, in the development of such terms as "mathematics" or "physics," fields of inquiry of increasing autonomy, also taking their names from an adjectival forerunner. I have, therefore, *in extremis*, adopted the bold solution of introducing a made-up English term, *mystics* . . . to render *la mystique*, a field that might have won (but never did, in English) a name alongside metaphysics, say, or optics.[17]

For our present context, I have added to Smith's neologism *mystics* the qualifier *comparative* to indicate a discourse that undermines the doctrinal claims of individual religions by setting them beside the claims of other religions. The purpose of such a comparative mystics is to expose all doctrinal claims as historically and culturally relative expressions of a deeper mystery or ontological ground (the gnostic Pleroma) that nevertheless requires these relative expressions for its self-revelation. Through comparative mystics (as a disciplinary field or practice) and its comparative mystics (as historical exemplars), I want to question whether it is the case that, as Latour asserts, constructivism has no opposite.[18]

My thesis, baldly stated (but developed in some detail below), will be that cultural differences and local knowledges are socially and politically important but not ontologically ultimate, and that the gnostic deconstruction or saying-away of cultural and religious "essences"—which flourishes especially in the subversive countercultures of the mystical traditions—is the level at which deep communication may be realizable. Before starting on this argument, however, I need to list a variety of reservations, lest I be misunderstood and dismissed out of hand.

I am not suggesting, for example, that this potential role of the mystical in our own day would repeat or return to some past revelation or some complete religious truth, or that the mystical traditions are without their own serious ethical liabilities and intellectual failures. On the contrary, I would say that modern social and intellectual forms (democracy, science, individualism, human rights, capitalism, globalism) themselves represent a fundamentally new revelation of human spirit with which the religions and their mystical countercultures must come positively to terms.

Nor do I want to suggest that a turn to the mystical should be equated, as it so often is in popular literature, with vacuous thinking about "experience," "unity," and "purity" (this last term usually a stand-in for prudery, sexual ignorance, and misogyny). Searing self-criticism, critical fury, eros, and the hard intellectual labor of repudiation are more what I have in mind. In this same apophatic spirit, I will not presume to intuit a common essence to the world religions that can offer a stable basis for diplomacy. I do think that mystical traditions bear uncanny resemblances to each other, but I locate these similarities primarily in the methods employed by these traditions to subvert their religions' local knowledges and practices. In short, I do not want to lose sight of the historical fact, so often forgotten, that many of these mystical traditions are *counter*cultures that have been persecuted, sometimes quite violently, by their own orthodox religious authorities.

I recognize, of course, that mystical traditions have served conservative, even violent ends. And I am aware too that, as Mark Sedgwick reminds us, the idea of a universal mysticism or "perennial philosophy" has buttressed an antimodern traditionalism that has had fascist and terrorist expressions.[19] In other words, mysticism can become simply another religious nightmare, another fundamentalist pathology. But this is hardly the norm; hence the radically liberal and socially reforming gnosticisms of the American counterculture and the human potential movement that are so often misunderstood and demeaned by both the left and the right.[20] It is countercultural manifestations of the mystical like these that I highlight here. What I am offering, then, is heresy—heresy as a hidden mode of discourse between civilizations, as a means of cultural transfer.[21] More precisely, I offer an academic gnosticism that can stand up against the petty and violent demiurge-gods that rule so much of our religious worlds.

I have few illusions about how such words might go over with orthodox religious believers: my own writing has been the object of Internet hate campaigns, media attacks, and two organized ban movements in India (the last of which ended in the Rajyasabha, the upper house of Parliament).[22] I would only insist that countercultures are inconceivable without normative cultures, that every orthodoxy must produce its own balancing heresies, and that the ethical relationship between mystical and orthodox forms of religiosity are exceedingly complex, dynamic, and structurally symbiotic. To invoke the paradoxical language of Elliot Wolfson and his understanding of religious tradition as a kind of "path," mysticism is the path that leads beyond the path by walking the path.[23] Even in my "transgressions" and "subversions," then, I deny that there can be any such final thing—to deny a tradition by gnostically engaging it is entirely traditional. As we shall soon see, what makes my own method untraditional perhaps is the fact that I finally recognize no ultimate barrier or boundary between the historical traditions. My comparative path thus takes me from tradition to tradition, and my point is to deny the logical and final ontological status of dualism and difference themselves.

Toward this end (it is really more of a beginning), I will proceed in three related movements: the first two treat two very different historical periods and their defining contexts (British colonialism in nineteenth-century India and the twentieth-century American counterculture); the third turns to more theoretical discourse in an attempt to link them.

I will begin in nineteenth-century Bengal with the archetypal Hindu example of East-West encounter, Sri Ramakrishna Paramahamsa (1836–1886), examining in some textual detail his comparative, deconstructive, and dialectical experiments with religious difference, that is, his own comparative mystics.

In the second part, I will return to the present and the historical genesis of that unique ritual place in Western culture where the mystical and philosophical experiments of Ramakrishna are carried out in some of their most sophisticated and widely practiced forms: the American Academy of Religion, academic publishing, and the standard college course on "comparative religion." In effect, I will creatively use the Indian archetype of Ramakrishna in order to explore the analogous mystical acts of contemporary Western intellectuals, students, and practitioners. In the process, I will suggest that whereas it was British colonialism that generated and made necessary the religious experiments and mystical subversions of Ramakrishna, it was the American counterculture that generated the personalities, research foci, and general spirit of the modern comparative study of religion, at least as it is presently practiced in the States.

Finally, in the third part of the essay, I will explore the theoretical categories of counterculture, gnosticism, and apophaticism as fruitful places to look for creative ways to better understand our own comparative mystics. The same categories, I will suggest, could serve us well still in our tasks of deconstructing our dysfunctional religious pasts (and they all *are* dysfunctional within our present social circumstances) and constructing new ones, particularly if we can join our countercultural and deconstructive projects across cultural and religious boundaries. Indeed, it is this very comparative project across time and clime that is structurally "mystical" in the sense that it recognizes the importance of cultural particularity but denies the ontological ultimacy of difference itself. To compare, after all, is to refuse both the fetishization of difference and the dangerous hegemonies of identification and conflation.

Ramakrishna: Colonialism, Universalism, Mysticism

My prime example of deep cross-cultural communication and cross-religious transgression is that of the nineteenth-century Bengali Shakta mystic and Hindu saint Ramakrishna Paramahamsa. I could turn to other remarkable Indian figures for similar reminders of the fluidity of culture and the mystical denial of religious difference. The fifteenth-century devotional poet Kabir, for example, sang of a God beyond all Muslim, Hindu, ritual, and caste differences. Guru Nanak (1469–1539) envisioned a God who united Muslim and Hindu in a monotheistic mystical theology that would recognize neither caste nor race and would soon develop into a new religion called Sikhism. Perhaps most spectacularly, we could also turn to the Mughal emperor Akbar, whose Sufi sensibility inspired him to create a small college of comparative religion at his court and to establish in 1582 a new universal religion later dubbed (by his critics) the Divine Faith (*Din-i-Ilahi*). To this same end, Akbar commissioned translations of classical Hindu scriptural texts and invited Sufi shaiks, Sunni ulama, Hindu pandits, Zoroastrian and Parsi scholars, Jains, and even Catholic priests from Goa to argue their points together in his presence. Akbar's Sufi experiment with religious difference would die with his great-grandson, Dara Shikoh (1614–1659), who was accused of heresy by orthodox Muslims and executed for, among other various political reasons, his embrace of mystical doctrines.

Indian history would have to wait another century and a half before this vision was picked up again and developed into a distinctly modern or comparative way of looking at religion. The place and time was nineteenth-century Bengal. The religious context of this new experiment was again a distinctly mystical and unorthodox one, carried on in a social environment imbued with debate and reform inspired by the dominating presence of Western religious and social thought.

Ramakrishna was born in 1836 to a poor family in a rural district and grew up in a very traditional, very orthodox Brahmin household.[24] His father died when the boy was six or seven. Soon Ramakrishna began falling into strange trances, which others interpreted as a sign of precocious religious abilities, and he began as well to entertain fantasies of being reborn as a girl. When his eldest brother, Ramkumar, moved to Calcutta, the British colonial capital, in an attempt to rescue the family from destitution, Ramakrishna joined him. They found work in the new Dakshineshwar temple, dedicated to the Tantric goddess Kali, north of the city. Ramkumar, however, soon died. Ramakrishna responded to this second major loss in the same way he had responded to his father's death—with trance and vision. A period of intense emotional suffering followed. Desperately seeking a vision of Kali as Ma (or "Mom") and frustrated with his visionary failures, Ramakrishna reached for a sword to cut his throat (the ritual sword used to decapitate goats offered to the goddess). But Kali intervened and submerged the young priest in an ocean of radiance and bliss: this was to be the first of hundreds of ecstatic unions that would become a defining feature of Ramakrishna's sanctity and fame. Even as an adult, he experienced himself (and was perceived by others) as a child of the Mother Goddess.

Over the next few years, Ramakrishna would pursue a remarkable religious experiment, worshipping and identifying with in turn a broad range of deities and experiencing the altered states of consciousness that they brought upon him. Within the broad and generous Hindu fold, for example, he engaged in Vaishnava, Shakta, and Advaita Vedantic *sadhanas*, or spiritual disciplines. Or as he put it himself, he practiced and thought "according to the Puranas," "according to the Tantras," and "according to the Vedas," three classes of Hindu scripture that represent the ways of theistic devotion, erotic transgression, and philosophical deconstruction, respectively (and very roughly). A series of gurus filed through the temple in these years, guiding, prodding, encouraging, sometimes forcing Ramakrishna through various rituals and meditative practices.

The young priest, for example, "became" Hanuman, the monkey god and paradigmatic devotee of Rama, and ecstatically sang to the beautiful blue god Krishna, often as the latter's female lover, Radha, "according to the Puranas." He cross-dressed as a handmaid of Kali's for a full year, in effect becoming a woman in order to conquer *kama*, or sexual desire.[25] He would also practice versions of the Five Ms, the five forbidden substances and antinomian acts that are ritually engaged in Shakta Tantric practice, and he learned of other mystico-erotic techniques with his female Tantric guru and the many local Tantric sects "according to the Tantras." Then he denied the existence of these same gods and goddesses in order to meditate on the formless *brahman* "according to the Vedas," under the tutelage of Tota Puri, a naked wandering ascetic whose departure (or presence—it is not clear which) sent the young priest into a dangerous six-month trance that is celebrated as exemplifying the pinnacle of yoga ("enstatic absorption without trace," or *nirvikalpa samadhi*).

Ramakrishna also came to experiment with Islam and Christianity before settling into life, within the temple precincts, as a teaching guru and local saint. With a Hindu convert to Sufism named Gobinda Ray, who expressed his faith in secret and may not have been a practicing Muslim, Ramakrishna took up Islam.[26] He repeated the name of Allah, wore Muslim clothes, prayed the daily Muslim prayers, and even refused to visit the Hindu deities. After three days of this discipline, it is said that he underwent a vision of a brilliant human figure with a long beard (that is, a male) and then merged into "the Fourth" state of the unconditioned *brahman*.

Ramakrishna also took up Christianity. Perhaps because the presence of Christianity was more salient than that of Islam and much more problematic in colonial Bengal, biographers generally concentrate on Ramakrishna's Christian practices. They tell us, for example, that he often visited a friend who would read him passages from the Bible and that on the friend's wall hung an image of the infant Jesus with the Virgin Mary (that is, another child/mother goddess icon). One day, we are told, the picture came alive and a ray of light issued from it and entered Ramakrishna's body. Another transformation had begun, this one centered on what a biographer terms the "Jesus state" (*jishu-bhava*). In a different version of the story, a foreign man of fair complexion approached Ramakrishna and identified himself as the greatest of yogis, Jesus Christ. Jesus then embraced Ramakrishna and disappeared into his body.

Partly as a result of these comparative experiments and the ecumenical teachings that would soon flow from them, admiring visitors and students began arriving at the Kali temple. From the mid-1870s through the mid-1880s, an impressive community of disciples formed around Ramakrishna, and the expression "Hindu saint" came to be applied.[27] Disciples learned from him about the many paths of various religions (or mental conditionings) leading to the same goal and debated whether Ramakrishna was an avatar or "incarnation of God." In 1886 he died of throat cancer after a long battle with the disease and passed into what the tradition calls "the great union" (*mahasamadhi*) beyond and beneath all local colors—into that level of being, consciousness, and bliss about which nothing can be said (KA 5:151).

Doctrinal and Historical-Critical Analysis

After his practices according to the Puranas, according to the Tantras, according to the Vedas, and according to Islam and Christianity, Ramakrishna eventually settled down into the more stable role of guru and began to develop the implications of his previous experiments through a series of memorable metaphors. In a series of fascinating appendixes to his *Kathamrita*, or *Nectar Talk*, that dialectically alternate between Ramakrishna's Bengali teachings and Swami Vivekananda's English lectures, Mahndranath Gupta nicely summarizes this comparative mystics and links it to the guru's primary disciple and the latter's famous missionary efforts in America and Europe, where he helped found numerous Vedanta centers and prepared the cultural ground for the hundreds of Hindu and Buddhist missionaries that would soon follow his successful example. "We have drawn from our diary these conversations on the harmony of all religions [*sarva-dharma-samanvaya*]," Gupta writes (KA 5:161). As a way of focusing our discussion, I will in turn draw on Gupta's appendixes.

To my knowledge, no long technical expression like "the harmony of all religions" ever appears in Ramakrishna's mouth, at least in Gupta's central text. The saint's *katha*, or "talk," as recorded there was pithy and catchy: his famous *mata-patha* was a kind of sound bite, meaning something like "perspective-path," or "as one's view, so one's religious practice." This same *mata-patha* doctrine is usually taken as the essence of Ramakrishna's teaching, and many metaphors of his do point to this basic conviction. In a teaching adapted from the Upanishads, he would liken the religions of the world to different rivers of the land, which flow finally into the same ocean. Or he would compare the social reality of religious difference to a pond to which Hindus, Muslims, and Christians all go to obtain water.

Whereas Hindus call what they draw out *jal* and Muslims call it *pani*, British Christians call it "water," but it is all the same fluid. Ramakrishna thus insisted on the relativity of the terms, practices, and beliefs that constitute religions and customs (*dharma*): these were means toward a common end or culturally relative descriptions of a universal ground (or better here, water). As such they should not be confused with that end, ocean, or pond.

Ramakrishna's teaching is, however, not as simple as is generally assumed. While he taught that "all religions are true" (KA 1:161), he did not confuse truth with God. "Religion itself is not God," he said, though "it is possible to get to God through various religions" (KA 1:161). By "true," then, he did not mean "without error"; on the contrary, he was clear that all religions err, just as no one's watch perfectly reflects the sun's movement (KA 1:162). By "true," he most likely meant "effective" or "conducive to the experience of God." Moreover, despite his own experimentation, he consistently taught that it is best to stay with one path or religion; people can reach the same roof by different means (stairs, ladder, rope), but no person can use two means at the same time (KA 5:161). Still, one must never imagine that the necessity (whether cultural or psychological) of following a single path renders that path singular. One must never make the mistake of thinking that one's own path is the only possible or effective way to the common roof and its grand vista. Ramakrishna thus stood solidly against what the Bengali text calls *matuyar buddhi*, which Gupta (and it is probably his term rather than Ramakrishna's) glosses in English to mean "Dogmatism" (KA 5:162).

It is also important to realize that Ramakrishna's tendency to compare religions did not prevent him from criticizing positions that he found dubious or dysfunctional in one religion or another. He was particularly hard on the orthodox Vaishnavas and the Christians,[28] whose doctrines of sin struck him as useless and ultimately destructive.[29] He would thus quote approvingly his Tantric friend, Vaishnavacharan: "Why do you only talk about 'sin' and more 'sin'? Be blissful" (KA 5:41). Atheists, Tantrikas, Brahmos and Muslims also received their due share of Ramakrishna's disdain. His attacks on atheists are particularly interesting, for those he refers to were in fact Brahmos (JU 102) and Vedantins (JU 62). Both Saradananda and Datta, for example, record scenes in which Ramakrishna describes a group of meditating Brahmos, those famous social and religious reformers of nineteenth-century Bengal, as "a troop of monkeys" (LP 5.1.1.6; JV[5], 72), acting out a religious practice for which they have no ability or promise. His treatment of Tantrikas was not always much better. He seems in these passages content simply to ridicule (KA 2:142) or make fun (KA 2:141) of those "branded thieves" (KA 3:52).

Obviously, then, Ramakrishna's comparative mystics cannot be accurately represented as the simple ecumenism or universalism that it is usually understood to be. Combining a remarkable appreciation of diverse religious systems and a critical edge derived from his own Hindu sensibilities, he developed a sophisticated dialectical ontology that allowed for both appreciation *and* critique. The ontology is fundamental. What is the ocean into which all rivers empty, the water about which all languages speak, the roof up to which all passageways lead, or the sun that all timepieces erringly follow? Ramakrishna is maddeningly complex on these questions; and commentators, myself included, have argued for over a century about his answers. In my own understanding, Ramakrishna generally rejected the *mayavada,* or "doctrine of illusion," of Advaita Vedanta, preferring instead to see the phenomenal world as a physical embodiment of the divine. *Tinii sava hoechen*—"She herself [or He himself] has become everything"—he often taught. Hence, the world could be called a "matting of illusion" only in the middle stage of spiritual practice; further down the path, one would learn to see the phenomenal world as a "mansion of fun" in which to take delight in the omnipresence and essential bliss of the divine. This was the "dialectical gnosis" (*vijnana*) of the Hindu Tantra that embraced both transcendent Consciousness (the god Shiva) and immanent Energy (the goddess Shakti) as ontologically bound or—more traditionally, in iconography and meditation—sexually united.

Still within this same erotic, bipolar, or dialectical gnosis, Ramakrishna was enamored of the tradition of Ramprasad, an eighteenth-century Shakta poet whose lyrics were constantly on Ramakrishna's lips and who famously sang that he had no desire to become sugar but would rather taste its sweetness. So too, Ramakrishna much preferred the sweet states of divine-human encounter—devotion (*bhakti*) and love (*prema*)— over the metaphysical absolutes of *nirvana* and *brahman,* though he recognized these latter as fundamental dimensions of the divine Pleroma.[30] He would sometimes make this case in terms of the traditional categories of form (*sakara*) and formlessness (*nirakara*): the formless waters of consciousness take on distinct forms through the freezing force of devotion and are melted by the hot "sun of gnosis of *brahman*" (KA 5:170–171). He did not, then, simply recognize devotional differences. He preferred them, even as he recognized that only *brahman* is absolute.

Still another approach to this point—the approach taken in Vivekananda's English lectures as quoted in these same appendixes—is by way of the modern category of *experience.*[31] Here, the argument is that differences in doctrine flow at least partly from psychological differences and the stunningly various subjective experiences that individuals have had of the divine. The bottom line is personal religious experience, to which Ramakrishna referred in Bengali as *anubhava* (experience or experiential replication), *bhava* (state, mood, mode of being, ecstasy, or spiritual orientation), *ishvaradarshana* (vision of God), or *ishvaralabha* (attainment of God). Vivekananda and the English commentators tend to translate these terms as "spirituality" (KA 5:156), the "realization of God" (KA 5:157), or simply "these experiences" (KA 5:159). When Ramakrishna or Vivekananda, then, claims that "all religions are true," he is asserting that all religions provide effective means to experience subjectively and directly the divine ground of all religions. As Vivekananda writes, "[R]eligion does not consist in doctrines or dogmas. . . . The end of all religions is the realization of God in the soul. Ideals and methods may differ but that is the central point" (KA 5:156). With this logic, one religion has no grounds on which to accuse another of malpractice—of "idolatry": "If a man can realize his divine nature most easily with the help of an image, would it be right to call it a sin?" (KA 5:172). Furthermore, "if one creed alone were to be true and all the others untrue, you would have again to say that religion is diseased. If one religion is true, all the others must be true. Thus the Hindu religion is your property as well as mine" (KA 5:153). In the end, it is experience, and not creed, that matter.

It is necessary now to step back from hagiography and the canonical tradition in order to better understand Ramakrishna's experiments with Hindu, Muslim, and Christian devotion and to isolate aspects that may be applicable in other times and contexts. The canonical reading of his comparative experiments grounds them in a form of Advaita Vedanta or, perhaps, neo-Vedanta that Vivekananda privileged in his lectures as the orthodox hermeneutic for reading his guru's life and as the basis for his own social reforms. However, there is little, if any, historical precedent in India for grounding either a universal ecumenism like Ramakrishna's or a social consciousness like Vivekananda's in classical Advaita Vedanta; quite the contrary, this particular philosophical tradition has historically been quite polemical toward competing religious visions and has been fundamentally ascetic in its attitude toward the social world, which it generally seeks to renounce along Indian lines rather than reform along Western lines.[32] We need to look elsewhere for the immediate sources of Ramakrishna's comparative practices.

Those immediate (Bengali) sources are Hindu and Tantric. Ramakrishna's teachings were part of a long Shakta tradition that drew on ancient tendencies in Indian thought to relativize opposing beliefs and traditions by including them in a more encompassing hierarchical framework. Ramakrishna was fully aware of this legacy when he paraphrased the Rig Veda to support his own position: "The Lord is one, though his names are many" (KA 5:14). But while this legacy was ancient, the manner in which Ramakrishna appropriated it owed much to more contemporary influences, especially the Bengali Shakta tradition and its poet-singers. Thus his Shakta reworking of the ancient Vedic ideal: "The Power [*shakti*] is one, its names are many" (JV 91). For example, Ramprasad in the eighteenth century sang to his unkempt Kali as the essence of all the gods and goddesses: "Kali, Krishna, Shiva, and Rama—they are all my

Wild-Haired One." [33] He sang as well of the "madhouse" of the world where "Jesus, Moses, and Chaitanya were unconscious in the ecstasy of love." [34]

That Shakta poets such as Ramprasad saw Kali as the actress behind the world's religious masks suggests that, even in his universalism, Ramakrishna was a Shakta, a child of the Goddess. The same lesson could be learned by considering this version of his *mata-patha* doctrine: "There are as many paths as there are opinions. All religions are true, just as the Kali Temple can be reached by different paths" (KA 5:161). [35] Where the paths lead, it seems, is as important as their obvious number. They are all "true," after all, because they all lead to the same place—to the Goddess. Again: "That which the Vedas call Parabrahman, he calls Kali. He whom the Muslims call Allah and the Christians call God, he calls Kali" (KA 1:236). This is she "who makes love to Shiva," the latter being formless *brahman* (KA 5:170) (rather like Barbelo and the Father in the Apocyphon of John). Even Ramakrishna's canonical biographer, Swami Saradananda, acknowledges the Shakta roots of Ramakrishna's universalism by asserting that it was Kali who "produced in his mind the liberal faith, 'as many faiths so many paths.'" [36] There is, then, something profoundly Tantric—and thus context specific—about Ramakrishna's universalism. It is hardly the blissful but abstract *brahman* of Vivekananda, his most famous expositor. The universal ground of Ramakrishna is closer to the midnight darkness where "black forms blend with one another" and "all jackals howl in the same way" (LP 4.4.30). [37]

The Shakta nature of this spirituality is "deeper," more "inward," than its common Shaiva or Vaishnava expressions. As a popular Bengali proverb puts it, "[I]nside a Shakta, outside a Shaiva, on the mouth Hari, Hari," which might be paraphrased: "Speak as a devotee of Krishna and act like a devotee of Shiva in public, but in your heart worship the Goddess as a Shakta." [38] This Shakta nature of Ramakrishna's experiments also becomes evident when we notice that he consistently prays to Kali before taking up any foreign path; he asks for her permission and also prays to her while engaged in foreign practices. Early (and largely ignored) biographers such as Satyacharan Mitra are clear about Ramakrishna's Shakta orientation: "Ramakrishna Paramahamsa practiced according to many teachings, but the view of the Tantras was his primary view. He was really in the tradition of the Tantras! This *sadhana* was the marrow of his *sadhana's* body" (JU 72). [39] Mitra also tells us that Ramakrishna saw and understood the "Kali-state [*Kali-bhava*], not the Krishna-, Rama- or Shiva-states" (JU 61). According to such early observers, Ramakrishna's universalism was an expression of his Shaktism; the neo-Vedantic reading of Vivekananda and the canonical tradition come later. [40]

Ramakrishna's own visions often follow the same pattern. He was reported as seeing Kali in the form of a disciple's mother, a woman whom he described as an orthodox and closed-minded Vaishnava. [41] The woman's

Vaisnavism and bigotry are superficial. "Inside" she is a Shakta, indeed
the Goddess incarnate, despite her outward or surface Vaishnava self-
understanding.

The same logic is at work in another scene, this one recorded in Mitra's
Jivana o Upadesha (JU 145–146). "At this time," Mitra tells us, "the big [Chris-
tian] preachers of Calcutta were going with Keshab Chandra Sen to see
Ramakrishna." The scene is thus set in a context of religious confrontation. Mitra opens the story by relating how a guileless Englishman
named William told Ramakrishna that "Jesus showed us many miraculous
things." Then William asked: "Can you show us any?" In the *Kathamrita*
scenes, Ramakrishna is quite clear about his inability to perform such
feats, but here Mitra has him obliging his Christian inquirer in spectacu-
lar fashion. Ramakrishna asks William to "come and see my Kali-Ma from
a distance just once." When William obliges his host, he is amazed to see
that "the image of Jesus appeared in the place of the Kali image." After this
display, Ramakrishna asks the astounded Christian, "How is that? Did you
see that my Kali is what your Jesus Christ is?" The scene ends with William
grabbing Ramakrishna's feet—an act of humble devotion—and taking up
the Hindu "*dharma* of renunciation" somewhere in the mountains. William's taking refuge at Ramakrishna's feet is the ritual expression of what
amounts to a conversion story: the story of a conversion from Christianity
to Hinduism. Once again, the Shakta goddess is the focus of confrontation
and symbolic resolution. She dissolves religious forms into their deeper
(Tantric) energies.

Alongside these Tantric visionary resolutions of religious difference
we can also easily detect a set of indigenous deconstructive techniques
that function to melt down the stiff boundaries of all the gods and goddesses into a deeper and more fluid unity, and here the debt to Advaita
Vedanta is a real one. Ramakrishna may have found these apophatic techniques too dry or boring for his own personal devotional tastes, but this
does not mean that he dismissed them as unimportant. Quite the contrary,
in numerous places in the Bengali texts, Ramakrishna's metaphors and
teachings employ a kind of radical deconstruction, suggesting in effect
that all religious beliefs or attitudes are products of the environment and
the mind's ability to take on the "color" or "dye" of its immediate sur-
roundings: "The mind takes on the color of whatever color it is dyed
in. The mind is the cloth of the dyer's room" (KA 5:119). Hence, if one med-
itates on God, the mind takes on the colors, as it were, of God, and if one
engages in worldly activities, the mind changes accordingly. What we have
here, in other words, is a metaphorical understanding of what we would
today call constructionism. What separates Ramakrishna's constructionism, however, from most contemporary forms is that he saw a deeper
"mind" or "heart" (*mana*) beneath all of these "colorful" constructions, a
mind-heart that was in turn ultimately rooted in the nature of a universal

consciousness (*chit* or *brahman*) that transcends and undergirds all forms of human culture and religion.

In accounting for Ramakrishna's religious universalism, we must add to the Tantric and Advaita Vedantic influences on him a distinctively Western catalyst, effective for some decades in Bengal. Stimulated by strands of Western social and religious thought, and also by Islam, Rammohun Roy, a Bengali reformer (often called "the father of modern India"), argued that Hinduism had in the time of the Upanishads experienced a golden age of monotheism that had since been corrupted by polytheistic practices.

In 1828 Roy instituted a Society of Brahman (the Brahmos) that would function as a monotheistic religion for middle-class, English-educated Indians and serve as their reply to Christian condescension. Roy's brand of Brahmoism displays real similarities (and some later historical connections) to Christianity, and especially to Unitarianism, which was developing in Boston at roughly this same time. Satyacharan Mitra, for example, writing in 1896, argued that the primary "state" or "mood" (*bhava*) of the Brahmos was the "Christ-*bhava*" (JU 87). Though Roy's advent as a Hindu reformer is said to have put fear in the hearts of Christians (JU 107), it is clear that Western Transcendentalists and Unitarians found in Roy's religion an exemplar of their own faith, one of the most impressive before Ramakrishna. Mitra, for example, insisted that the influence of Roy and other Brahmo monotheists on Ramakrisha was immense and went so far as to call anyone who denied the influence "ridiculous" (JU 108).[42]

This seemingly obvious connection between Brahmo universalism and Ramakrishna's religious experiments (not to mention American Transcendentalism) gave rise to a very long controversy between the Brahmos and Ramakrishna's followers over who influenced whom. Keshab Sen (a leader in the Society of Brahman, who broke away to found his own group) so identified Christianity with religious authority that he claimed Ramakrishna was a reincarnation of John the Baptist (a claim that implicitly identified Keshab himself as the new messiah) (KA 2:102). The textual evidence, however, is far more humble, even as it affirms Mitra's observation that Ramakrishna was affected by Roy and Christianity, although Ramakrishna was, as I have already observed, resistant as well as open to non-Hindu religious forms. Keshab, it turns out, was sometimes more open to the religious other than Ramakrishna. Ramakrishna, for example, actually pressed Keshab to return, late in life, to "the names of Hari and Ma" (KA 4:239).[43] As for himself, Keshab had set up an impressive academic program in which he assigned disciples to prolonged textual study of various religious traditions in their original languages, a much more extensive version of Ramakrishna's simpler, if more famous, comparative experiments.[44]

While the Brahmos and the Calcutta culture they did so much to form provided the context for Ramakrishna's experimental universalism, he himself led the Brahmos away from their "Christ-*bhava*" and its social gospel back to the "Mother-*bhava*" and worship of the Goddess (JU 87). This implicit rejection of Brahmo universalism for a more traditional Hindu identity appears again in a story about the Brahmo whom Rama-krishna converted: "He left the Brahmo [Society] and practiced *sadhana* according to the Hindu way" (JU 94). It was later canonical interpreters who identified Ramakrishna's inclusivism and religious tolerance as the primary reason he had "descended" into the world as the modern incarna-tion of God (*avatara*). He came to combine the Hindu, Christian, and Mus-lim into a single harmonious community in the very center of all the world's religions, even if that center was already an unstable one.

Ramakrishna and the Comparativist

Certainly the modern comparative study of religion cannot be reduced to a ritual repetition of Ramakrishna's visionary explorations, since in histori-cal truth, Ramakrishna's Indian experiments were products of the same broad global forces that resulted in the earlier Indian experiments of Ram-mohun Roy, Keshab Sen, and the Brahmo Samaj, or "Society of Brahman," and of the earlier and simultaneous Western phenomena of European and English Romanticism, American Transcendentalism, the Theosophical So-ciety (founded in 1875 in New York), the grand comparative theorizing and cross-cultural editing work of Max Müller and his *Sacred Books of the East* translation series, and the 1893 World Parliament of Religions in Chicago (significantly, it was this latter event that more or less created the fame and public persona of Swami Vivekananda, Ramakrishna's missionary to the West).

As for the sense that all religions share a common core, that was an ancient idea in India and a very old idea in Europe, articulated by such figures as Nicholas of Cusa (1401–1464) and Agostino Steuco. Steuco artic-ulated his version of this doctrine in 1540 in conversation with the neo-Platonism of Marsilio Ficino. Ficino held, Steuco believed, in Sedgwick's words now, that "all religions shared a common origin in a single peren-nial (or primeval or primordial) religion that had subsequently taken a variety of forms, including the Zoroastrian, Pharaonic, Platonic, and Christian."[45] If we take Steuco's system as emblematic, what I am calling comparative mystics and modernity were born more or less together in the West, interestingly at the precise same time that they were being similarly explored in north India at the court of Akbar.

The European project would crash on the rocks of historical criticism: in 1614 Isaac Casaubon showed persuasively that the *Corpus Hermeticum*, which perennialists read as a Mosaic text prophetic of their own Christian-Platonic synthesis, had been written centuries after Platonism and Chris-tianity became established worldviews.[46] For the next century and a half, perennialism would linger, surviving in French Masonic lodges, before its renewal in an explicit linkage with Hindu inclusivism. This move was announced first in 1799 when Reuben Burrow connected Hinduism, Hermes, and Moses in a deeply eccentric essay in *Asiatick Researches*, the journal of the Asiatick Society of Bengal, which had done much to introduce India to the West.[47] That Indo-Hermetic-Mosaic synthesis (Sedgwick terms it a "Vedanta Perennialism") is still with us. For our present purposes, perhaps what matters is that this stream is the one into which Mircea Eliade waded (he wrote his MA thesis on Ficino and Giordano Bruno and his PhD dissertation on *la mystique indienne* of yoga) in order to create space for a modern study of religion that is neither answerable to Christian (or any other) theology nor reducible to the social sciences. Eliade, in other words, did more than any other comparativist to transform perennialism into scholarship and a new way of thinking about religion.[48]

Obviously, we are not dealing here with a cause-and-effect relationship or a debate over what culture created which; rather, we are dealing with a shared global history and a set of verisimilar responses. Still, it is also the case that the legacy of Ramakrishna in the history of religious studies is both originary and intimate. Max Müller, the founding father, or perhaps grandfather, of comparative religion, for example, corresponded with Vivekananda and wrote the first English biography of Ramakrishna, though it would take nearly a hundred years for Müller's historical-critical questions and doubts about the hagiographical tradition to be taken seriously.[49] The second major Western biography was written by Romain Rolland, the Nobel laureate in literature, who initiated the psychoanalytic theory of mysticism by sending his dual biographies of Ramakrishna and Vivekananda to Sigmund Freud.[50] A bit later, a young Joseph Campbell would help Swami Nikhilananda edit his 1942 English translation of the *Kathamrita*, the now-classic *The Gospel of Sri Ramakrishna*, a modern Tantric-Gnostic gospel, if ever there was one. Campbell would also make Ramakrishna's Shakta Tantra the teleological summation of Indian philosophy in his ghostwriting of Heinrich Zimmer's influential *Philosophies of India*. Little wonder, then, that to this day Ramakrishna's presence is invoked as exemplary of a type of spiritual pluralism championed by a wide range of popular writers and practitioners. He has been a gnostic presence in American religious history for well over a century now.

Perhaps then I can be forgiven for employing Ramakrishna's famous comparative experiments here in this second section neither as an ambiguous textual complexity to unravel with historical-critical and psychological methods (as I have done in part 1 and, to a much greater extent, in *Kali's Child*) nor as the last word on the relationship of the religions (as Swami Vivekananda and his tradition have tended to do), but rather as a kind of cultural archetype of a certain type of comparative mystics that simultaneously denies the ultimacy of cultural and ethnic differences and celebrates their psychological necessity, even as it grounds both moves in an ontology of human being, however the latter is conceived in the displacements and receding semiotic patterns of language and the relativisms of culture.

Certainly every one of Ramakrishna's archetypal experiments (with the various theistic traditions of Hinduism, with Advaita Vedanta, with Tantra, with Christianity, and with Islam) possess fantastically rich and elaborate histories in Western scholarship. Ramakrishna's Shiva, Krishna, and Kali, for example, have each enjoyed a long history of engagement and hermeneutical encounter with Indology within a kind of intellectual devotion. Moreover, scholarly work on Hindu-Christian and Hindu-Muslim relations has deepened in insight as volume after volume has appeared on the violent injustices of British colonialism in India, on various Christian and Hindu experiments in dialogue and global theology, on the rich history of Sufism in India as a mediating force between Islam and Hinduism, and on the historical, structural, and psychological animosity that has defined relations between Hindus and Muslims and, to a lesser extent, Hindus and Christians in historical and contemporary India. Modern historical-critical scholarship has arrived at some new answers to all of these questions and cannot finally agree with Ramakrishna's belief that "all paths lead to the same goal." Yet scholars have nevertheless chosen to engage all of the religious forms represented in Ramakrishna's archetypal experiments. The saint may not always convince us with his particular metaphysical solutions, but he knew where the problems lay (and still lie), and he was not afraid to confront them head-on as specifically problems of religion.

The Critical Study of Religion as a Modern Mystical Tradition

The origins of the discipline of religious studies in nineteenth-century Europe are not primarily mystical or even religious. A highly developed secular sense is a sine qua non of the discipline and its social sustainability anywhere on the planet (hence its virtual absence outside the Western academy). I would like, though, to make a restricted and heterodox case that regarding the discipline as a modern mystical tradition could be useful in approaching the constructive tasks being explored in these reflections. In this, I am not suggesting that the discipline must or even should be read in this way. Rather, I wish only to make the much more restricted, but no less unorthodox, case that some of the discipline's practices and practitioners (that is, those that are capable of forging a tensive mystical-critical practice out of the discipline's dual Romantic/Enlightenment heritage) *can* be read in such a way, and that, moreover, such a mystical-critical rereading of the discipline might be useful for the constructive tasks under discussion here, namely, the cross-cultural influence of religious systems toward a safer, more humane, and more religiously satisfying world.

Scholars of religion, it turns out, often have profound religious experiences reading and interpreting the texts they critically study, and these events have consequences for the methods and models they develop, the conclusions they come to, and even for the traditions they study.[51] Given what is often personally, professionally, and religiously at stake in these events, it perhaps should not surprise us that such writers commonly hide these secret (*mystikos*) experiences from their peers and readers through a variety of rhetorical and esoteric strategies. Historians of religions, in other words, are often closet mystics, if we allow ourselves to redefine *mystic* in an untraditional—that is, (post)modern—way. Steven Wasserstrom substantiated a thesis of this kind with respect to Eliade, Henri Corbin, and Gershom Scholem, three giants in the field, although his personal assessment of this gnostic phenomenon, unlike mine, is almost entirely negative: we see some of the same gnostic patterns but evaluate their meanings and possibilities very differently indeed.[52]

Eliade, for example, hinted that he had stepped "out of space and time" while studying yoga as a young Indologist and had later camouflaged his mystical experiences in a supernatural novella about the *siddhi*, or superpower, of invisibility.[53] Scholem too "longed for mystical experience"[54] and spoke of his own "genius" as an "inner compass," like Socrates' *daimon*, that guided his spiritual quest.[55] Scholem saw his massive scholarly output in mystical terms, as the expression of a desire to penetrate "through the wall of history" and "into the essence of things."[56] But the atemporal mystical truth, "whose existence disappears particularly when it is projected into historical time," became visible for Scholem solely in "the legitimate discipline of commentary and in the singular mirror of philological criticism."[57] As for Corbin, he followed the example of his mentor Louis Massignon, who during a suicide attempt in the desert of Iraq converted back to Catholicism in the ghostly presence of his dissertation subject, the tenth-century Sufi al-Hallaj. Corbin similarly claimed that an eleventh-century Sufi master, Suhrawardi, had personally initiated and transmitted teachings to him while he was absorbed in Suhrawardi's writings.[58]

Daniel Gold has recently studied for us some of the aesthetic dimensions of writing and reading in the modern study of religion and what he calls the "religiohistorical sublime," that is, that experience of the abyss or the transcendent-as-limit often evoked by the writings of historians of religion and commonly experienced by their sensitive readers. Invoking Kant's notion of the sublime, Gold argues that the ambivalent experience of beauty and fear readers often experience in works of scholarship arise from their (correct) sense that something profound is being communicated, and that this something, if taken seriously, will effectively deconstruct or dissolve the assumed certainties of the reader's own lifeworld. There is a kind of "high" here, and there is a subsequent fear. This same ambivalence is doubled, moreover, by the ambivalence of the scholars themselves, who, more often than not, are both attracted to the beauty and depth of religious language and profoundly uncomfortable with its unjustified claims to absolute truth. As heirs of both Enlightenment reason and Romantic imagination, such scholars are being true to their deepest cultural legacies and intellectual conclusions.[59] They are being rational gnostics.

Another way of observing this pattern is through a genealogy of the category of mysticism itself. This eminently modern category—or rather, construction—amounts to a celebration of premodern forms of consciousness and writing as reviewed (to quote Wouter Hanegraaff) "in the mirror of secular thought."[60] Although the category of mysticism has precedents reaching back as far as the eighteenth century in England (where, in its very first English appearance, it already signaled a kind of sublimated feminine eroticism),[61] the seventeenth century in France,[62] and—at least in adjectival form—in the ancient Mediterranean world,[63] the noun as used today was more or less born in June 1902, when William James published his Gifford Lectures, *The Varieties of Religious Experience: A Study in Human Nature.*[64] Significantly, James wrote this text in part out of his own experiments with nitrous oxide and psychical phenomena, which he approached with great philosophical seriousness, and insisted on the *noetic* quality of mystical experience. That is, he saw that mystical states routinely engage nonordinary or alternative epistemological domains, and that these are worth taking very seriously.

Put more baldly, then, "mysticism," rather than being an ancient category easily found in all religions in all times, derives its modern salience from a mystically inclined Harvard professor and psychical researcher speaking in Scotland whose published lectures have since been read by countless other scholars of religion (and practitioners) and subsequently developed into a coherent, often quite popular idea we now call "mysticism." It should hardly surprise us, then, that the modern study of religion displays numerous qualities or dimensions that can be classified as a kind of modern or postmodern "mysticism": the discipline, after all, created that very term, partly no doubt to capture its own implicit interests, goals, and forms of consciousness. Put most simply, then, "mysticism" and the modern study of religion are inseparable because they are largely about the same set of modernist and now postmodernist convictions, forms of self-reflexivity, and theoretical approaches to religious plurality. "Mysticism," in other words, is our semiotic response to the same global forces and epistemological problems that produced Ramakrishna's experiments. It is our chosen *sadhana*, our own comparative mystics.

But I do not myself want to define the term "mystical" as replicating *bhava, brahman,* or *samadhi* as Ramakrishna used those words.[65] Rather than a particular state of consciousness or a collection of psychological experiences reserved for extraordinary individuals, I would prefer, with the theologian Don Cupitt, to define mysticism as a discipline of writing, that is, as a necessarily subversive hermeneutical practice that works in the here and now to "melt down" the dualisms of orthodoxy established to delay salvation, liberation, or enlightenment interminably. So defined, the mystical is fundamentally opposed to all forms of institutional mediation. The religious and implictly political critiques advanced by mystics, of course, tend to be compromised as their writings are appropriated by the orthodox authorities of their traditions. Censorship, including self-censorship, is a part of any writing practice that describes itself as secret, esoteric, or *mystikos*. But the radicalism remains, as the censorship is usually incomplete or halfhearted, and the secret is often more or less public. We have, then, a pair of explanations for the esoteric nature of mystical discourse:

> [T]he reason why mystics use language in the strange ways they do is twofold: on the one hand, they are trying to play games with language in such a way as to destabilize structures of religious oppression that are firmly built into language.... But, on the other hand, they are acutely conscious of being surrounded by enemies who will seize upon a careless word and use it to destroy them.... If a mystic's writing sometimes appears far-fetched or fanciful, the reason is not that he or she is a soulful eccentric with idiosyncratic ideas about heavenly matters, but rather that religious utterance is surrounded by very severe pressures and threats of a political kind.[66]

Among the most striking examples of this phenomenon is the writing of William Blake, that "witness against the Beast" whose weird poetic-political visions literary critics have read as a radical's coded critique of imperialism and monarchy.[67] At the end of his long history of religious studies, Walter Capps turns to consider "what turmoil William Blake's insights would create for the methodological conceptualization of standard religious studies. How could any of them be fitted to any coherent scheme, or, if they were, would they remain what they were originally? Why is the mentality of the technician sanctioned in religious studies while the attitude of the artist is treated with suspicion?"[68] In light of the above remarks about mystical writing as a form of art and esoteric politics, we should perhaps be asking a different question: In what ways and modes is the modern study of religion *already* Blakean in character?

A standard way of resisting the visionary tendencies of scholarship in this field is to pose still another question as the basis of wholesome training and methodology: What is the proper relationship between the study of religions and the religions studied? Historically, this question has been asked (and unfortunately answered) with reference to the categories of the "insider" and "outsider." Who makes the better scholar? The insider has been acculturated into the ritual, doctrinal, and mythical intimacies of a religious tradition and so can better describe its feel and meanings; and yet because of that intimacy, the insider can often lack the critical edge or emotional distance necessary for reductive analysis and the embarrassing question. The outsider, on the other hand, may lack a natural feel for the tradition studied and so miss much of the detail and subtleties, but distance provides resources for asking questions and for arriving at independent answers.

Back and forth the discussion has gone for nearly a century, with no resolution in sight.[69] I do not want to enter, at least not directly, into this debate here, as I think its very terms preclude its resolution: "insider" and "outsider," after all, are binary categories that imply opposition and thus tension. Dialectical tension may be basic to intellectual or ethical progress ("without Contraries [there] is no progression," Blake writes in *The Marriage of Heaven and Hell*), but I would suggest that we understand the tension as emblematic of a deeper relationship—as a *marriage*, to use Blake's metaphor again. Ironically, the metaphors of the "inside" and "outside" themselves already imply a resolution, as they suggest a single container that may be experienced differently from different viewpoints.

The study of religion occupies a liminal and problematic place in the modern university because, as a hermeneutic discipline suited to understanding and appreciating religious experience, it often looks (and sometimes really is) religious. But as a social-scientific practice suited to observing the political, social, economic, psychological, and sexual aspects of religious phenomena, the academic study of religion will appear irreligious to pious believers. Remove either pole of this paradox and the discipline collapses.

For the sake of simplification, I would put this in counterstructural terms; that is, I see the relationship of the critical study of religion to religion to be very roughly analogous to that of the apophatic mystical traditions to the religions from which they developed and in which they historically flourished. In other words, the critical study of religion is to religion as mystical deconstruction is to orthodox creed, ritual, or law. Early Christian antinomianism (in relation to first-century Jewish purity codes), the psychologized biblical hermeneutics of early Jewish and Christian gnostics (in relation to the more literal readings of the Jewish and Christian orthodox communities), the transgressive erotics of the Hindu Tantra (in relation to the Brahmanic *dharma*, caste, and purity codes), some forms of radical Sufism (in relation to the Islam of the ulama), medieval Kabbalah (in relation to rabbinic Judaism), and the academic study of religion today (in relation to the religions studied) appear to share a set of practices. Each mystical mode evidences a type of intellectualism bordering upon a type of nihilism, and each prescribes transgressive acts designed to reveal the socially constructed nature of presumed religious reality. Each mode, moreover, sponsors an erotic hermeneutics (gnostic, Tantric, Sufi, Taoist, and kabbalistic erotics make Freud's insights into the connection between sexuality and religion appear prosaic), and each mode mounts a philosophical critique of dogma, the result of which is often censorship or actual persecution by the orthodox authorities of its own culture. In a single word, the study of religion and the mystical traditions are all *countercoherent*. They echo one another not so much in their teachigs as in their counterings.

Scholars of comparative religion have grouped these countercultures under the heading "mysticism" because they intuit in all of them a not-yet-fully articulated or understood form of consciousness that they themselves to an extent share. The structural resonances between mystical and critical hermeneutic practices explains why the study of mysticism has been central to the modern study of religion. In effect, modern scholars have privileged what they have identified with themselves and thus understood. But the comparativist's unacknowledged normative aim—a kind of esoteric universal humanism—is also at work in this context. The differences between the orthodox forms of Hinduism, Buddhism, Judaism, Christianity, and Islam are very great, and their mystical subcultures are inextricably involved in the traditions from which they emerged. But those subcultures can seem to be uncannily similar to each other, at least in structure. Each, after all, routinely transgresses the binary categories of its own orthodox culture. The mysticisms are thus viewed by modern scholarship as similar in hermeneutic practice, if not in metaphysical substance.

This perception on the part of religious comparativists may help explain why nineteenth-century Western intellectuals were so attracted to the "mystic East": certainly not always to colonize it, as is often assumed (although that was happening too), but more often to draw inspiration and strength for their own countercultural subversions of normative Western culture. And indeed, what in the end could be more subversive of Christian exclusivism and the cultural arrogance of Christendom than the realization that there are other great world religions—"other Europes," as Schwab put it—with dramatically different deities, forms of salvation, and coherent ethical systems? The plurality of high cultures and great religions was established as a fact of social science, and as a result ideas like "saved," "chosen," and "damned" became suspect within even insular varieties of Western religion.

Here too we can better understand why the comparative study of religion grew markedly in the countercultural 1960s (the American Academy of Religion, by far the largest organization of its kind in the world, was founded in 1964), and why so many Asianists who grew up in this climate ultimately turned to Hindu and Buddhist forms of Tantra—that is, to Asian countercultures—as their chosen specialization: echoes of counterculture answer one another and then harmonize across space and time. Perhaps not accidentally, this period also signaled the high point of Freud's popularity in American intellectual life, the blossoming of the civil rights movement, the beginning of the gay rights movement, and the definitive entrance of feminism into popular consciousness; sex, race, and gender justice were the order of a New Age. Finally, the same decade (it was 1965) saw the lifting of the Asian Exclusion Act (passed in 1924), which allowed Asian families to immigrate in large numbers and so transformed the shape of American religious pluralism.[70] Most established scholars of Asian religions, I would hazard, were first introduced to Hinduism, Buddhism, and Taoism (often in their Tantric forms) in this countercultural, existential, and highly eroticized context. Little wonder, then, that so many contemporary Buddhist practitioners found their first taste of enlightenment in psychedelic states or that Tantric studies have flourished primarily in America among baby boomers.[71] In the end, it is American counterculture, not British colonialism, that best explains the origins, dynamics, and eros of the academic field of comparative religion, our own comparative mystics.

The Scandal of Comparison

There is one sense at least in which the modern study of religion is more radical than its mystical precursors. And it is this: the academic field of comparative religion recognizes no specific orthodoxy for subversion: it cannot recognize the authority of any particular religion. A Christian who is offended by the Jesus Seminar and its historical-critical methods ("Jesus probably said almost none of this") would scarcely blink at scholarship of the kind applied to the Qur'an or to a Hindu scripture. Similarly, the Muslim or Hindu who rejects psychological or sociological methods applied to Islamic or Indic materials as "neocolonialist" or "Orientalist" is either unaware that the same methods have been applied very extensively to Christianity and Judaism for nearly two centuries or else, if aware, could not care less. In either case, the believer himself may selectively use critical-historical methods to debunk other religious worldviews.

   The true scandal of religious studies lies not in what any particular work of scholarship has to say about any particular religious belief, practice, or community, but rather in the discipline's implied insistence that all religious phenomena, without exception, are fruitfully approached as human products and studied with the same literary and social-scientific methods. The egalitarianism of religious studies, as currently pursued (especially in the United States), denies the ultimacy and authority of any local truth or practice and the primacy of any religious community, and academic religious scholarship finds all claims to primacy or authority interesting subjects of historical, anthropological, and psychological investigation. While each religious orthodoxy denies the claims of other orthodoxies, and while mystical countercultures subvert many claims of the religions from which they derive, academics in religious studies today subvert the claims of *all* religions, first and foremost the Western monotheisms of Judaism and Christianity from which the critical study of religion historically arose.

Framing the modern study of religion as a counterculture with nothing in particular to counter is not unproblematic, of course. Wasserstrom has expressed suspicion of the paradoxical phenomenon he calls "religion after religion" and has criticized what he describes as the discipline's "mystocentrism." Academic religious studies, in other words, are in his view fixated inappropriately on mysticism and mythology while showing inadequate interest in orthodox creeds, as well as ethics, ritual, and the mundane workings of religion in society.[72] Still, how *does* one go back to believing the unbelievable? The virgin birth of Jesus, the childhood exploits of Krishna, the night journey of Muhammad, and the burning bush of Moses may be central truths of Christianity, Hinduism, Islam, and Judaism, but they are rather obviously myths to those who stand outside those traditions. How is a scholar of comparative religion to forget this simple and obvious point?

On the other hand, I do want to affirm, and affirm loudly, Wasserstrom's other key argument about the ethical liabilities of mysticism and the troubling political affiliations of many who have made it their life's study: the absolute collapse of difference within mystical monism does not lend itself to an adequate ethics or to vibrant social critique.[73] Wasserstrom has rightly reminded us that mysticism and fascism are by no means incompatible.[74] But these dangers should be remote so long as we keep the premodern elements of mysticism tied to the critical and reductionist methods of the social sciences (something Eliade, Corbin, and above all René Guenon failed to do).[75] It bears repeating: the gnostic epistemology I am exploring in these meditations works, and works *only*, through a tensive but creative unity of radical criticism and ontological openness. Remove either pole, either mode of being, and the gnosis disappears.

Whereas Wasserstrom and other like-minded colleagues, then, want to move the discipline more fully toward pure reason—to make it more academic in every sense—my interest is more in moving it beyond the faith-reason distinction into a new kind of gnosis and into less predictable forms of argument and expression. What I have in mind is the kind of work done by the French literary critic Abdelwahab Meddeb in his recent *The Malady of Islam*. Here the author consistently turns to the Sufism of the Indian Akbarian tradition,[76] particularly as it was elaborated in the framework of the esoteric sciences of Ibn al-'Arabi (1164–1240)—"the Andalusian master who recommended being '*hyle* so that all beliefs can take form within you' . . . [and who had] the capacity to internalize all forms of beliefs and to progress with their truth without trying to reduce them or make them disappear"[77]—in order to deconstruct the archaisms, criminal monstrosities, and gross contradictions of Islamic fundamentalism, a move that only furthers the point being made here, namely, that one of our best hopes for cross-cultural influence lies through our religions' mystical traditions and their radical hermeneutical practices and pluralistic sensibilities.

The same, moreover, could also be said about the kabbalistic inspiration and literal title of Rabbi Michael Lerner's *Tikkun* magazine and community, which has worked so hard through various activist programs over the years to address the Israeli-Palestinian conflict, often through the invocation of distinctly mystical themes linked to hard-nosed political criticism and commentary. Lerner, in fact, is explicit about his debts to Jewish mysticism.[78] Here, then, is a "Spiritual Left" poised to counter (as another mystical counterculture) the "Religious Right" of contemporary American culture and politics.

This is hardly to suggest, however, that such moves are in themselves fully sufficient, or that we should neglect the hard work of analyzing and correcting the grossly obvious injustices and imbalances of international relations, or even take off the table the ominous card of military intervention. Meddeb, for example, is highly critical of American foreign policy in the Middle East, but he does not exclude the possibility, even necessity, of military action in some cases, nor does he ever make the mistake of laying all the blame on America and Europe for what he calls "the malady of Islam," a double entendre for both Islam and Islamic fundamentalism, the latter representing a "sickness" that has done so much to lay waste to a once gorgeous, sensual, pluralistic, and sophisticated Islamic civilization, the latter now merely resentful and "inconsolable in its destitution." Meddeb rather understands and embraces the broader historical context (that is, the rise of modernity and the Enlightenment and the internal failures of Islam to answer or fully participate in them) and then goes on to develop a richly dialectical model of Islam as an intimate part of the West and its history. In other words, he enacts another mystical denial of difference.

Perhaps, then, what I am really offering here, to continue with the political or diplomatic context, is a kind of "track-two diplomacy," a term first coined by the diplomat Joseph Montville to evoke all those "unofficial" cultural, scientific, and personal exchanges between nations that seldom make the news but nevertheless have their own real effects. In an important essay that Montville coauthored in 1982 with William Davidson in *Foreign Policy*, Davidson and Montville defined track-two diplomacy as "unofficial, non-structured interaction. It is always open minded, often altruistic, and . . . strategically optimistic, based on best case analysis. Its underlying assumption is that actual or potential conflict can be resolved or eased by appealing to common human capabilities to respond to good will and reasonableness."[79] Although certainly no substitute for traditional track-one diplomacy with its very real "carrots and sticks," track-two diplomacy has its own genius and role to play in international relations. It is clear, I hope, that I am not offering a cure-all solution here, or even a primary response to religious violence and enmity. What I am suggesting is a kind of gnostic "track-two" spiritual diplomacy that can loosen the armor on all sides through deep explorations of one another's deconstructive hermeneutical traditions and countercultural resources.

Professional Heresy: The Gnostic Study of Religion

Specific aspects of the Asian traditions (particularly certain nationalist or communal dimensions of contemporary Hinduism) may presently be suffering a kind of historical amnesia with respect to their own subversive and erotic dimensions, no doubt brought on by the historical trauma or sickness of colonialism against which they still feel a need to be sufficiently immunized, but all of these Asian traditions are in fact astonishingly rich in precisely these kinds of mystical resources. If this is even approximately true, it would appear that for any cross-cultural bridge we construct much of the most difficult foundational work will need to be done on the Western side, and in particular with the Western monotheistic tendency to "smash the idols" and deny the truths of the other; that is, we will have to continue to struggle with Western exclusivism in all of its modes: theological, cultural, and political.

Such a task, however, will require better-informed cultural memories and less belligerent intellectual and imaginative practices. Christians, Muslims, and Jews need to approach the problem together with cultural resources that, happily, they share in the interrelated mystical traditions of the Bible, gnosticism, and Neoplatonism. The potential of a modern critical gnosticism seems especially worth exploring. As already noted, Gilles Quispel has suggested that Western culture possesses three ways of understanding—faith, reason, and gnosis—and that the third (knowledge that comes from intuitive, visionary, or mystical experience of the divine, rather than from either faith or reason) has been the least developed.[80] The study of religion shares in a dual heritage deriving from the Enlightenment, with its suspicious and rational approach to religion, and from the Romantic movement, with its apotheosis of the imagination; and there are many forms of study that privilege one or the other of these modes. But there is a third epistemology, largely untapped even in religious studies, and, following Quispel, I suggest that we think of it as fundamentally gnostic.

Perhaps what most sets apart the modern academic gnostic from his or her premodern precursors is the academic's secure home in a central institution of Western liberal society: the college or university. This relatively new fact of sociology, combined with the historical implausibility, social dysfunction, and increasing violence of traditional religious systems, has made the usual strategies of dissimulation and concealment less necessary. Thus, the gnostic critique of orthodoxies is now available in thousands of classrooms and on innumerable library shelves in Western vernacular languages.

I do not mean only that the *Zohar* and the gnostic gospels have been translated and are popular on undergraduate reading lists. I mean also that the masters of suspicion (to use Paul Ricoeur's term) in modern philosophy and social science are invoked within religious studies as heroic figures whose ideas are as necessary to mature religious faith as the disillusionments of childhood are to growing up. Put mystically, the reductionistic methods of religious studies often function as apophatic techniques to deconstruct a fraudulent demiurge posing as God. They thus free us for more genuine, more mature, and less dangerous forms of spirituality. They tell us what "God" is *not* and how human, all too human, so many of our religious ideas truly are. Perhaps this is why the great Protestant theologian Paul Tillich insisted on the radical rationality of mystical writers, saw mysticism as an important component of the world's religions, and chose to define the category of mysticism as "God fighting religion within religion."[81]

I am fully aware that humanities disciplines, apart from comparative religion, are now basically contextualist in orientation. But radical knowing (gnosis) disappears where contexts are said to be incommensurable and cultures are not subject to criticism by criteria other than their own. Gnosticism is therefore, among the milieus that dismiss epistemological doubt, perhaps the most mistrusted. Not only does the kind of academic gnosticism I am proposing here question the infallibility of modern epistemology, but it also refuses—adamantly—to ground itself in any one tradition, context, or regime of truth. It is notoriously comparative, countercultural, and even (it might be added) anticultural. Still, contextualists should not reject the gnostic stance automatically. Our present historical context, after all, indicates that contextualism operates politically to Balkanize the human species and hinder efforts to establish standards for a much-needed global morality. Moreover, contextualists—who tend to be trained in history and historical method—know that there have long been people who, on the basis of claims to gnosis wider and deeper than local knowledge, have risked their lives to expose cultural, national, and religious myths as such. If there is hope for our religious worlds—and there may not be—it may well reside in this attitude of openness, dissent, and (finally) open heresy.

While reflecting on the literal etymology of *heresy* (as *hairesis,* or "choice": the choosing of personal conviction over the authority of tradition or group), Elaine Pagels quotes to good effect the early church father Irenaeus against himself. Irenaeus, she writes, "mocked his Gnostic opponent for encouraging his fellow Christians to seek experiential confirmation of their beliefs and ever-new visions: 'every one of them generates something new every day, according to his ability; for no one is considered "mature" [or "initiated"] among them who does not develop some enormous lies.'"[82]

In an implicitly humorous aside, Pagels goes on to point out that Irenaeus's description of gnostic Christians precisely describes the kind of free thinking that artists and writers cherish today. Indeed, our entire system—from undergraduate Socratic discussion (Socrates, recall, was condemned by Athens for corrupting its youth), to the mandatorily original PhD dissertation, to the ever-new lists of our university presses—is designed explicitly to "generate something new every day, according to [our] ability." And the newer, the more provocative, the more "controversial," the better. In effect, we are professional heretics, paid to choose and propagate our own truths and visions in the public free marketplace of ideas.

This, of course, may not always bode well for our relationships with the religions some of us love and study (for they are all filled with people like Irenaeus who claim to know the truth already), but at least such a gnostic model offers us one possible way through the culturally creative but ultimately unbelievable dualisms that we are struggling through now (faith/reason, sacred/secular, tradition/modernity, East/West, Christian/Muslim, Hindu/Muslim). In this gnostic light, anyway, it is quite possible to be both an "insider" and an "outsider," to draw on the symbolic and ritual resources of a tradition without being slavishly bound to it, to love a religion and be deeply, publicly critical of its lies, to choose a form of consciousness that participates in both "faith" and "reason" but moves beyond both to a kind of modern "gnosis," even to imaginatively internalize and unite the depths of other religious traditions in one's own mystical body and its erotic energies. This is something similar to what Ibn al-'Arabi wrote toward in fourteenth-century Andalusia, what Kabir, Guru Nanak, and Akbar attempted in late medieval India, what Ramakrishna experimented with in nineteenth-century colonial Bengal, and it is what we try now again in our own historical contexts.

It is a depressing historical fact that all of these previous experiments failed largely because the orthodox cultures in which they were embedded were ultimately successful in domesticating, taming, even suppressing the countercultural forces of their own mystical thinkers and writers. It remains to be seen what will happen to our own mystical denial of difference in this more secular and global context. When I originally wrote this essay (in the fall of 2003), many of us in Indology were under some rather severe political pressures from both a nationalist-controlled central government in India and some wealthy, ultraconservative segments of the Hindu diaspora to censor our own writings and publicly recant and apologize for our published forms of intellectual gnosis. Ban movements were organized against our books, lawsuits and imprisonment in India were entertained in the Indian media, and at least one of our Indian colleagues had to travel to and from campus for ten months under police protection, as religious activists burned his book in front of his home, petitioned the government to arrest him, and called his work "sheer blasphemy."[83]

Sadly, similar assaults on the intellectual and civil liberties of scholars of religion could be easily repeated within other subdisciplines of the field, from biblical studies to Sikh studies. In short, many of us work and write each day under political pressures similar to those that have always created esoteric forms of radical deconstruction, moral protest, and mystical counterculture. This is why, I believe, so many of us have found some measure of inspiration and even hope in the mystical-critical texts of Ibn al-'Arabi, Meister Eckhart, William Blake, and Ramakrishna. Their remarkable texts, if not always their traditions, stand to this day and for us as powerful witnesses to the not-impossible.[84]

Logoi Mystikoi;
or, How to Think like a Gnostic

I am Protennoia, the Thought that dwells in the Light. . . .
I cry out in everyone, and they recognize it, since a seed indwells them. . . .
Now the Voice that originated from my Thought exists as
    three Permanences: the Father, the Mother, the Son. . . .
I am androgynous. I am Mother (and) I am Father since I copulate
    with myself. I copulate with myself and with those who love me. . . .
Trimorphic Protennoia

We consider the bibles and religions divine. . . . I do not say they
    are not divine,
I say they have all grown out of you and may grow out of you still,
It is not they who give the life. . . . it is you who give the life;
Leaves are not more shed from the trees or
    trees from the earth than they are shed out of you.
Walt Whitman, Leaves of Grass

To savor the mystical intuition of the divine as the coincidence of
being and nothing—what may be considered for the kabbalist, as his
counterpart in medieval Islamic and Christian mystical speculation, the primary ontological binary that comprises other binary constructions, the binary of binaries, we might say—one must reclaim the
middle excluded by the logic of the excluded middle, for it is only by
positioning oneself in that middle between extremes that one can
appreciate the identity of opposites in the opposition of their identity:
that a thing is not only both itself and its opposite, but neither itself
nor its opposite. *Elliot Wolfson*, Language, Eros, Being

I RECOGNIZE THAT THE PRECEDING three meditations do not
always proceed in neat linear lines, that, in effect, they circle around and
around a common set of themes, in this case, those of eroticism, humanism and comparativism. The reader, then, may feel some need for clarity
at this point, or perhaps desire some simpler set of formulas with which
to translate such a rambling gnosis into a more stable and solid gnostic
reason.

This seems like a good idea, the more so because the present text is at something of a transition point or crossroads. My fourth and final meditation, "Mutant Marvels," is of a different order from the first three. It certainly treats related gnostic themes—the ritual structure of the study of religion and the social reception and politics of its initiatory gnosis—but it does not work in quite the same way as the first three essays. It functions rather as a self-conscious allegory through which the reader can try out and think with the conclusions of the first three meditations. Certainly its claims are more speculative and its rhetorical forms more playful. Hence, it should be read in a somewhat different state of mind. An interlude seems in order to signal and help effect this shift in consciousness.

Here, then, between theory building and application, seems like a good point to stop for a moment and take stock, to crystallize what it is I think I am saying here. We thus arrive at three fundamental *logoi mystikoi*, three "hidden sayings" or, if you prefer, three "mystical reasons," followed by a brief note on the common three-formed, dialectical structure of gnostic thought. I will not fully develop these three theses or this dialecticism here.[1] That is not the purpose of this interlude. Moreover, I will add a fourth *logos mystikos* in the conclusion that in many ways encapsulates or encompasses these first three.

For now, however, here are my three *logoi mystikoi* on the subjects of eroticism (chap. 1), mystical humanism (chap. 2) and apophatic comparativism (chap. 3), respectively:

Whereas male heteroerotic forms of the mystical generally become heterodox or heretical, sublimated male homoerotic forms generally become orthodox.

All sacred attributes, powers, or acts recorded in scripture, narrated in myth and folklore, portrayed in sacred art, or reenacted in ritual are projections of human attributes, powers, or acts (often of an exaggerated sort) that nevertheless suggest hidden dimensions, states, or potentials of human being that have historically been expressed by magical, mythical, or mystical language.[2]

The comparative method constitutes a form of apophatic mystical thought in the sense that it both implies a shared human nature or ground (both psychologically and physically construed) across all known cultures and recorded times and simultaneously relativizes the specific cultural and religious expressions of this shared humanity as historically constructed and as nonultimate.

These three theses should not be pondered separately, as if they did not together constitute a greater gestalt or whole. As I intend them here, they mutually imbricate one another, that is, they are all connected. So, for example, when I assert something like "the mystical is the erotic," I do not mean, "all religious experiences can be fully explained by hormones and sex organs." Rather, I mean, "some types of religious experience (of which there are many historical forms) draw on the energies of human sexuality (of which there are many historical forms) to express and reveal an astonishing range of human being that can well be poetically described as 'divine' or 'of mythological proportions.'" In other words, such a brief claim as "the mystical is the erotic" involves complex and essentially dialectical claims about eroticism, humanism, *and* comparativism that simultaneously engage both rational and religious, universal and relativistic epistemologies. It is neither a matter of pure reason nor a statement of simple faith. It is a (post)modern form of gnosis.

Whereas the first mystical reason is an example of a kind of Platonic "form" or "comparative pattern" seen with the mind's eye,[3] the second and third mystical reasons display what we might call the poetic and metalogical structures of gnostic thinking.

Poetically speaking, gnostic thought recognizes that religious expressions function as symbols and, as such, are simultaneously true and false, that they both reveal and conceal. Reductionism and revelation lie down together here in a (post)modern form of what the Sufi tradition understood as the paradox of the veil (*hijab*), that is, the psychological and linguistic necessity of cultural forms that reveal the divine light (which is in itself beyond all representation) precisely by concealing it behind veiled symbols and signs. Within the paradox of the veil, that is, within any linguistic system, there can be no revealing without a simultaneous concealing. Every appearance of true reality (*al-haqq*) is also a relativism. Every religious truth is a literal lie. Given the inherently symbolic and referential nature of language itself, it can be no other way.[4]

Metalogically speaking, this same gnostic thought is rigorously dialectical, and this in at least three senses. First, it is dialectical in the sense that it recognizes that the grammatical flow of thought can often be reversed and reflected back on itself, "transformed," as Feuerbach put it so beautifully, like a snake biting its own tail. It recognizes, in other words, that a predicate can often become a subject. We saw this most clearly with Feuerbach's anthropological reductionism, but most of my earlier work on mystical forms of eroticism performs an essentially identical move with respect to Freud's psychoanalysis (much along the lines of Feuerbach's "God is love" becoming "Love is God"). So, with respect to Feuerbach, if the divine can be reduced to the human, then the human can also be celebrated as divine. And, with respect to Freud, if the sacred can be explained by the sexual, then the sexual can be read as encoded by or expressive of the sacred. Hence my two gnostic categories of mystical humanism and the erotic.

Second, such thinking is dialectical in the sense that it embraces both sameness and difference. There is room here, ample room, for both nature and nurture, both genetics and culture, both universalism and contextualism, both modern essentialism and postmodern constructivism. Truth is reached not by erasing one of these poles, but by *relating* them and tracing their elaborate interactions, all the while recognizing that this constant dance of sameness and difference is no illusion without effect, but that it produces a genuine transfiguration of being, as in the Marxist insight into the real transformation of human consciousness via socioeconomic change or the genetic alchemy from primate to human being traced by evolutionary science.

Third, such gnostic thinking is dialectical in a traditional, mystical, or mythological sense. Indeed, such a pattern is so common in the history of religions that the depth psychologist C. G. Jung and, probably following him, the historian of religions Mircea Eliade identified and labeled this pattern the *coincidentia oppositorum*, that is, the "coincidence of opposites."[5] In a somewhat more rigorous key, the structuralist anthropologist Claude Lévi-Strauss and the comparative mythologist Wendy Doniger have demonstrated that mythological systems are manifestations of human cognitive processes that attempt through various narrative, ritual, and psychosexual techniques to resolve or transcend what are essentially irresolvable paradoxes of human experience created by the binary processes of the human brain (good and evil, life and death, matter and mind, sex and spirit, sacred and profane, being and nothingness, male and female, etc.). Something similar is true, I think, of mystical systems as well, with the important exception that these systems claim to transcend or resolve the paradox, something the myth never does (and cannot do) in the structuralist systems of Lévi-Strauss and Doniger.

Whether or not they are truly successful, both religious styles, the mythical and the mystical, seek to push their storytellers, listeners, and thinkers beyond every sort of dualism or Two into a realm of being—that is, a One that is also a Three—that simply cannot be captured by our normal binary modes of thinking. What they seem to be saying, if I may translate the mythological and mystical systems into modern code, is that because reality overflows or surpasses the cognitive and adaptive abilities of the human brain, which have evolved over millennia in order to allow the species to survive and flourish, it is a serious mistake to confuse what the human brain can process with what actually exists in and as the cosmos. Evolutionary adaptation and cosmic reality are certainly related (since it is exceedingly doubtful that adaptation and survival would be served by misperception and gross cognitive error), but they are hardly the same thing, and any cognitive system that is adaptive almost certainly filters out *far* more of reality than it lets in. We should never confuse, then, what we can think with our on-and-off, dualistic, binary computer-brains with the full range and depth of cosmic being. We should also expect that, were an immediate or unmediated experience of reality possible, such an experience would shatter and violate these same dualistic forms of thinking. This, of course, is exactly what we find in the history of mystical literature.

We might finally summarize this form of gnostic thought through a kind of mystical mathematics, that is, a set of simple integers that appear to lie at the center of the history of religions: One, Two, Three.[6] We might also note that this most basic of all dialectical structures finds its most obvious and probably most ancient experiential base in the phenomenology of sexuality: the Two who ecstatically unite to produce a Third, a One who is both the same and not the same as the original Two. It thus no accident at all that when Jung and Eliade sought to explicate the *coincidentia oppositorum*, they turned quickly, like the erotic gnostic angels, to the classical confluence of sexuality and spirituality—what Elliot Wolfson so beautifully calls the eros of consciousness and the consciousness of eros[7]—and, more specifically, to the paradigmatic example of Indian Tantra.[8] Gnostic thought, in other words, is also fundamentally erotic thought. It is thinking having sex with itself.

Mutant Marvels

Mutants have an extra power, extra ability, some extra facet or quality denied a normal man. The word "extra" was the key. Mutants are, in a sense, people with something extra. And, if we think of the word "extra" in phonetic terms, we might think of that phrase as "people with something x-tra." And a man with something x-tra could conceivably be called an x-man! *Stan Lee on his creation of* The X-Men

[I]f scholars were to analyze carefully the structure of that peculiar mode of being that accompanies the out-of-body experience, they would discover therein the key to understanding why mystical experience so often goes hand-in-hand with a proclivity for supernormal powers of perception and action. . . . *—all these seemingly disparate phenomena can have a common genesis in the recollective act.* . . . When the empowered imagination objectifies itself, something extra, some overplus, attaches to that objectification that prevents one from saying that the subject is only externalizing the contents of his own mind. *Jess Hollenback,* Mysticism: Experience, Response, and Empowerment

IN 1963, A YOUNG COMIC BOOK WRITER named Stan Lee (born Stanley Lieber) imagined a school for the gifted in Westchester County just north of New York City, not far from where he himself actually worked for Marvel Comics in Manhattan.[1] There in Westchester a psychic professor, a telepath by the name of Professor Xavier (or Professor X, as he would sometimes be called) gathered around himself a small group of talented "mutants" whose strange powers needed to be nurtured in a safe environment and safely hidden from the gaze of the public, a public that would certainly pursue and persecute these gnostic souls were their strange secret powers to become widely known. Although a young woman named Jean Grey, another psychic, was among their elite membership, Lee was writing slightly before the consciousness raising of the feminist revolution, and so he called this small troupe of gifted individuals the X-Men, the letter "x," Lee tells us, suggesting "people with something x-tra."[2] One such X-man, Angel, could fly with a set of literal wings. Another, Iceman, was made entirely of ice that he could manipulate to various offensive and defensive effects. A third, Cyclops, possessed eyes that could emit powerful beams of energy. And a fourth, the Beast, possessed remarkable animal-like strength, gymnastic abilities and an acute intellect. The lovely Jean Gray, constantly hit on by her four male admirers, completed the five-member team, now rife with sexual tension.

The X-Men have been well known to comic book readers since their first appearance in the early 1960s. Their stories have morphed considerably over the decades through different combinations of characters, writers, and artists, but the basic mythology has always revolved around the central motif of the evolutionary mutation that is at once an astonishing gift and a social curse—the uncanny power that sets one apart from the rest of the crowd. Interestingly, unlike most other superheroes, the X-Men generally have no secret identities. They may seclude themselves and their students in their own ivory tower institution, but they are who they are, and they do not hide that fact with a fake public persona.

More recently, Twentieth Century Fox made some of these characters household names with its film adaptations, *The X-Men* and *X2*, with Patrick Stewart of *Star Trek* fame playing the bald and wheelchair-bound Professor Xavier. The films, especially the first, do a marvelous job of capturing the mythological universe of Marvel Comics, where superpowers always come at a heavy price—"With great power comes great responsibility," Peter Parker as Spider-Man learns in another blockbuster remake—and where every hero is also a fault-filled human being who fears, bumbles and blunders, swears a lot, falls in love, and, perhaps most important, maintains a playful, often quite sarcastic, sense of humor through it all. Put too academically, the Marvel superheroes are postmodern embodiments of self-reflexivity, doubt, and ironic wit.

In *Unbreakable*, another film in this same comic book genre, M. Night Shyamalan spins an eerie tale of a boy born with a rare condition that renders every bone in his body eminently breakable—a skeleton of shattering glass. In a moment of both desperation and inspiration, his mother gives her son, now a depressed and despairing adolescent, a comic book and so introduces him into the fantastic world of superpowers, evil villains, and superheroes. More or less imprisoned in his home by his innately fragile physical condition, the boy does his reading and grows up to become a successful comic book art collector named Elijah Price, played by Samuel Jackson (who in real life, by the way, is an avid collector of comics). Elijah, or

Mr. Glass, as he is also known, believes that comic books encode a secret history of supernormal powers that in fact exist in the real world: "I believe comic book heroes walk the earth," he tells a baffled David Dunn, played by Bruce Willis.

To prove it, Elijah stages a series of catastrophic accidents—a plane crash, a hotel fire, a train derailment—as sick but sure means to search for the man who would emerge unscathed, unbroken, that is, as his mythical opposite, his archhero who will complete the nondual spectrum of good and evil that is his mystical world. Through a dramatic train accident, Elijah in fact finds just such a hero in Dunn, who must learn from his unknown archnemesis about his own still-unconscious powers before he eventually discovers the terrible truth about this mysterious teacher and turns him in to the authorities. Mr. Glass, like so many other charismatic teachers, is both a wisdom figure and a criminal.

I begin this final gnostic meditation with these comic book figures and popular films, partly because I grew up in the late 1960s and early 1970s with some of these same beloved characters (hence, I have never quite shaken the conviction that I may be Spider-Man), but mostly in order to allegorize, popularize, and finally radicalize my own basic mythology, namely, that the (post)modern study of religion—by virtue of its subject matter, the nonordinary epistemologies this subject matter encodes, and the dual critical-intuitive or gnostic methods the discipline employs to engage these unusual states of mind and body—remains to this day a kind of hidden, even forbidden, knowledge within American public culture that feels, at least to me, like both an astonishing gift and a social curse, an uncanny power that sets one apart. Such an open esotericism, paradoxically embedded in one of America's central cultural institutions, the university, in turn constitutes the discipline as one of the most poorly understood, least appreciated, and, in many ways, just plain weirdest branches of American higher education, the Area 51 of the university, as one of my mischievous colleagues at Rice University likes to call it: that secret place of alien contact, misinterpreted truths, and metaphysical conspiracy, imagined or real.[3]

My gnostic reflections on the basic esotericism of the discipline here work on at least four different levels: that of an *educational, sexual,* and *political allegory* and—for the really brave—that of a certain *radical empiricism.* The latter expression, as we shall see, is borrowed from the American psychologist and philosopher William James for that radical open-mindedness that refuses to ignore anomalous psychological events—what James called "wild facts"—simply because they cannot be fitted into the reigning worldview or epistemology of the day.

On the level of educational allegory, I want to suggest that Professor X can be read as Everyprofessor, his talented mutants as undergraduate and graduate students, and his private school for the gifted in Westchester

County as every institution of higher learning that specializes in plumbing the depths and complexities of "religion" just outside the public gaze within the nurturing confines of an elite minisociety. Here I will also note that the college or graduate experience is in effect one of American culture's most developed initiation rituals, and that it can be read and experienced as a hero myth.

On the level of sexual allegory, I want to point out that the initiation rituals, the hero myths, and the modern college experience are all located in the life cycle just after the remarkable psychophysical transfigurations of puberty, that is, just after the appearance of forms of life energy that are complexly connected—as both gift and curse—to the various creative powers that set our young X-Men and X-Women on their personal quests for vocation and vision. Here I will also name a single psychohistorical fact that has wide-ranging implications for how we read comics or watch their cinematographic virtual visions, namely, the fact that the superhero comic has, from day one as it were, been connected to desires for and fears of sex and the latter's still essentially mysterious and gnostic "superpowers."

On the level of political allegory, I want to suggest that, partly because of this initiatory or heroic structure and its intimate (and erotic) connection to youth, the university remains one of our best resources for new life and new ideas, and that the health and welfare of our modern world may depend at least partly upon how fully we can integrate both the analytical and intuitive powers of the study of religion into our social practices, public policies, and legal and political institutions. Put mythically, I want to ask why Professor Xavier's school for the gifted must traditionally remain a secret and, more important, whether this is really such a good idea. Put more theoretically and abstractly, I am interested in exploring the relationship between the professional study of religion and American popular and political culture and how, or whether, these cultures can be brought more fruitfully together.

But be forewarned: although my juxtaposition of material from American popular culture and ancient mystical literature—"comics and gnostics" for the vaguely rhyming—expresses a sincere wish that they can be brought together, I am not persuaded that this is so. I am, moreover, fully aware that sometimes a wish is another name for an illusion. It is not for nothing that Professor Xavier had to hide his young students behind the walls of a secret educational institution, or that one of the overriding themes of this mythology is the cruel incomprehension of politicians and the public. And what *is* all that talk about ivory towers that academics hear so often, if not a form of faint praise mixed with resentment, a touch of jealousy, and perhaps even a bit of fear? We are indeed mutants.

Along the same ethical-political lines, I have no desire to paint a simplistic good-versus-evil picture of the world in which the study of religion is an entirely positive force of unqualified goodness unrelated to the colonial and imperialistic histories of Western political life, or where all the good guys are among us and all the bad guys are, well, somewhere or somebody else. The metaphors of mutation and evolution should warn us immediately here. Mutations, after all, are much more likely to kill an organism than they are to gift it. And biological evolution is by no means a linear process of unqualified development and progress toward greater and greater complexity; indeed, much of evolution is more of a meandering or even a regression, and most of its patient paths are literally dead ends.

When I suggest, then, that the modern study of religion functions like both a cultural mutation and a form of secret knowledge, I am not romanticizing. I am trembling. I am also seeking to place the field within a long and quite serious history of mythological, literary, and ethical reflection on the psychology and politics of secrecy in Western thought. I have in mind everything from the ancient myths of Adam and Eve and Pandora's "box" (a misogynist myth of the vagina, if ever there was one), to Goethe's Faust and Shelley's Frankenstein, to our present ethical struggles over the human genome project, the wisdom of genetic engineering, and the constitutional limits of national security in an age of global terrorism.[4] Secrecy and forbidden knowledge, it turns out, are perennial features of the human desire to wonder and to know, and to *not* want to wonder or to know.

Finally, on the level of radical empiricism, I want to suggest that the superpowers of the comic book heroes are not as fantastic or as fictional as the most rational among us might assume, and that in actual empirical fact they participate in a general phenomenology of the traumatic, the mystical, the magical, and the psychical that is very familiar to the historian of religions, particularly one schooled in the psychology of dissociation. Put mythically, that is, in the terms of the film *Unbreakable,* I want to suggest that, if the history of religions means anything, it is indeed true that "comic book heroes walk the earth."

I am not quite suggesting that there are literal superheroes here, unless, of course, someone wants to show me his cape or her golden lasso. So far, no one has been willing to do either (although I did see the Batmobile as a child once, at a car show with my dad). What I am suggesting, rather, is that, once we take the data of the history of religions seriously—that is, as empirical features of human consciousness and energy that have been exaggerated as mythology and projected as theology but nevertheless point to a human ontological ground that is quite real and quite literally cosmic—the human being to which all religious phenomena are rightly reduced in the study of religion begins to appear as far more fantastic, amazing, incredible, and uncanny than any strictly rationalist method can possibly imagine, let alone explain.

Reductionism and mysticism thus meet again, and the colorful and beautifully illustrated gnostic mythologies of the American comic book turn out to be closer to the truth of things than we first thought. As

Mr. Glass insisted, such myths may indeed exaggerate everything, but they do so in order to advance in an unconscious or esoteric fashion what is essentially a true and in the end quite empirical point or wild fact: the human being is often empowered by forms of consciousness and energy that, in relation to the conscious ego or social self, are indeed literally "super" or "x-tra."

Educational and Sexual Allegory

A rather long time ago, about one hundred years to be inexact, a Belgian anthropologist by the name of Arnold van Gennep noticed something special about many of the initiation rituals of different cultures. They tended to follow a tripartite pattern. In van Gennep's language, these rituals moved from an initial state of separation from society through a transitional period and into a final state of incorporation back into the community.[5] Much later, the British anthropologist Victor Turner took notice of van Gennep's tripartite structure and decided to focus on what we might call the existential and social transformational possibilities of this movement. He thus extended the model into his well-known reflections about the "liminal" qualities of van Gennep's transition state, a chaotic but creative condition for Turner defined by paradox, ambiguity, and bivalency, and an attending, often radically egalitarian social experience that Turner called *communitas*.[6] The liminal state for Turner was that magical place "in between," neither here nor there, where transformation is effected through ritual actions designed to break down one's previous identity in order to form it into something new and more adequate to the demands and mystery of life.

The experience of the traditional shaman or native healer might follow a similar structure, even as it takes on more extreme, spontaneous, even psychopathological features. As a young man, he might begin experiencing visions, suffer a whole range of symptoms that can take on initiatory qualities, or come to know his sexual powers as mysteriously "third," that is, as somehow being different from those of others: he is a marginal, liminal being down to his very flesh and bones. He is being "called." Terrifying visions of dismemberment might follow, in which he is ritually torn apart before he can be magically put back together again and can return to his community as a new being, that is, as a respected shaman, miracle worker, and healer capable of traveling in ecstatic trance to the world of the dead.[7]

Here too we can place all those world mythologies that scholars of religion such as Otto Rank, Lord Raglan, C. G. Jung, Joseph Campbell, and Robert Segal have identified as following a pattern they have chosen to call the hero's quest.[8] In this general pattern, the hero is marked at birth by strange events or anomalous features. He leaves his society at some point, often quite unwillingly, to depart on a kind of vision quest through which he must meet many dangers and battle many monsters in order to prove his worth and find some hidden treasure, holy grail, wisdom teaching, or secret identity. The hero's quest is complete, however, only when he returns to his original community with the treasured wisdom in hand to share with others. Even if his community greets him with incomprehension, misunderstanding, or even violence (and it often will), his is a quintessentially social task, a personal quest for the sake of the community and its eventual transformation. From the ancient Mesopotamian story of Gilgamesh on his poignant search for the secret of immortality, to the classical lives of Hercules, Moses, the Buddha, Jesus, and Muhammad, to our modern cinematic mythologies, our *Star Wars*, *Spider-Man*, and *The X-Men*, the hero and his quest are an astonishingly consistent and popular pattern in the world of comparative mythology. Indeed, even some of our most common religious patterns and popular mythologies—the near-death experience and the alien abduction, for example—follow this same basic pattern of calling, separation, struggle, and return.

If we could but learn to take our own cultural practices with the same seriousness and metaphysical depth with which we routinely treat those of other "foreign" or ancient cultures, we might see that the same models apply quite well to the college experience—that classical American liminal period between adolescence and full adulthood—and even more to its more extreme version, the vision-seeking, vocation-granting ritual of graduate school. The graduate student, especially in the humanities, is on a kind of modern-day vision quest, and she is likely to suffer the same fate as the traditional initiate, shaman, or hero: a vague sense of calling or vocation, a willed and extended separation from society (often this may involve some rather significant sacrifices involving extreme degrees of solitude, self-reflection, and the suspension of income-generating activities), an eventual vision quest in the form of an original idea or project that will define her, perhaps for the rest of her life, and the relative miscomprehension of her family, friends, and society in general.

Who, outside the students themselves and the Professor X of every professor, *really* understands why a young bright adult perfectly capable of law, business, or medical school (and hence a sizable income) would give this all up and dedicate five to ten years of her life to a pursuit that in many cases will have no financial payoff (that is, there will be no job) and probably win her little else, on the surface at least, than the patient forbearance of her family and friends? Who truly understands what is at stake, personally, socially, and spiritually? The truth of the matter is that the initiatory structure and rituals of the graduate experience often effectively dismember and reconstitute the initiate just as effectively and completely as any shamanistic trance.

And although such transfigurations happen all the time in intellectual practices from the study of literature or the history of art to philosophy and anthropology, nowhere, I would suggest, is this more true than in the study of religion, for here these same "callings" are often quite conscious and literal, these vision quests sometimes constitute actual visions, and the miscomprehension, indifference, even occasional hatred of the community can be quite extreme. The knower in the study of religion is indeed a hero: he has left, he has battled his demons and doubts, he has known, and he has returned with a gift of gnosis that no one seems to want, much less understand. Part of the problem is that his is an essentially forbidden knowledge, a gnosis or secret identity that can never be fully revealed, no matter how hard he tries to communicate it or how much he would like others to understand. Even if they chose to remain within the dominant scientific register of our modern culture, the filmmakers of *The X-Men* had it right: the dark, misunderstood heroes, it turns out, are "in real life" actually *students*, young people with dreams and strange gifts that they themselves do not quite understand and cannot quite accept.

On Puberty and Powers

Part of the secret that these young people sense in themselves and cannot quite integrate into their lives just yet is sex and, in particular, male sex. It is, after all, the pubescent male that has always overwhelmingly defined the main audience of the American superhero comic book. *The Rough Guide to Superheroes* gets it right, then, when it comments on Umberto Eco's analysis of the anonymity of Clark Kent as a very good approximation of the average reader: "Without a nondescript alter ego, these stories would not strike so resounding a chord, especially with those who have never completely outgrown their adolescence. In other words, men."[9]

This should make us laugh, but it should hardly surprise us. The hero mythologies of almost any culture on the planet are masculinist narratives that focus on separation, courage, and battle of some sort, all features of a socially constructed masculinity as it has been studied by such anthropologists as Thomas Gregor and David Gilmore.[10] One is born male, but not a man. The former is a biological given; the latter a cultural and individual accomplishment often involving initiatory structures of some sort.

We are also dealing with a kind of coded eroticism in both the traditional mythologies and the American comic book. With respect to the latter, note, for example, the exaggerated curves of all those tightly, and often barely, costumed bodies. The female characters are inevitably full-breasted, tight-waisted, and stunningly beautiful. The men have six-packs for stomachs and immense biceps, thighs, and pecs. The bodies are essentially perfect, at least as that physical perfection has been imagined in modern American culture. We are dealing with ideal body types, certainly not real bodies. We are dealing, that is, with male *desires*.

And probably frustrated, or at least confused, desires at that. Indeed, some have speculated that the superpowers of a comic book hero and the sexual powers of its creator (or most devoted readers) are sometimes inversely related: the more powers, the less sex; the less powers, the more sex. This rule certainly holds for two of the earliest and most archetypal figures of the American comic book genre: Superman and Batman. Whereas the two young Jewish Cleveland men, Jerry Siegel and Joe Shuster, who created the almost invincible Superman were nerdy, shy, and confessedly awkward around the opposite sex, Bob Kane, who dreamed up a Batman without any supernatural powers whatsoever, was tall, handsome, and dashing.[11] Who needs x-ray vision when one lives in what is basically a playboy mansion?

It also seems hardly incidental here that it is around early adolescence, that is, around puberty and the onslaught of the "secret" and largely misunderstood powers of sexuality, that both traditional initiation rituals and the American comic book revolve. This, I would suggest, is precisely what in real life is x-tra about real X-Men and X-Women and why the myths speak most deeply to adolescents: what simultaneously gifts and curses the young adult is the mysterious x-tra of sexual maturation, understood (quite correctly) here not simply as a biological instinct but also as a potential occult energy or "superpower."

Thus, the history of the American comic book is also the history of sex. Indeed, much of the inspiration for the earliest superheroes came from eroticized pulp magazines, and the earliest publishers and distributors of the genre also dealt in soft porn (and prohibited liquor and the birth-control devices and radical literature of Margaret Sanger, an early proponent of women's sexual rights and safety).[12] Little wonder, then, that the comic book has always been hounded by accusations of "obscenity." Similar patterns carry through from the beginning of the genre down to the present. So, for example, Jack Cole, the creator of Plastic Man (the sunglassed pink guy who can stretch his body to any shape) in the 1940s, also happened to be the first and probably most famous cartoonist for *Playboy* magazine—all that pink stretching wasn't for nothing.[13] And the psychologist William Moulton Marston, who invented Wonder Woman in 1941 after the Greek Amazon myths (under the pen name of Charles Moulton), got into trouble with his editor, Sheldon Mayer, mostly because he was always trying to get Wonder Woman (or any other woman, for that matter) tied up. One of his stories involved a contest to see who could rope up the most girls, and another illustrated some form of bondage in seventy-five panels! Mayer did his best to edit out Marston's fantasies, but the original bondage fetish remained coded in Wonder Woman's golden lasso.[14]

More recently, we have a blockbuster film like *Spider-Man 2*, whose central narrative revolves around Peter Parker's love life and his troubling inability to, well, shoot his white stuff, in this case, gooey webs out of his wrists.[15] As Peter's love life collapses, so too does his superpower to spin webs and leap from tall buildings. As he learns to love, he simultaneously regains his confidence and his mystical powers, white stuff and all. Similarly, in the recent *X2: X-Men United* movie, when a young mutant boy finally breaks the news to his parents about his own supernormal gifts, the event is framed around a classical "coming out of the closet" scenario: to be a mutant and to be gay are more or less interchangeable here.[16] Whether framed in a heteroerotic or a homoerotic code, these latter films thus make a rather transparent linkage between the erotic and the mystical and work at the same time against the superhero asexual norm as manifested in such archetypal characters as Superman. As Umberto Eco has noted, to become a superhero is also often "to take an implicit vow of chastity"[17] (which also links, this time via repression and sublimation, the forces of sexuality and the superpower). Not here in the movies, though. Here, sexual expression and superpowers manifest themselves *together*, suggesting in the process that their energies are in fact linked on some profound level.

None of this is meant to reduce the traditional initiation, hero myth, or American comic book to simple sexuality. It is not to return to Fredric Wertham's hysterical psychoanalytic rant, *Seduction of the Innocent* (1954),[18] that form of psychological McCarthyism that almost sank the comic book industry in the 1950s and led to the Comic Book Code Authority of 1954, which included such memorable lines as, "Females shall be drawn realistically without exaggeration of any physical qualities," and "Passion or romantic interest shall never be treated in such a way as to stimulate the lower and baser emotions."[19] The latter code was designed, in direct response to Wertham's attacks, to appease the fearful public through acts of self-censorship and moral control. Wertham, for example, had seen lesbianism in Wonder Woman and a homosexual fantasy in Batman and Robin (whose young legs, he pointed out correctly, were often shown bare), and he wanted it all stopped.[20]

And it was stopped, at least for a while. Within a few months after the appearance of Wertham's widely read book, Congress was calling hearings and the comic book industry was censoring itself. Batman, for example, would be given a (heterosexual) love interest in Batwoman, and soon Robin would even have his own Batgirl. Most publishers, however, simply went out of business, their markets now destroyed by the righteousness of the new moral code. Things were straighter now, and presumably safer.

At least until ABC got a hold of the Batman mythology and in 1966 aired its first episode of the wildly popular *Batman* television series, thereby transforming the Dynamic Duo into what would become the veritable archetype of gay camp.[21] Over three decades later, this pattern would become even more exaggerated with *Saturday Night Live*'s animated series "The Ambiguously Gay Duo," featuring things like a "Batmobile" that looks pretty much exactly like a penis and the Ambiguously Gay Duo grabbing each other's ankles and assuming a "69" position in order to tumble into their villains. Alas, the repressed *always* returns; it also usually gets the last laugh. Not that it was only the homoerotic that returned from repression in ABC's *Batman*. The series also included any number of memorable heterosexual episodes and lines, like those uttered by the gorgeous and leathered Catwoman to a sexually naive Robin, that Boy Wonder: "Hi, Robin, my name is Pussycat, but you can call me Cat!"[22]

Cat indeed.

But this is not quite what I am suggesting here. I am not suggesting that the comic book mythologies are simply sexual codes for adolescent boys (although they are that too), or that Spidey's shooting webs suggest ejaculating sperm (although they psychologically function in exactly that way in the second film), or that "Cat" really means "Pussy" (although it does), or that the Dynamic Duo can easily function as a male homoerotic fantasy (although it certainly can). Nor am I pointing out that the historical origins of the superhero comic book are tied up (forgive the pun) with soft porn and the "girlie magazine" (although they are). What I *am* suggesting is that in order to understand properly the hero motif in world mythology, and in American mythology in particular, we must be willing to mythologize sexuality as an originary expression of a kind of mystical humanism and recognize that hidden within human sexuality lie real "secret identities" and "superpowers" that continue to sublimate and morph throughout the life cycle into multiple forms of consciousness and energy as wild and various as any superhero team. In other words, instead of simply reducing the mythical to the sexual, I want to imagine *raising* the sexual into the mythical. Hence Dr. Kavita Rao's rather matter-of-fact observation in a recent issue of *Astonishing X-Men* that "[a] child's mutant power usually manifests at puberty."[23] My point exactly. What is x-tra is the seXual.

Denying the Demiurge

If we carry through our educational and sexual allegory of the superhero, what cultural mutations, what x-tra powers are catalyzed and stabilized in a typical college or graduate initiation within the study of religion? What altered forms of consciousness, which we call "theory," are entered and realized to a degree that they dismember and then re-member the initiate? Put most simply, that is, nonmythically now, what is it exactly that scholars of religion claim to *know*?

I would name nine such altered states of consciousness, nine forms of theoretical knowledge. Mythically and mystically put, these are nine protognostic techniques of apophatic deconstruction, that is, nine intellectual rages against the demiurge of religion itself. Such forms of "hidden" or forbidden knowledge are commonly found in the academy but seldom discussed, much less understood, in public formats. That is, one will seldom, if ever, hear a commentator on the Middle East deconstructing the violent exclusionary structure of monotheism itself or hear an analyst of American Evangelicalism note that biblical literalism was abandoned two hundred years ago by the knowing, or that Christian fundamentalism was originally a rejection of biblical scholarship in the universities. One will never hear, that is, that monotheistic fundamentalism, of any variety, is a form of historical and textual ignorance, a rejection of higher education, and a very good way to set up a dysfunctionally violent world.

I can only summarize these nine forms of ignored knowledge here. If we wanted to be *really* gnostic (or Blakean, which amounts to the same thing), we might stick to eight (an Ogdoad) and give each a strange-sounding mythological name—Yaltabaoth, Urizen, Luvah, Saklas, Barbelo, Pronoia, that sort of thing—but I will resist that temptation here and simply describe them in their more usual prosaic terms:

1. THE GNOSIS OF THE MANY. We know that the truth claims of the religions, taken together and as literal truth claims, cancel each other out. Despite the oft-mouthed anecdotes of the street, there simply are no clear or obvious universal religious positions. God either has a Son, as in Christianity, or he does not, as in Judaism and Islam. The soul is either eternal and divine, as in some forms of Hinduism, or it is an empty and dangerous illusion, as in many forms of Buddhism. We either live once and are judged by an external personal God, as in the Western monotheistic religions, or we live many times in a cycle controlled by the forces of karma and rebirth, as in many of the Asian traditions. And this is only the beginning. Every religious teaching, to quote the late Ioan Culianu, is literally unbelievable; that is, whereas each religious truth seems obvious enough to those who espouse and practice it, this very same truth will inevitably appear unbelievable, even ridiculous or blasphemous, to cultural actors who were not socially conditioned into its constructed plausibility. There are, of course, many mechanisms to deny, resolve, or transcend this plurality, from perennialist universalism and Hindu inclusivism to fundamentalist exclusivism to psychological metaphorization, but all of them share a common insight into the basic and still-irresoluble scandal of religious history, the scandal of religious pluralism.

2. THE GNOSIS OF THE AMBIVALENT SACRED. We also know that the great diversity of human experiences of the sacred can never be framed as a single experience of unqualified goodness. Rather, the sacred has consistently manifested itself in ways that have been both profoundly positive and horribly negative. The same deities and traditions that heal, include, and save some also demean, exclude, and kill others. Nor are the latter negative dimensions something external to religion, as if religious behaviors that harm people are "not really religious." No, this internal ambiguity of

beauty and violence, of good and evil, seems to be rooted in the ambivalence of the sacred itself, to which Rudolf Otto spoke so eloquently at the
beginning of the twentieth century with his notion of the sacred as a *mysterium tremendum et fascinans*, that is, as a mystical order at once terrifying
and alluring.[24] The French sociologist Émile Durkheim intuited the same
basic truth with his notion that the sacred is divided within itself, that it
is a polarity: "on the one hand, a pure, noble elevated, life-giving form (the
'right' sacred); on the other, an impure, vile, degraded, and dangerous
form (the 'left' sacred)."[25] The terrifying truth of the matter that few religionists, much less politicians or policy makers, seem willing to face,
much less critically respond to, is that the sacred has always been a deeply
ambivalent force in human experience, as capable of producing an Osama
bin Laden as a Martin Luther King, Jr.

3. THE GNOSIS OF SOCIETY. We know that the power and salience of
religious myths, rituals, and institutions derive partly from their ability to
actively dissimulate; that is, religious traditions provide coherence and
meaning to people's lives precisely by disguising their own human origins
as divinely inspired or revealed. In a word, *religions lie.* In the oft-quoted
and more gentle words of the sociologist of religion Peter Berger, "Every
human society is an enterprise of world-building. . . . Institutions, roles,
and identities exist as objectively real phenomena in the social world,
though they and this world are at the same time nothing but human pro-
ductions."[26] Berger, of course, is writing within the same sociological tradition as Émile Durkheim, whose thought was famously captured in the
sociological sound bite "Religion is society worshipping itself." Now all of
this, as Berger himself suggests, may in fact be based on something more
fundamental, something external to human society, perhaps even something divine that we might detect within humor and other "rumors of angels," but religion remains nonetheless a quintessentially human produc-
tion that can, and must, be studied as such.[27]

4. THE GNOSIS OF POWER. We know that power is endemic to religious
systems, that it extends into and through every level of society and social interaction, and that the rich and powerful in any society tend to dominate
the poor and the relatively powerless, often through religious institutions
and mythologies. Religious systems, in other words, are never innocent of
physical, practical concerns that determine how goods and resources are
distributed in society and between societies. This is not to say, however, that
religion always functions as a conservative status quo force in society, as an
opiate, as Marx so memorably put it in another famous sound-bite. Religion, after all, can just as easily function as a powerful revolutionary force
in society, as a language of protest, and as a means of subversion. Either way,
however, as protest or as opiate, religion is never devoid of the political, the

ideological, and the economic. On some level, no doubt a deep one, religion is about naked power clothed with the divine.

5. THE GNOSIS OF THE BODY. We also know that many forms of religious experience and practice are imbued with sexual forces and gender patterns that may be, and often are, vehemently denied by the practitioners themselves. Once again, religions dissimulate or lie, and one of their favorite dissimulations is the illusion of the genderless, sexless religion; in truth, there is no such thing. If there is a universal in the history of religions, it is the human body and its physiological shaping of religious practice and experience. Not everyone believes that God has a Son (a profoundly gendered belief, by the way), or that there is something we can call a soul, or that ritually killing an animal or human being somehow removes impurities and sins (more violated bodies), but every single human being who has ever walked this earth began in an orgasm, gestated in a woman's womb, and was born in a bloody, violent event. Most of us, moreover, came into this world, as Tertullian so sarcastically put it, "inter faecem et urinam," that is, "between feces and urine." The body, its desires, its needs, and its fluids, then, are religious universals precisely because they are also physiological universals, and for all our talk of cultural difference and relativism (all true enough), the interior of the human body, any human body of any race, language, or culture, is virtually indistinguishable.

6. THE GNOSIS OF HISTORY. We know that religious systems, like all cultural forms, develop from previous cultural systems, that they develop through history, and that they eventually die or morph into other systems. We know, in other words, that religions are historical phenomena that can be studied, tracked, and understood as any other historical phenomena. The seeming eternal verity of religious forms, in other words, is another dissimulation, believable only because the temporal span of our lives is so short and hence gives us only the most meager snapshot of the history of religions. We are like the ant colony beneath the oak tree that imagines, falsely of course, that the oak is eternal and does not change. In truth, what human beings are forever taking as "the way things really are" is little more than a snapshot or single frame on the fast-running film of time and its elaborate social constructions. The oak tree can be cut down, it is constantly changing, and it will most certainly die. So too will all religions.

7. THE GNOSIS OF THE OUTSIDER. Methodologically speaking, we know that certain insights into religious systems are generally unavailable to the practitioners themselves, so determined are their thought processes by religious ideas and practices, part of whose raison d'être, as I have already pointed out, is to conceal all sorts of things in order to justify their own "obvious" truths. Moreover, within any particular community or tradition

there is an entire sociology of knowledge, that is, a social construction of truth and reality that determines what ideas seem plausible, even thinkable, and to whom. In short, our imaginations and our very thought processes are socially determined to a quite remarkable extent; hence, it is crucial to privilege the perspective of outsiders in order to assess, understand, and interpret a religious worldview that would otherwise prevent this very project from happening on its own terms and conditions. Occasionally, cultures even honor this same gnosis. Hence the Chinese proverb "Pang guan zhe qing," or "Outsiders have clarity [of vision]."[28]

8. THE GNOSIS OF THE INSIDER. Conversely, we know that certain insights into religious systems are generally unavailable to outsiders who have not fully internalized the linguistic practices and ritual forms of the religion being studied. Life is short, our cultural and linguistic experiences are always limited, and hence it is impossible to know a religious or cultural system the way someone who was raised in it knows and feels it. Any adequate comparative study of religion, then, must also rely on the gifts and perspectives of insiders as well.

9. THE GNOSIS OF REFLEXIVITY. This penultimate tension between the insider and the outsider in turn leads to our final and perhaps most important methodological point. As many interpreters have pointed out, what sets apart the study of religion from the religions themselves is its unique willingness and ability to apply all of the above hermeneutics, not only to every religion it encounters, but also to itself and its own practitioners. Moreover, what binds the discipline together is not its varied subject matters (which are as different as the religions and the doctrines), but its dedication to theory and constant self-criticism. The study of religion, as is constantly and rightly pointed out, is a thoroughly historical phenomenon deeply rooted in a set of cultural practices and histories, all of which are themselves in turn imbued with sexual, economic, political, and social forces. Hence the immense literature psychoanalyzing Freud, historically situating and correcting Marx, and studying every detail of Nietzsche's life and writing, from his obvious indebtedness to Greek mythology to his repressed, tortured, and philosophically fecund homosexuality.[29] To study religion, in other words, is not only to study religion: *it is to study ourselves.* This is what makes it one of the quintessential disciplines of the humanities. In the end, what we are studying is human beings, and any methods up to that task will have to apply not just to the other but to the self. In some profound way that has yet to be fully appreciated or plumbed, then, the discipline represents, embodies, and puts into practice a specifically new form of human consciousness that cannot be found in any stable fashion in any previous culture or historical period.

This, I would suggest, is our deepest and most important (post)modern gnosis, our serpent's gift to the modern world still depressingly stuck in the imagined gardens of myths that never really worked and now threaten any truly sustainable global future.

Toward a More Radical Empiricism

Because they are publicly replicable and relatively easy to communicate within the bounds of an adequately trained reason, the nine analytic or de-constructive dimensions of the discipline outlined above are probably the best place to begin building a gnostic methodology. Unfortunately, their metaphors are primarily negative ones, and they thus lend themselves easily to aesthetically ugly, if quite accurate and perfectly legitimate, words like "reduction," "false consciousness," and "illusion." Moreover, their truth claims hardly exhaust and in truth do not yet really reach what I am calling the gnostic, which is much more positive, if not actually ecstatic, in tone and experience. Put in the allegorical terms of our comic book meditations, they do a very good job of exposing the villain that is religion, but they do a very poor job of revealing the hero that is religion. This is why I have referred to these altered states of consciousness as *protognostic*. They are an important and necessary beginning, but they are only a beginning of a movement toward a more constructive, positive, and radical vision of things. A dialectic is necessary, then, between deconstruction and construction, between reductionism and mysticism.

One way to begin envisioning such a gnostic dialectic and to catch a glimpse of the hero alongside the villain of religion is to turn to that broad spectrum of altered states of consciousness and energy framed as "magi-cal," "mystical," or "psychical" and to ask how we might begin to theorize out of such paradigm-shattering states. Again, I am certainly not pro-pounding a return to a literalizing faith here, nor am I abandoning reason. I am simply asking for a more expansive, imaginative, and attractive vi-sion of what it means to be human, which, or so I am suggesting, looks a lot more like the X-Men with their mutant powers than it does the social scientists with their statistical analyses or the pure rationalists with their social constructivism and Marxist methods, whose conclusions always somehow manage to be negative and depressing.

Let us admit the epistemological "catch" up front and immediately, though. The X-Men scenario implies altered forms of consciousness and energy that are not normally available to healthy functioning egos, schol-arly ones included. The X-truths are *state-specific* truths; that is, they ap-pear to be restricted to specific states of mind that are rare, unpredictable, and unquantifiable—hardly the stuff of respectable science and just barely accessible to the humanities. Rationalism and reductionism, of course, are also state-specific truths (that is, they are specific to highly trained egoic forms of awareness), but their states of mind are more easily reproduced and communicated, at least within our present Western cultures.[30]

We are left, then, in something of an embarrassing situation as far as rational public discourse goes. How, after all, can we adequately communicate forms of knowledge that rely on states of consciousness and energy that are not normally available to us? We are confronted with the problem of how to articulate an epistemology that is based on what amounts to a type of esotericism and a set of secret identities. Humorously put, we are dealing with phenomena not unlike that superpower of Invisible Boy in the comedic movie parody *Mystery Men*. Alas, Invisible Boy was only invisible when he was completely alone.

Dissociation and the Release of Nonordinary Energies

It is one of the central features of most comic book mythologies that the real identity of the superhero is kept hidden or secret. In most cases, this is a ruse necessary to protect the hero's loved ones or simply to allow him to live an approximately normal life. Similarly, in most traditional forms of religious esotericism, there is a clear understanding that most people are not ready for the hidden knowledge, and that one would do well to keep one's secret secret for practical political or social reasons. In Jesus's cruel but realistic language, it is a foolish thing to throw pearls before pigs.

Along related lines, serious literary critics interested in the comic book genre have noted that the comic books work their magic partly through a particularly clever ruse, namely, the mask. By putting a mask on the hero, the comic book artists and writers implicitly encourage the reader to identify with the hero and imagine that it is *his* face that is really behind that mask. The reader-as-hero thus defines much of the comic book reading experience; hence every little boy's fantasy that he is Spider-Man or Batman or whoever.

What the contemporary critics do not realize, perhaps, is that the mask has long served similar functions in the history of religions, and that human beings have been donning ritual and dramatic masks, reading fantastic stories about heroes and villains (or gods and demons), and identifying with this or that cultural hero or god (many of whom look remarkably like the comic book superheroes) for millennia. Indeed, the English word *personality* is derived from the Latin for "mask": a *persona* is quite literally a "mask" that one speaks (*sona*) through (*per*). The implications seem clear enough: we are not who we think we are, life is a stage, and there is a god (or superhero) in each of us. The virtually universal phenomena of possession, an altered state in which a divine or demonic being temporarily takes over the body of the possessed, speaks to a similar notion of the human as multiple, as do the common psychiatric phenomenon of multiple personalities, various mythologies of the incarnation or *avatara* in Christianity and Hinduism, and a large technical literature documenting children around the globe who accurately remember their previous lives as someone else (more on this below). All of these diverse forms of human experience boil down to the same basic truth: "There is an other in here."

Such possession states enter the comic book world through such characters as the Mighty Thor. A frail American doctor named Donald Blake finds an ancient cane in a secret cave chamber while vacationing in Europe. When he strikes the cane against a rock, it becomes a powerful hammer and he is physically transformed into the Norse god Thor through what can only be called an exaggerated possession state. Thor's mighty powers are now his.[31]

There is a sense, I would argue, in which our social selves really are masks, and that each of us truly possesses a secret identity, a superself, even perhaps a Norse god. Or is Nietzsche the only one who gets to philosophize "with a hammer"?[32] Little wonder, then, that anthropologists, historians of religions, pilgrims, and travelers have all been known to become possessed by local deities and indigenous spirits, much like the vacationing Dr. Blake in pagan Europe.[33] The human person really is not identical to the social ego, to the everyday awareness of the name. I will expand on this basic bimodal psychology in my conclusion. For now, it is enough to point out that one of the most efficient (if also unfortunately dangerous) ways to realize this Thor behind the Dr. Blake is through the psychological mechanism of dissociation, which itself is usually triggered by some form of physical, psychological, or sexual suffering.

The traumatic model certainly works well with the American mythologies. Mythically put, it is suffering and a psyche's subsequent dissociation that often grant access to the super- or x-tra of the hero. Thus it is the early horrible event of a little boy witnessing the murder of his parents outside a theater that psychologically produces the figure of Batman, and it is the trauma of watching his father accidentally murder his mother that produces the rage that triggers the transformation of Bruce Banner into the Hulk in the Hollywood movie.

The mainstream comics, still wary of the McCarthyism (really Werthamism) of the 1950s, have tended to stay far away from any explicit mention of sexuality, so they have also avoided any significant discussion of sexual trauma (but then, so too do most religious texts). What they have chosen to narrate instead is an elaborate Cold War mythology of the trauma of the atom, of nuclear energy and of an always possible nuclear holocaust. Thus, what we might call an *atomic mysticism* defines the entire silver age of the American comic book (1958–1975). Indeed, it is very nearly an industry joke that virtually every early Marvel Comics character achieves his or her powers from some kind of atomic or radioactive accident. Hence, the Fantastic Four were astronauts battered with cosmic rays. Peter Parker was bitten by a radioactive spider. Bruce Banner was bombarded by the energy of an atomic bomb test (changed to a nuclear medicine test gone awry in the movie). Daredevil was empowered by a radioactive chemical accident. And so on. At first glance, the X-Men may appear to be an exception to the rule here. After all, their superpowers are derived from evolutionary mutations, not nuclear accidents. But when Stan Lee first wrote about a mutant superpower in a minor story called "The Man in the Sky," he could only imagine it in an atomic scientist who had absorbed small doses of radiation in his work.[34] Moreover, when the X-Men later took center stage in Marvel's mythological universe, they were introduced as "children of the atom."[35] This, I think, in the end is what constitutes whatever possible religious wisdom the comic book mythologies might possess, consciously or unconsciously, that is, their implied insistence that the mystical and occult transformations of the human being are never simply matters of "the soul" or even of "the spirit." They are also and always matters of *energy*, which is another way of saying of *the body*.

The superpowers of the comic book mythologies, then, are not as fantastic as many of the more rational among us might wish to assume. Indeed, their most basic atomic mysticism is in many ways an imaginative exaggeration of real science, which long ago abandoned any simple materialism (since "matter" is actually a kind of frozen light) and reintroduced consciousness, will, and intention (that is, *experience*) back into the heart of reality through quantum mechanics (why, then, some scholars in religious studies want to commit themselves to both materialism and a rejection of experience as somehow unreal or unimportant is somewhat puzzling and certainly behind the times). Just as significantly, this same atomic mysticism also encodes, enacts, and explores a very real and very wise ambivalence concerning nuclear weaponry and America's role in the Cold War period as a "superpower": as the heroes become self-reflexive and doubtful about their own powers, so too does America. Many of the origin stories are based, moreover, on a well-known psychological mechanism with deep roots in the history of religions, that is, dissociation and spirit (or hero) possession. Psychologically speaking, such dissociative states can indeed release overwhelming and often healing states of consciousness and energy that historically have been mythologized as descending gods, spirits, or, in our contemporary case, superpowers catalyzed by the trauma of some nuclear accident.

On Death as Dissociation

The ultimate dissociation, of course, is death. And just as the dissociations of physical or sexual trauma produce elaborate mystical and psychical phenomena, so too does the experience of the dissociation of death. Here too, moreover, the texts are filled with what we can only call "superpowers," from imagined Superman-like flight to seemingly accurate Professor

X–like precognitive and clairvoyant abilities that are simply impossible to fit into any strictly materialistic worldview. The literature is immense here. For the sake of illustration, we will consider just one case, that of a nineteenth-century near-death experience that somehow manages to prefigure the powers of not one, but three late twentieth-century superheroes: Spider-Man, Plastic Man, and Richard Reed of the Fantastic Four.

The year is 1889. The place is a little town in Kansas called Skiddy. The dissociation is death. And the real "superhero" is a medical doctor named Dr. Wiltse, who is dying, or so it seems, of typhoid fever. Dr. Wiltse is without a perceptible pulse for four hours. The church bells are tolled to signal his passing, although his attending doctor, Dr. S. H. Raynes, continues to perceive, just barely, tiny little gasps of air at long intervals.

From Dr. Wiltse's internal perspective, the events of these few fateful hours are considerably more dramatic. He passes through a state of "absolute unconsciousness" and emerges on the other side awake and luminous, still in the body but with a clear sense that the body is no longer exactly himself; that is, he recognizes that he is now Two: "I looked in astonishment and joy for the first time upon myself," he writes, "the me, the real Ego, while the not me closed it upon all sides like a sepulcher of clay." But it is not all sepulchre here. Indeed, this real Self seems utterly fascinated with "the wonders of my bodily anatomy, intimately interwoven with which, even tissue for tissue, was I, the living soul of that dead body."

But not for long. By some mysterious force, the Ego or true Self begins to be rocked back and forth like a baby, "as a cradle is rocked," Dr. Wiltse tells us, and the soul finds itself "unzipping" from the body, beginning at the soles of the feet and moving toward the top of the head. While this is happening, the dying doctor hears "the snapping of innumerable small cords" until his "whole self [is] collected into the head."

It is at this point in the narrative that Dr. Wiltse begins to act like the later comic book characters Plastic Man or Reed Richards of the Fantastic Four, both of whom can stretch out his plastic body to fit through any crack, crevice, or internal space. Wiltse is worth quoting at length in his own fantastic-plastic narrative: "I passed around the brain as if I were hollow, compressing it and its membranes, slightly, on all sides, toward the center and peeped out between the sutures of the skull, emerging like the flattened edges of a bag of membranes. I recollect distinctly how I appeared to myself something like a jelly-fish as regards color and form."

After emerging from his own skull, retaining his normal form (at first naked, then magically clothed), and finding his way to the door, he decides to walk out into the street and do a little exploring. In terms of my running comic book analogies, we now switch from the Fantastic Four to Spider-Man. Dr. Wiltse: "I discovered then a small cord, like a spider's web, running from my shoulders back to my body and attaching to it at the base of the neck in front." As he walks on—with this spider cord stretching along with him, we can only assume—he eventually encounters a mysterious cloud of lightning and black vapor that communicates with him telepath-ically in a manner that would be at home in any number of comic book (or biblical) plots: "This is the road to the eternal world. Yonder rocks are the boundary between the two worlds and the two lives. Once you pass them, you can no more return into the body. If your work is complete on earth, you may pass beyond the rocks. If, however, upon consideration you con-clude that . . . it is not done, you can return into the body."

The spirit of Dr. Wiltse decides that his work on earth is in fact finished and that he would like very much to cross over the boundary between the two worlds. The black cloud apparently disagrees, however, since as soon as he puts his foot over the line, he feels himself paralyzed and unable to go forward. The next thing that Dr. Wiltse knows is that he is awake, very much alive, and in his body again.[36] Apparently, the spiderweb had suc-cessfully pulled him back into his body so that his straying soul could be resewn with the same subtle cords that had earlier unzipped to free him.

Real X-Men

One need not exactly or even nearly die, however, to obtain such powers. Intense physical suffering can accomplish similar transformations in a human being. Consider, for example, the case of Mollie Fancher (1848–c. 1899), the blind Baptist woman from Brooklyn who spent over thirty years confined to her room and bed after two serious falls left her legs and arms largely paralyzed. Mollie's reported powers were as extraordinary as they were carefully examined by family members, friends, doctors, and even journalists (the New York newspapers were filled with articles on her abilities in 1878). Among other "superpowers," she demonstrated dramatic precognitive and clairvoyant abilities, and she claimed to commune with the dead. She also demonstrated hundreds of times that she could "see" colors of yarn or other objects by holding them behind or on top of her head, read letters sealed in envelopes, and speed-read books or other texts with the tips of her fingers.

As if this were not enough, a throat condition prevented her from eat-ing for years, and her body was inhabited by four distinct personalities, each of which was assigned a different name and personality and one of which completely took over her consciousness for nine years, a period Mollie later referred to as "the great trance." Humorously, the moment "Mollie" emerged from this trance, she picked up right where she had left off nine years previously: "Well, Doctor, were you in time for your 'chicken-pot pie'?"[37]

The Fancher case appears in Fr. Herbert Thurston's *The Physical Phenom-ena of Mysticism*, a quite remarkable text whose combination of open-mindedness, close readings of archival material, and use of the church's own legal method of doubt concerning all such "miraculous" matters (the famous *Promotor Fidei,* or "devil's advocate") sets it apart as virtually unique in the literature. Seriously engaged with both modern psychiatric models of hysterical suggestion and comparative ethnography, Thurston is finally able to produce a gnostic text that can take seriously but also suspiciously a wide range of physical phenomena ranging from stigmata and telekinesis to seeing without eyes and levitation. The book, for example, opens with a long discussion of levitation in the saints, with a particular focus on Teresa of Ávila and Joseph of Copertino, whose numerous floats and flights in broad daylight, personal efforts to hide their embarrassing, even terrifying abilities, and convincing external witnesses make them difficult to ignore (Joseph's recorded levitations, for example, number into the hundreds and were allegedly witnessed by thousands). Although there is much to be devilishly suspicious of here, there is also much that is eerily suggestive, if not actually convincing. Why such material has been almost completely ignored in the contemporary study of religion is an open question, but one worth asking.

It is certainly not for lack of precedent, as even the briefest trip through the literature can demonstrate. The American psychologist William James, for example, who is widely considered to be one of the founders of the modern study of religion, worked closely with a very convincing Boston psychic named Mrs. Piper and wrote extensively on psychical matters.[38] His was, as we have already seen, a radical empiricism that refused to look away from phenomena simply because they offended common-sense or scientific notions about what is real or possible. It is also well known that C. G. Jung, another major force in the field, wrote his dissertation on the psychology of séance phenomena and pursued related occult themes and even actual experiences throughout his gnostic life.

What is less known is that Freud was also open minded about such matters as thought transference and telepathic communication, as his skeptical (really horrified) friend Ernest Jones has documented in his canonical three-volume biography of Freud.[39] Among many other stories, Jones relates how Freud was fond of keeping him up past midnight to tell him uncanny stories about his patients involving clairvoyance, dead spirits, and other occult phenomena. When Jones reproached Freud for such seeming nonsense, Freud replied: "I don't like it at all myself, but there is some truth in it." Jones, who is obviously bothered by all of this, nevertheless feels it necessary to record Freud's quizzical expression and desire to shock when he uttered such things: "But there was something searching also in the glance, and I went away not entirely happy lest there be some more serious undertone as well."[40] More seriously still, Hereward Carrington, who had asked Freud to coedit three different periodicals on occultism (he refused every time), related that in Freud's response to his invitation, Freud had actually admitted that "[i]f I had my life to live over again I should devote myself to psychical research rather than to psychoanalysis." Interestingly,

Freud would later deny writing such a thing, despite the fact that the letter was later produced and the passage in question confirmed: he had indeed written exactly that.[41]

Freud, it turns out, was probably convinced that there was a "kernel of truth" in occult matters, particularly telepathy, for had not dreams, another classical occult subject, proven to possess actual meaning in his own system of thought, indeed, had the altered states of dreams not help *found* his thought? But if telepathy were now admitted and allowed to form psychoanalytic theory, then what? Where would such a line of thought lead, or more important, where would it end? Whatever he thought in his heart, Freud, at least the public Freud, could not bring himself to allow such dangerous things into public consciousness. Hence he counseled Sándor Ferenczi not to relate his telepathic researches to the Homburg Congress of 1925 with these telling words: "By it you would be throwing a bomb into the psychoanalytical house which would be certain to explode."[42] In other words, such gnostic matters are probably true on some level, but they must be denied for the sake of intellectual consensus and the stable future of a young, and still vulnerable, movement. No doubt, Freud was right. On some level, however, the fact remains that Freud actually believed in the telepathic "superpowers" of Professor X. But the times were simply not ready. Neither, of course, was Freud.

F. W. H. Myers was ready, though. Trained as a classicist at Trinity College, Cambridge, Myers abandoned Christianity after an exposure to science and turned to psychical research after meeting the famous medium and preacher Stainton Moses (in 1874) and losing to death a woman he deeply loved (he would later communicate with her through a medium). At the encouragement of his teacher Henry Sidgwick, an eminent professor of moral philosophy at Cambridge University, Myers founded, with Edmund Gurney, Mr. and Mrs. Sedgwick Myers, and some other colleagues, the London Society for Psychical Research in 1882. He was also one of the earliest figures to introduce Freud's psychology to the English reading public. Alongside these psychoanalytic interests, Myers would dedicate most of his adult years to the systematic study of psychical phenomena, often by placing ads in newspapers asking for letters of evidence and following these up with interviews and cross-checks (more than ten thousand letters were written in 1883 alone by a six-member committee). He also would become a close friend of William James, the most eminent member of the American Society for Psychical Research, which was founded two years after the London Society, that is, in 1884. Myers died in Rome in 1901, fully convinced that the human spirit does indeed survive the disintegration of the body and that, moreover, the phenomenon for which he coined the term *subliminal self* was the secret of genius, dream, hypnotism, automatic writing, ghostly apparitions, telepathic communication with the living and dead, trance, possession, and religious ecstasy.

Myers, in other words, left the world the basic elements of an entire gnostic psychology of religion. Two years later, in 1903, his colleagues Richard Hodgson and Miss Alice Johnson completed and published his greatest work, *Human Personality and Its Survival of Bodily Death*, a two-volume, 1,360-page work that stands to this day as a remarkable testament to Myers's ability to combine a sensibility to religious phenomena with an unwavering, unflinching insistence on exposing these experiences to both critical psychological analysis and a comparative method through which truth is progressively advanced not through traditional authority or revelation, but through the careful collection of case studies, systematic classification of patterns that emerge from this evidence, consideration of a wide range of naturalistic and religious explanations, and finally theory building, itself always recognized as necessarily tentative and open to further qualification, development, or rejection. The case of Dr. Wiltse summarized above is one of hundreds of cases recounted and analyzed in *Human Personality*.

Myers's research agenda has been taken up more recently and advanced in a more cross-cultural direction by Ian Stevenson, a psychiatrist working in the Division of Personality Studies at the University of Virginia. For the past forty years, Stevenson has churned out hundreds of elaborate case studies of past-life memories, particularly in Hindu and Buddhist South and East Asia (India, Sri Lanka, Thailand, and Burma), Shiite Lebanon and Turkey, West Africa, and Northwest America.[43] As of 1997, Stevenson had collected 2,600 reported cases of past-life memories and had published 65 detailed reports on individual cases, including a massive and eerily suggestive study of 225 cases of what he calls "the biology of reincarnation," that is, the phenomenon of birthmarks or birth defects as physical "marks" from a previous life's violent ending by knife, rope, or bullet wound.[44] It is worth noting that this remarkable research, whose implications clearly violate both the materialism of modern science and the reigning constructivist contextualism of the humanities, has been taken very seriously by professional skeptics and debunkers such as Carl Sagan and positively reviewed in such intellectually weighty venues as the *Journal of the American Medical Association* and the *Journal of Nervous and Mental Disease*. The latter professional organ actually dedicated an entire issue to Stevenson's work. The conclusion of Harold Lief in the latter issue seems an apt one: "Either [Stevenson] is making a colossal mistake, or he will be known . . . as the 'the Galileo of the twentieth century.'"[45]

Also of interest here, particularly with respect to our X-Men allegory, is the work of Michael Murphy. Murphy is the cofounder (with the late Richard Price) of the Esalen Institute in Big Sur, California. For the past forty-five years he has explored what he and George Leonard in 1965 named the *human potential*, that is, the notion that the human being possesses immense untapped potentials that can be accessed, activated, and stabilized through specific transformative practices, integral philosophies, and enlightened institutions. Long before Shyamalan's *Unbreakable*, Murphy had argued that the human potential includes all sorts of "supernormal" powers, from clairvoyance and telepathy to extraordinary feats of physical prowess, all of which have been framed and exaggerated in religious literature, folklore, and modern fantasy as supernatural but that are better understood as foreshadowings or intuitions of natural potentials of evolution and of our own quantum biology. Quantum physics and the mystery of the atom thus become prime sources of esoteric thought in Murphy's novels and analytic writings. Just as the X-Men are announced in the comics of the late 1970s, we are all, quite literally, physically, scientifically, "children of the atom."[46] Indeed, in 1992, Murphy even named the superhero mythologies and the comic book genre as possible foreshadowings of what he called "the future of the body."[47]

In my own present theoretical terms now, Murphy's notion of the human potential is fundamentally a gnostic approach to religious phenomena in the sense that it insists on the human referent of all religious phenomena but reads human being in ways that affirm both the basic unity of the species and the rich ontological possibilities that the history of religions gives witness to in such fantastic abundance. As something entirely *human*, the phrase locates meaning in and as human nature and so quickly embraces the reductive sciences as entirely within its purview and range; as a *potential*, however, the same phrase simultaneously suggests that human nature is fundamentally open, instinctually plastic, and that it might be more, much more, than we typically imagine it to be in our premature foreclosures. Reductionism and mysticism thus meet and merge again in the category of the human potential.

It bears repeating, so also do the X-Men. Murphy's most developed thought as systematized in his eight-hundred-page magnum opus, *The Future of the Body*, is essentially an evolutionary mysticism that argues, in effect, that it is biological evolution that drives these mutations and thus produces these strange, usually misunderstood, if not actually demeaned, supernormal phenomena. Psychical abilities and the bodily transfigurations of the mystical literature in this model are not temptations of pride and power to avoid, as the faith of the religious traditions usually has it, or absolute fantasies, as the reason of the skeptics insists, but possible "evolutionary buds" that may gnostically hint at the further evolution of the species. Murphy, not unlike Professor Xavier, thus encourages his readers to accept, nurture, educate, and develop their own nonordinary experiences of consciousness and energy as integral features of both the religious and scientific quests. In short, if we were looking for a real-life analogue to Professor X and his mutant academy for the gifted, Murphy's vision of Esalen would be a very good place to begin.[48]

Perhaps not surprisingly, Murphy is not a professor, although, true to my gnostic reading of the modern study of religion, he found his first mystical inspiration in a Stanford classroom of comparative religion with his own Professor X, Frederic Spiegelberg. Indeed, none of these writers have been located within the professional study of religion. For the most part, they have either been psychologists working on the margins of their discipline (and it is significant that Stevenson's Division of Personality Studies survives only on donations and is not supported by the state of Virginia, as the rest of the university is) or independent writers pursuing their research agendas well outside the traditional academy. The only contemporary writer located within the professional study of religion who has treated this material with real seriousness in any systematic way appears to be Jess Hollenback.

For Hollenback, psychological and ritual techniques that focus consciousness and lead the mind into deeper and deeper states of contemplative concentration somehow catalyze remarkable transformations of psychic functioning, which in turn can lead to the traditional visionary landscapes of the mystic, to noetic insights into the interpretation of scriptural texts or traditional doctrine, and to distinct parapsychological phenomena (precognition, telepathy, out-of-body flights) that appear to grant accurate information about the external world and even the content and states of other minds. Noting the central phenomena of nonordinary forms of energy or power often reported in mystical literature (which the comic book mythologies also highlight through their atomic mysticism), Hollenback explicitly links consciousness and energy in his notion of the *empowered imagination*. Hollenback, in other words, argues that something special or "x-tra" happens to the human mind when it is intensely focused, and that this concentration, this fascination, somehow literally empowers or energizes the mental processes to perform at greater speed, with more insight, and with greater creativity and cognitive reach. Often, the results are quite literally ecstatic (*ek-stasis*, a "standing outside") and result in supernormal or psychic abilities.

At least three things are important to keep in mind here. First, Hollenback is not making a psychologistic argument; that is, he is not reducing the noetic content of such recollective acts to internal subjective states or to the projection of unconscious dynamics (neither, however, does he avoid or deny the crucial insights of depth psychology).

Second, he is not claiming that this content can always be adequately explained by the cultural context in which the state occurs, even if he also insists on the enculturation and context-sensitive nature of all mystical states. In his own words, "various sorts of supernormal experiences, such as clairvoyance, telepathy, and precognition that sometimes accompany mystical states of consciousness, do not appear to be explicable in terms of the contextualist paradigm."[49] Hollenback is thus arguing that "the imagination can function noetically,"[50] and that "[w]hen the empowered imagination objectifies itself, something extra, some overplus, attaches to that objectification that prevents one from saying the subject is only externalizing the contents of his own mind."[51]

Third, "there is no radical discontinuity between the paranormal processes that occur during ex-stasis (such as traveling clairvoyance and extra-ocular vision) and those ordinary mental processes that take place while one dreams or engages in idle imaginings."[52] In other words, "mystics are not a species set above the rest of humanity. They simply appear to exaggerate, temporally compress, and consciously control processes that are always taking place slowly and quietly, in a more attenuated form and more or less unconsciously, whenever human beings are engaged in those activities that create and sustain a cultural or religious tradition."[53] Empowered mystics, in other words, consciously play with the cultural codes that others take for granted and so leave alone. Through their empowered imaginative acts, they dissolve and create new patterns of meaning and so create new culture, only faster. Hence, hermeneutics and mystical experience (which for Hollenback is always and already an interpretive act) can be understood as psychologically related, and each can become empowered with nonordinary states of energy.

Essentially what we have here is a gnostic hermeneutics, that is, a form of interpretation that embraces reason and all the insights of the constructivist and contextualist paradigms but then moves on from there to a radical empiricism that recognizes that human creativity can become empowered by noetic states of consciousness and energy. Mythically speaking, that is, in the terms of the present essay, Hollenback is suggesting that the X-Men are real.

On X-clusions and X-ceptions

The question remains, however: Why are the psychical researches and x-tra interests of such figures as James, Jung, Freud, Thurston, Myers, Stevenson, Murphy, and Hollenback almost completely ignored in the contemporary study of religion? Why do so few read, much less comment, on Ian Stevenson or Herbert Thurston, for example? There are exceptions, of course, mostly among the anthropologically inclined, who either have had dramatic experiences in the field that effectively initiated them into other realities or have been persuaded by the ethnographic literature that the Western ego is only one of many cultural variations of the species. Anthropology and parapsychology, it turns out, are not so far apart.[54]

This relative silence is particularly odd in the study of religion, where one would think we could find a bit more openness to nonordinary or at least non-Western models of reality. Again, there are exceptions. In 1937, for example, Mircea Eliade published a little essay (in Romanian) entitled "Folklore as an Instrument of Knowledge," in which he argued for the empirical or experiential reality of folkloric beliefs and psychical phenomena.[55] Behind at least some of these "miraculous" stories, Eliade argued, lie a series of actual concrete human experiences, which are then exaggerated and mythologized by the religious imagination. Eliade thus explores the critical literature on such things as the fluid link said to exist between an object and its previous owner assumed in various magical rituals and psychical practices (hence "contagious magic," relics, and the psychical perception of persons via their possessions), the incombustibility of the body widely reported in the anthropological literature (which includes but also goes beyond fire walking), and the phenomenon of levitation in Catholic hagiography (Joseph de Copertino again) and Indian yoga.

As a way of concluding the essay, Eliade takes the historicists to task for claiming faithfulness to the historical documents, until of course these documents violate their own positivistic worldviews. Then they simply ignore them or brush their data aside as "primitive," "mistaken," and so on. Bryan Rennie has suggested to me that this essay and its early rejection of historicism as inadequate to the task of explaining occult, psychical and magical events may explain Eliade's later, more developed, and much more famous rejection of the adequacy of historicism in *The Myth of the Eternal Return* (1949). I suspect that he is correct. I also suspect that there is a kind of radical empiricism at work in Eliade's entire analytic and literary corpus, and that this empiricism, much like folklore in his model, is based on a series of actual concrete experiences of the occult. [56]

Other than this single essay by an admittedly paradigmatic pen (tucked away, I must add, in a Romanian journal for all these years) and a few other exceptions I have no doubt overlooked, I believe it is fair to say that the modern study of religion has generally failed to engage this type of material at all. Indeed, I am aware of only one academic writer published in a major university press who has mentioned Stevenson's remarkable corpus and pursued its implications in a radical empirical fashion: Richard Shweder of the University of Chicago. "What are we to make," Shweder asks, "of those cases in which a child claims to have memory of a former life in another family at another time and many of the details in the child's account of that family turn out to be accurate?" The facts, as he rightly notes, seem "resistant to either genetic or environmental explanations." [57] That is putting it mildly.

Along similar lines, I am aware of only one social scientist, Fred Frohock of Syracuse University, who has written about psychical material in what I would consider a radically empirical fashion. Frohock's unique combination of his own mystical experiences and a rigorous rationality to explore the philosophical and scientific implications of modern-day psychics and healers is emblematic of the gnostic methodology I am calling for here.

Indeed, he even manages to invoke an evolutionary X-Men-like scenario to explain these unusual but entirely natural powers. He suggests that psychical, and particularly telepathic, abilities may very well be operative, largely unconsciously, in the experience of "luck" and in the uncanny ways some individuals manage to negotiate so successfully through life. In explicitly evolutionary terms now, such abilities are highly beneficial and so may have been naturally selected out by millions of years of human evolution.[58]

The mutant x-ceptions of Shweder and Frohock aside, there are both some very understandable and some very dubious reasons for this near total neglect, for this radical x-clusion of the "superpower" in the study of religion. On the understandable side, there is the looming and very real intellectual threat of the popular literature, the grocery-store-line booklets on "how to be a psychic" and the megabookstore section labeled "New Age" or "Metaphysical." The latter contains enough fallacies and fantasies to make any serious intellectual weep, or perhaps simply sneer and turn around to the "Philosophy" shelf, which, equally disturbing, is often right next to or even on the other side of the "Metaphysical" shelf.

On the dubious side, this same psychical and occult material, if it is even occasionally (or even once) accurate or genuine, puts into serious question the final reach of the Kantian, political, and materialistic epistemologies that undergird the professional study of religion. As Hollenback has noted, once one begins to take these empowered cognitive capacities seriously, it is exceedingly difficult to hold absolutely to a contextualist or relativist paradigm, let alone to a strictly political or social one. The psychical material is thus conveniently and necessarily ignored in order to preserve the illusion that the reigning paradigms of materialism, historicism, constructivism, and reductionism are sufficient.[59] Illusions aside and as Shweder has correctly noted, the facts suggest strongly that such paradigms are exceedingly useful, indeed crucial, but hardly sufficient.

In the end, then, what I think we are left with alongside James's radical empiricism, Murphy's human potential, Eliade's folklore, and Hollenback's empowered imagination is what I would call a *super naturalism*, that is, an epistemology that rejects any kind of simplistic supernaturalism or recourse to literal faith but remains radically open to the possibility (likelihood, really) that psychical, magical, mystical, or occult events, when they are genuine and not faked (and, admittedly, they often are), may be both empirically real and entirely consistent with natural, though as yet unexplained, laws or patterns. Thus, a number of renowned and respected scientific writers have seriously suggested that paranormal phenomena—from precognition and telepathy to psychokinesis—are actually implied by quantum physics, and that contemporary physics makes no sense unless we accept consciousness as an irreducible dimension of the universe itself. Professor X may be real. The anomalous nature of "occult" or "paranormal" events, in other words, is most likely a function of our inadequate models of consciousness and energy, not a sign of these events' final un-

reality or fiction. It is not that the uncanny is unreal; it is that our conceptions of the real are not uncanny enough.

In making such a move via modern American mythology, I hope I have
not presented an argument that appears to reduce the history of religions
or the study of that history to the fictional world of the comic book. I hope
readers do not now begin thinking that I have a cape in my closet or a Batmobile in my garage. It has not been my intention to reduce the history of
religions to the comic book. It has been my intention to raise the comic
book—with or despite the intentions of their writers and artists—into
the history of the religious imagination, where these mythologies find
some of their deepest and most tangled roots.

Political Allegory; or, How (Not) to Be an X-Man

What would happen were we to attempt to make both these rational protognostic and these more speculative, gnostic, and radical empirical
forms of truth more widely known to the American public, which in fact
is also a global public? Would it help or hurt us in forming public policy?
In forging international relations? In dealing creatively with religious violence, religious conflict, and religious terrorism? Would our often struggling academic programs lose their funding, much of which no doubt
comes from sources that would be horrified by the specifics and implications of such a doubly forbidden knowledge? Or would it help us gather
new sources of support and funding from both secular and religious organizations? What would we say on CNN? What *should* we say? Can we
move beyond our present politically correct bows to faith, embrace a vibrant critical reason, and call *all* the major religions on their gross and
patently obvious gender inequalities and misogynies? Can we comment
openly on the textual absurdity of any Bible-based "family values" cam-
paign, on the racist dimensions of the Hindu caste system, on the foundational violences of the Torah, and on the horrifying anti-Semitism of
much of the Islamic world? When exactly will we begin calling a spade a
spade? And once we have publicly embraced and finally practiced reason
with respect to religion on CNN, what of gnosis?

I recognize fully that there have been many individuals and academic
organizations that have taken up the mantle of the public intellectual and
provided real leadership. For example, the admirable work of the Jesus
Seminar and its remarkable ability to make the cover of *Time* or *Newsweek*
almost every year should provide the academy with a real model to ponder
and attempt to emulate. I also cannot help but think of the Scholars at Risk
program that for the past nine years has identified harassed and threatened scholars from around the world working in a wide variety of fields
from economics to theology in order to place them in American host
universities for physical and emotional protection and further professional development. "Around the world today," the 2006 Scholars at Risk

brochure observes, "scholars are attacked because of their words, their ideas and their place in society. Those seeking power and control work to limit access to information and new ideas by targeting scholars, restricting academic freedom and repressing research publications, teaching and learning." Academic freedom, it turns out, is a very real human rights problem, and the harassment of intellectuals, wherever it is found, is inevitably an accurate marker of important thought and real challenge to oppressive social practices. Our mutants need protected.

Certainly such a list could be expanded for a very long time. But I also know that the more common answer to all of my above questions goes something like this: "We do nothing. We say nothing. Or better, we say what we think to ourselves, that is, to other specialists who will understand us and read us fairly. But to speak what we know in the public square would be both foolish and dangerous, as it would certainly be misunderstood, twisted beyond recognition, and probably virulently rejected by both the religious and the secular." Let me say immediately that the latter observation is perfectly true, as many scholars of religion know from extensive experience. This, no doubt, is why, mythologically speaking, Professor X's Westchester academy was kept secret—to avoid persecution, harassment, and the violence of ignorance. But is this really the best long-term solution, and does not our present world literally cry out for a sensitive *and* critical analysis of "religion" in all its forms? And are we not manifesting here precisely what scholars such as Russell McCutcheon have analyzed as a failure of intellectual nerve?[60] I think so.

The present geopolitical and religious outlines of our world, however, raise an even deeper and more troubling issue, one that concerns the effect our rational gnosis can have on non-Western cultures not culturally prepared for its truths. As we have already had occasion to note, the historical fact of the matter is that the modern study of religion is a cultural child of Western European history, particularly of those historical moments we conveniently label the Reformation, the Enlightenment, and the Romantic movement. Without any one of these three political and intellectual revolutions in Western thought, the study of religion would not be. Whereas the Reformation sufficiently weakened the premodern structures of authority and truth of the medieval church and laid the religious foundation for a modern individuality and the individual interpretation of scripture, the Enlightenment and Romanticism furthered this development and, in the process, produced what can only be described as the paradoxical or gnostic structure of religious studies scholarship, a structure I have delineated throughout these essays within the two poles of the analytic and the mystical, which together form or at least strive for the gnostic.

Here, though, is the historical catch. This paradoxical practice of sympathy and suspicion relies on a full five hundred years of Western cultural development, none of which has occurred, spontaneously at least, in any non-Western culture, and all of which arose simultaneously with another broad Western cultural phenomenon: colonialism. Moreover, and more dramatically, when such developments have occurred in non-Western cultures, they have often occurred through a violent imposition of these structures by Western colonial powers. This historical fact of Western colonialism has become, if you will, the catch-22 of the field.

India is a perfect example of this. Certainly Indian religionists and intellectuals know more than a little about Enlightenment thought and suspicion of religious phenomena, particularly in their Marxist forms, but many associate this thought with colonial oppression and so reject Western methodological and historical conclusions, not necessarily because of their inherent benefits or weaknesses, but primarily—and quite understandably—because of this colonial history, or better, because they believe that the ideas and the history are inseparable or *are the same*. The search for some measure of social justice, humanist truth, or historical probability is thus often swept away by nationalist politics and the very real traumas of historical memory.

Similar cultural dynamics can be seen in the struggle for women's rights in the Middle East (where such rights are often equated with sinister Western influence and dominance), the call for human rights in places like China (where the discourse is read as an arrogant imposition of Western cultural values on ancient Chinese practices), or in the attempt to stop "female circumcision" in Africa (where such calls can be reframed and rejected through the notions of cultural relativism and, again, Western arrogance). In every instance, the charge of colonialism can be used as both a valid historical analysis or moral critique of the West and as a crude blunt instrument to beat back any and all ethical or intellectual advances. What does it mean, what *can* it mean, to be an American intellectual gnostically deconstructing religion when the United States is increasingly seen, and with good reason, as an imperial power without equal more or less forcing its will on the planet at the expense of local cultures, environments, and religions?

Whether or not they can actually help us think more creatively and boldly here, the comic book mythologies and their social histories illustrate similar existential dilemmas and concerns. It all seemed so simple in 1941 when Captain America punched Adolf Hitler in the face on the cover of *Captain America* #1 (before America actually entered the war). But things are different now. As Bradford W. Wright has demonstrated so powerfully, the Marvel characters who appeared in the 1960s emerged from the trials of the 1950s censorship campaigns, Cold War fears of an impending nuclear nightmare, the civil rights movement and, as the decades ticked by, an increasingly plural America. Not unlike the global superpower itself, the Fantastic Four, Spider-Man, the Hulk, and the X-Men were all essentially "reluctant superheroes who struggled with the confusion and ambivalent consequences of their own power."[61] As Wright points out, the Fantastic Four's Thing, for example, unlike any comic book hero before him, discovered that his superpowers alienated him from the rest of humanity; the Hulk became an antiauthoritarian symbol whose most common enemy was the U.S. Army; and Spider-Man, always doubting his own vocation and motivations, became a revolutionary hero on campuses across the country, along with Bob Dylan and Che Guevara.

Interestingly, Wright's *Comic Book Nation* begins and ends with similar problems and promises. In his preface, he tells the story of visiting East Germany with his father in the late 1970s at the age of nine. At the checkpoint, the East German border guard confiscated his most treasured possessions, his comic books. This disturbed him greatly, but it also caused him to begin to think more deeply about what comic books encode, about what it was that made them so objectionable and censorable to a communist society. He eventually realized "how they epitomized so much of what was attractive and possible in the advanced consumer cultures of the West."[62] He even eventually created his own fantasy about how the border guard took them home to his children, who grew up to help tear down the Berlin Wall in 1989.

Wright's book, of course, does not end with a now-defunct Soviet communism. It ends with Islamist radicalism and an epilogue entitled "Spider-Man at Ground Zero," in which Wright discusses the reactions of the New York comic book industry to 9-11. "'God. . . .' This is all Spider-Man can manage as he holds his head and stares in anguish at the smoking ruins where the World Trade Center stood only moments before."[63]

Artist Frank Miller could say a bit more, and in his three potent lines we can hear echoes of a kind of pure postmodern gnostic rage: "I'm sick of flags. I'm sick of God. I've seen the power of faith."[64] This is not quite Wright's reaction, however. He concludes, as I wish to conclude, on a note of metaphysical astonishment and creative hope. Mythology and reality, fact and fiction, have merged, Wright observes:

> When I read how Osama bin Laden schemed to plunge the free world into chaos so that radical Islamist governments could take over, it struck me as something that the Red Skull or Baron Zemo might have imagined. The real world has once again caught up to that of the comic books. In the most horrible sense, the fantasy of comic book nightmares has become our reality. Can comic books continue to balance escapism and relevance in this frightening post-9-11 world? Will superheroes still hold the power to stir our imaginations and inspire our dreams? I hope so. For we need them now more than ever.[65]

For the sake of my own mythical conclusions, I am reminded here of the final scene of *The X-Men* movie. Magneto, the villain of the story, is a Jewish man whose bitter experiences in the Nazi concentration camps have transformed him into a misanthropist (the theme of religious identity as object and generator of hate is a subtle but important one), a hater of all human beings who are not like him, that is, a mutant gnostic. He has kidnapped one of Professor X's mutant students in order to harness her powers to a machine that will emit an immense energy field over New York City and transform its every inhabitant into a mutant. The plan is simple: turn them all into us and they will quit persecuting us *because they will be us*. What Magneto doesn't know is that few human beings are in fact capable of such mutations, and that the forced mutations of his technological invention are literally deadly. Unwittingly but really, he is about to kill every human being in New York City, and, ironically, he is going to do it from *the* symbol of American freedom, the Statue of Liberty's torch, within which he has set up his deadly machine.

I take this cinematic myth as a potent reminder that cultural mutations cannot be forced, and that when they are, they easily turn destructive, if not violent and deadly. Not everyone is ready for this kind of freedom; not every culture is ready to leave its particular garden; not every human being can handle the mutant gnosis. And this in turn necessitates the secrecy and the scandal of the mutants who have gotten there, well, naturally. Such mutants are a danger, a scandal, a threat to "the way things are." They offend the moral order by their very existence and powers. They are monsters to be hunted down and destroyed, or at least quickly silenced. This too, of course, is heinous, as wrong and as misguided as Magneto's attempt to force transformation on people that are not ready for it.

As a modern parable for the study of religion, the analogies are transparent, even if the moral is hardly clear. What *are* we to do with our inescapable conclusions, our most heartfelt, our most honest knowledge, our historically unprecedented freedoms? Do our past European colonial histories, which none of us in fact participated in and which most all of us would recognize as immoral, delegitimate all that we think and are now in a new century? And even if we could recover our global image from such colonial memories, do not many of our present American foreign policies have the effect of delegitimating us further, justly or not, in the eyes of much of the rest of the world? Because others are not yet ready to accept the serpent's gift, whether ours or their own culture's, must we silence ourselves and stop writing, retreat back into our Westchester ivory towers? Do our religious, intellectual, and cultural mutations constitute us as freaks that deserve only censorship and harassment or, just as bad, as neocolonizing imperialists out to homogenize the whole world? Or do we, inspired, taught, *and joined* by the countercoherent gnostics of every culture, in fact possess secret powers that might be beneficial, even crucial, for the future social evolution of the species?

Again, the evolution metaphor certainly cannot answer this for us. Mutations may be the driving force of evolution, but most of them are also dead ends doomed to extinction. Moreover, and more dangerous still, the trope of evolution was central to many of the earliest comparative models of religion in nineteenth-century anthropology, where they inevitably functioned as barely concealed ideological devices to advance the supposed superiority of Christianity. Miraculously, thousands of years of cultural and religious development, through innumerable "primitive," polytheistic, and monotheistic religions, culminated again and again in a worldview that looked remarkably like the Lutheranism or Catholicism of the man (it was always a man) doing the comparing. Clearly, we do not want to return to this kind of evolutionary mythology posing as scholarship.

But neither need we deny our own sense of otherness, our own honest conviction that we are living through an *after,* a *post-,* as in *the postmodern* or *the postcolonial.* Nor should we miss the fact that the gnostic model I am proposing here relies explicitly on cross-cultural comparison to work at all, that is, that it relies on both the relativization of the hermeneut's own inherited worldview and a deep admiration for the worldviews of others, which are also relativized. The vocation of the gnostic comparativist is thus very similar to that of the cultural psychologist as outlined by Richard Shweder. Such a cultural psychologist, Shweder explains, is called to go "to some far away place" where he can "honor and 'take literally' (as a matter of belief) those alien reality-posits in order to discover other realities hidden within the self, waiting to be drawn out into consciousness."[66] "[R]ealities hidden within the self, waiting to be drawn out into consciousness"—this is precisely the language of both psychoanalysis and the human potential, and it can only lead to both a deep appreciation of other cultures as invaluable revealers of reality and to a willingness to criticize any and all cultures as inescapably limited: "For if there is no reality without metaphysics, and if each reality-testing metaphysics (that is, each culture or tradition) is but a partial representation of the multiplicity of the objective world, it becomes possible to transcend tradition by showing how each tradition lights some plane of reality but not all of it."[67]

Along similar nonethnocentric lines, it is crucial to point out that, although the specific analytic methods of the academy may be historically unique to the modern Western university (which is not at all to deny that other cultures have their own unique ways of deconstructing their own certainties, as we saw in chap. 3), the fully gnostic epistemologies of psychical and mystical experience celebrated and mythologized in the present meditations certainly show no preference for Western culture or Western actors. Quite the contrary, I have spent almost as much time with Ramakrishna as Jesus, and a corpus like that of Ian Stevenson on past-life memories implicitly leans to Asia, not the West, to explain its radical empirical findings. Moreover, whereas the mystical is a kind of repressed underground in the West, where it suffers all the distortions and pathologies of the repressed (denial, sickness, and criminality) and so becomes "the occult," similar dimensions of human consciousness and energy are socially tolerated and accomodated and so better integrated into daily life in most non-Western cultures.

In short, the full expression of my X-Men model in no way privileges Western culture, or any other particular culture for that matter. Quite the contrary, really. Little wonder, then, that the various X-Men teams of the comics, particularly since the late 1970s, have been veritable archetypes, if not actual parodies, of ethnic and cultural diversity. Hence the trope of *the team*, with each member gifted in some specialized and highly idiosyncratic way (very much like the academy again). One of the most famous X-Men teams, for example, that first introduced in *Giant-Size X-Men* #1 (in 1975), was constituted by a literally blue German Catholic mystic raised by a Gypsy queen (Nightcrawler), a Native American warrior (Proudstar), an immense Russian (Colossus), a Japanese man (Sunfire), an Irishman (Banshee), an African woman (Storm), an American (Cyclops), and a Canadian (Wolverine). Professor X's school of mutants, in other words, could be read into a thousand different versions of adolescence. And why not? As any good biologist will tell you, any successful biological community implies *diversity*. Feuerbach, it turns out, saw the same with his X-Men-like appreciation of the multiple, indeed practically infinite, powers of humanity: "Each new man," he wrote, "is a new predicate, a new phases of humanity. As many as are the men, so many are the powers, the properties of humanity." [68]

Certainly this same stunning diversity, this same multiple gift, has often been read within a sexual code. As one prominent contemporary scholar of religion put it to me with respect to his own early "consoling scripture," that is, his adolescent copy of *X-Men* #1, "For me, that [mutant] school appealed as a religious order—endowed with real magic, beholden to a truly mysterious creator—that welcomed *queers*." And so it always has: the queer, the uncanny, the mystical, *the sacred*.

In the end, what I suppose I am trying to say is that Jesus, Feuerbach, and Ramakrishna were all basically correct, at least in a symbolic sense. The divine is (in) us. But as the rational study of religion has taught us equally well, so too is the demonic. As with the human body, there is a "right" side to the sacred, and there is a "left," or sinister, side. We would do well to keep both in mind. The gnostic study of religion is important precisely to the extent that it can help us take off the mask, look in the mirror, and see both this villain and this hero, both a Magneto out to make everyone the same, whatever the cost, and a Professor X who understands that difference and diversity as well as sameness are the very secret to the marvels of mutation—biological, cultural, and otherwise.

Return to the Garden

Jesus said, "Let him who seeks continue seeking until he finds.
When he finds, he will become troubled. When he becomes
troubled, he will be astonished, and he will rule over all."
The Gospel of Thomas 2

His disciples [said, "Master], who seeks and [who] reveals?"
[The master] said [to them], "One who seeks [also] reveals."
The Dialogue of the Savior

This statement brings us to our most crucial point, the true
seat and source of religion. The ultimate secret of religion
is the *relationship* between the *conscious* and *unconscious*, the
voluntary and *involuntary in one and the same individual*. . . .
Man with his ego or consciousness stands at the brink of
a bottomless abyss; that abyss is his own unconscious being,
which seems alien to him and inspires him with a feeling
which expresses itself in words of wonderment such as:
What am I? Where have I come from? To what end? And this
feeling that I am nothing without a *not*-I which is at the
same time my *own* being, is the religious feeling. But what
part of me is I and what part is not-I?
Ludwig Feuerbach, Lectures on the Essence of Religion

THESE FOUR RATHER ECCENTRIC ESSAYS on the New Testament
and Nag Hammadi texts, a heretical nineteenth-century Lutheran theologian, a Hindu Tantric saint, and the superheroes of contemporary American popular culture were designed to communicate a self-confessed (post)
modern gnosis in an erotic, philosophical, mystical, and finally mythical
fashion. Certainly, they were not intended to be taken as exhaustive or

even as particularly faithful discussions of the historical Jesus, Ludwig Feuerbach, Sri Ramakrishna, or Stan "the Man" Lee. Rather, very much like the writings of the ancient gnostic authors with their wildly idiosyncratic appropriations of biblical stories, these were four creative misreadings, four heretical mistranslations toward my own still-developing thought. They were, if you will, publicly performed *seekings* not unlike those of which Jesus speaks above, that is, labored discoveries that moved, quite literally, from erotic scandal and troubling reductionism to genuine mysticism and marvel.

How might one now summarize these seekings and move on to envision a specifically hermeneutical version of Jesus's "and he will rule over all"? That is, how might we now come to an at once more objectively critical or distant and more subjectively satisfying or intimate understanding of the full scope of the human being as the latter is manifested in the history of religions? Finally, how might one now communicate such a gnosis in a more rational key for those who did not quite have ears to hear but now think, quite reasonably, that they might hear something?

Toward such ends, I want to return to the story of Adam and Eve in the garden, reread its mythical narrative, and then fashion it anew in an explicitly allegorical fashion; that is, I want to transform the precritical *mythos* of the biblical text into a postcritical *logos* of my own literary text— in this case, a fourth and final *logos mystikos*, or mystical reason. Actually, however, there are three separate movements to this final gnostic reason: (1) a bimodal model of human consciousness that can take seriously the altered states of consciousness and energy that constitute so many of the origin points of the history of religions, while staying true to the legitimate concerns and ethical commitments of Enlightenment reason; (2) an analysis of the role that bodily energies play in empowering the cognitive, moral, and imaginal capacities of the intellectual life; and, finally, (3) a specific bimodal empowered logic derived from (1) and (2) that can be fruitfully applied to contemporary theoretical debates within the study of religion.

As a further means of demonstrating what I intend, I will also offer along the way the examples of three modern gnostic intellectuals who have embodied different aspects of this mystical reason: Sigmund Freud, the French novelist Romain Rolland, and the Yale literary critic Harold Bloom. Together, such figures suggest that my gnostic model for the study of religion is neither anomalous nor unreasonable. On the contrary, such thinkers suggest that such a gnosis has always dwelled and still dwells at the very heart of Western culture's intellectual life.

But *caveat lector*, "Let the reader beware." What follows may be an attempt to render the unconscious of the present text more conscious, but it will never fully succeed. It cannot. Alas, pure transparency is a pure impossibility here, for the simple reason that I myself, the author of these words, am not fully conscious, even to myself. I am Two. I thus write to wake up, to be enlightened (in both the European and Asian senses), to make the Two One, but this does not mean that I am ever fully awake, enlightened, or whole.

Nor, reader, I suspect, are you.

The Other Tree

And out of the ground the Lord God made to grow every tree
that is pleasant to the sight and good for food, the tree of
life also in the midst of the garden, and the tree of the knowledge of good and evil. *Genesis 2:9*

The tree of the knowledge of good and evil focuses the Genesis creation myth, but it was hardly the only tree in the garden. There was also the tree of life, whose fruit, or so the story suggests, would grant immortality to any who could eat of it. The primordial couple, of course, was never able to taste the fruit of this second tree, as God exiled the human being from the garden, "lest he put forth his hand and take also of the tree of life, and eat, and live for ever" (Gen. 3:22).

Just as the first chapter of Genesis recognized something essentially divine about the human being, created, we are told, in the androgynous or bisexual image of the deity (Gen. 1:26–27), this passage implicitly recognizes that there is more to the fruit of the garden than moral awareness and sexual shame. There is also the possibility of *theosis*, or divinization. We saw something of this in Feuerbach and my second *logos mystikos*. The creation myth reminds us again, now in a mythical mode, that there is more to the human being than is commonly imagined, even more than the creator-deity himself is willing to imagine. This human potential, however, remains just that in the biblical myth: a *potential*. That is, the potential of divinization lies only in the future and beyond the pettiness and cruel jealousy of the banishing creator-god.

My final *logos mystikos* can be read as both a rational or psychological expression of these two trees and as an allegorized denial or de-projection of the petty god who banishes. That is, it can be read as a return to the garden and the two trees. Here, then, is the *logos* or saying:

> Each human being, each reflection of the Adam of Light, is Two, that is, each person is simultaneously a conscious, constructed self or socialized ego and a much larger complexly conscious field that normally manifests itself only in nonordinary states of consciousness and energy, which the religious traditions have historically objectified, mythologized, and projected outward into the sky as divine, as "God," and so on, or introjected inwards into the human being as nirvana, brahman, and so on.

I am not defining the precise ontological status or psychological structure of this second field of consciousness (whether it is personal, whether it survives physical death, whether it is structured by archetypes, whether *nirvana*, God, or *brahman* is the better descriptor). I frankly do not know the answer to any of these questions and so remain agnostic and open about such matters. Nor am I defining the precise relationship between the two fields of human consciousness, although, as I will note below, I do think that many of the theoretical problems that the study of religion suffers from stem ultimately from a failure to recognize these two separate but related fields of human being. I am simply arguing that the data of the history of religions suggest strongly that something like these two broad fields of consciousness exist and, moreover, that any adequate theorization of that history must take this general phenomenology of consciousness into account.

The latter point deserves some immediate elaboration. To the extent that the study of religion has concentrated almost exclusively on the minutiae of the socially constructed self, it has made immense strides toward understanding, analyzing, and deconstructing this first field of human consciousness. By the same measure, however, the discipline has generally failed even to recognize the existence of the second field, and so it has forfeited any possibility of offering a genuinely satisfying and truly radical theory of "religion." Certainly a great deal of valuable work can be done restricted to the level of the conscious socialized self, but in the end this will not be enough for the simple reason that such an exclusive focus cannot adequately explain or make sense of the full range of data, particularly that flowing from the altered states of trauma, trance, psychical phenomena, psychedelic states, certain types of erotic rapture, numinous dream, vision, and near-death events. It is like trying to understand the full spectrum of light by examining only the tiny sliver that the healthy human eyeball can detect. Or it is like trying to understand matter by ignoring the fact that matter is essentially frozen light, *regardless* of the everyday fact that our sense-based reason tells us that this is impossible.

If one desires an entirely secular key, we might say that to be conscious is also to be or rather, as we say, "to have" an unconscious (even though the reverse—that the unconscious has one—is almost certainly much closer to the actual truth of things). The Freudian key is hardly an accidental one, as Freud's psychoanalysis, even with its stunted materialistic ontology, remains the best rational model we yet have for how a particular knower might get from the pre- or nonrational to the rational and, moreover, how these two realms of human being are in fact intimately related and always informing, influencing, even actually determining one another. Quite despite himself, Freud gives us a way of having it both ways, not as a compromise, but as a bimodal statement of human being, which really *is* both ways.

This is why Freud, that modern archrationalist, was so committed to embedding reason and its socialized ego within a greater and immeasurably more complex psychic field. This is also why he so deeply admired the artist, the poet, and the creative writer as protoanalysts with unique powers to access these same normally "unconscious" fields. Moreover, and more radical still, this is why he was convinced that the "occult" powers of telepathy are quite real and need to be taken into account for any full model of the mind.

What Freud lacked, of course, is precisely what he himself recognized that he lacked, namely, an ear for the music of the mystical, as he openly admitted to his dear friend and correspondent, the French writer, social activist, and playwright Romain Rolland. As William Parsons has demonstrated so thoroughly, Rolland knew mystical states on an almost constant basis and pushed Freud to distinguish between the illusions of religion and the gnostic truths of certain altered states of consciousness that gave access to real knowledge or, as we might say, to real gnosis about the nature of the self as Two.[1]

Thus, Rolland admired Freud for his firm stand against the illusions of religion (that is, against the projections of the socialized ego) in his controversial and, for many, deeply offensive book *The Future of an Illusion* (like Freud, Rolland believed in neither the immortality of the soul nor the existence of a personal God).[2] This did not mean, however, that Rolland reduced the human being to the same illusory ego and its religious projections. Quite the contrary, he sought to convince Freud that there was another way of being religious, a way that could dispense with the common man's immature Feuerbachian projections and rest content with the innate beauty and pleasure of what he liked to call "an oceanic feeling" (*un sentiment oceanique*), which, interestingly enough, he linked with the biographies of Sri Ramakrishna and Swami Vivekananda that he was writing at that time (1927).

"I myself am familiar with this sensation," Rolland wrote to Freud. "All through my life, it has never failed me. . . . In that sense, I can say that I am profoundly 'religious'—without this constant state (like a sheet of water which I feel flushing under the bark) affecting in any way my critical faculties and my freedom to exercise them—even if that goes against the immediacy of the interior experience."[3] Romain Rolland, in other words, was a gnostic intellectual in precisely the ways I am calling for here. He knew all about faith (in his case, his native French Roman Catholicism), and he rejected its literalisms. He also knew all about Enlightenment reason, and with Freud he embraced its reason to the extent that it explained. But it was the paradoxical gnosis of a double field of consciousness that grounded his own worldview and transformed him into a great artist, a real mystic, a rational critic of religion, a social activist, and, perhaps most significantly for our present purposes, a dear friend of Sigmund Freud.

Freud's response to Rolland's intellectual gnosticism is interesting. In a private letter to Rolland, Freud pointed out that what Rolland liked to call intuition could tell us much about "an embryology of the soul when correctly interpreted," but nothing helpful for an "orientation in the alien, external world." Still, he admitted, "I am not an out-and-out skeptic. Of one thing I am absolutely positive: there are certain things we cannot know now."[4] In another context, this one an exchange with the Swiss poet Bruno Goetz, Freud compared the mystic to a kind of "intuitive psychologist" or protoanalyst who dives into the terrifying whirlpool of the unconscious to return with genuine psychological, artistic, or therapeutic insight.[5] In still another, this time in his *New Introductory Lectures on Psycho-analysis,* Freud went so far as to suggest that psychoanalysis and "certain mystical practices" share a common line of approach in that each seeks to gaze into and appropriate the hidden depths of the psyche by "upsetting the normal relations between the different regions of the mind."[6] Mysticism, in other words, was a kind of protopsychoanalysis for Freud, which implies that psychoanalysis can be read as a kind of secularized or rationalized mysticism, that is, as a kind of *logos mystikos,* or gnostic rationalism.

I invoke this deep friendship between an archrationalist and a modern artist-mystic not to dwell again on psychoanalysis or on mysticism. I invoke this friendship because it demonstrates in a paradigmatic and quite touching fashion the fact that reason and gnosis are not incompatible, and that, indeed, the two forms of consciousness and thought can mutually enlighten one another by meeting on common ground. What is that common ground? The awareness that human consciousness is much more than we commonly assume it to be, and that the secret of psychology, of art, and of religion itself lies precisely within that "much more."

The relative truth or falsehood of my four gnostic meditations depends largely, if not entirely, upon this "much more"; that is, it depends upon the nature of the human personality and the subsequent epistemologies that necessarily flow from different conceptions of this same multiple self. If one operates with a theory of consciousness that restricts human subjectivity to the functional awareness of the successfully socialized ego or to the cognitive programs of the adaptive brain, then one will identify human thought with reason, logic, and all the obvious benefits that accrue to such a model, including modern science. I have no qualms about any of this on its own level. I am not antireason, much less antiscience. But, exactly as Rolland pointed out to Freud, the fact that one embraces the socialized ego's reason and its astonishing science (or its astonishing psychoanalysis) hardly means that one thinks that the ego and rationality exhaust the full range of human being.

Freud taught us in a secular key what the mystical traditions, from ancient gnosticism to medieval Kabbalah (which is really an heir and transformation of ancient gnosticism and perhaps a precursor of Freud's psychoanalysis),[7] taught us in their own religious keys, namely, that human consciousness cannot be restricted or reduced to the ego and its specific forms of knowledge and experience. There is always a More, to use the language of William James now, and so any adequate model of the human being, and hence of human knowledge, will have to take this More into account.

This, again, is what the purely rational methodologies of the study of religion generally fail to do. This does not make thinkers who employ those methodologies any less valuable or less central to the enterprise of the study of religion. They are absolutely necessary to that enterprise. Indeed, there is *no* study of religion without their Enlightenment reason and reductive methods. They are not wrong, then. They are simply not enough.

Certainly, we have seen many examples, both implicit and explicit, of this doctrine of the human being as Two or More in these four meditations. We could easily read the orthodox Christological claim that Christ possessed two real natures, one human and one divine, as a kind of unconscious mystical anthropology or precritical bimodal psychology. I do, anyway. So too in the theology of Feuerbach: each human being is simultaneously a limited social ego and a specific instantiation of an infinite human potential. A similar, if by no means identical, doctrine is quite explicit in the Ramakrishna materials, where we find the ancient Indic claim that the *atman* is the *brahman,* that is, that the deepest core of the human being is identical to the cosmic essence of all things, despite the fact that the conscious ego (the *ahamkara,* or "I-maker") is normally completely unconscious of its own deepest field of consciousness. The superheroes, of course, play with a similar pattern through the secret identity trope. Clark Kent is not really the mild-mannered, bespectacled reporter his contemporaries think he is. Nor is Peter Parker the bumbling photographer and nerdy science major his friends poke fun at. Each of these surface egos, like each of us, possesses an alter ego, another superself with amazing powers. What sets the superheroes and mystics apart from the rest of us, of course, is that they already know that they are Two. They have become conscious of that which is unconscious in the rest of us. They have more fully actualized their own human potential.

It is thus literally true that we all have secret identities, and that these secret selves bear immense untapped potentials that have been mythologized in both the history of religions and in popular culture and fantasy. This is finally why, I suspect, we love these ancient and modern mythologies so. We see ourselves, quite accurately, in them. This is also why some of us finally remain unsatisfied with the purely rational and sociopolitical models of human nature and knowing that presently define the study of religion and, indeed, the humanities in general. We do not see ourselves in them, or better, we see only *a part* of ourselves in them. And not the most interesting part at that. In the end, we are not even allowed to catch a glimpse of the second tree in the garden, much less taste its sweet fruit. We are banished again.

The Forbidden Fruit

So when the woman saw that the tree was good for food,
and that it as a delight to the eyes, and that the tree was to
be desired to make one wise, she took of its fruit and ate;
and she also gave some to her husband, and he ate. Then the
eyes of both were opened, and they knew that they were
naked; and they sewed fig leaves together and made themselves aprons. *Genesis 3:6–7*

The biological, psychological, social, and cultural complexities of what we today call sexuality have been the focus of intense research for well over a century now. It would be difficult, if not impossible, to overestimate the importance of this corporate knowledge for how we have come to see "religion" over this same period. Our eyes have been opened, and it is now impossible to shut them again, despite all the efforts of conservative political and religious forces to do just that. We have tasted the forbidden fruit, *and we know.*

It is probably no accident that both the modern categories of *religion* and *sexuality* as signs marking fields of rational discourse and critical study were born more or less together within the same time period (the nineteenth and twentieth centuries) and within the same cultural institution (the Western university). In other words, our collective eye-opening to both sexuality and religion as fundamentally related fields of discourse amenable to rational analysis and hermeneutical insight is part of the same broad Enlightenment that sets Western critical understandings of religion and sexuality apart from (and often in serious and irresolvable conflict with) all previous Western and virtually all historical and contemporary non-Western understandings of the same. As a consequence of eating this fruit of knowledge, we really are different now. And, as a culture at least, we cannot go back and pretend otherwise.

Very much related to this same modernist sense of the unprecedented are the intensely ethical tone and far-reaching social implications of much of the discussion and the degree to which analyses of sexuality and religion tend to question or transgress an otherwise assumed intellectual ideal of cultural relativism. It is, for example, exceedingly difficult to read very far into feminist studies of the world's religious traditions without getting a saddened, if not actually enraged, sense that modern forms of consciousness defined by the most basic moral standards of gender equity are incompatible with the past (and present) structures, doctrines, and rituals of every major religious tradition on the planet.[8] This fruit, in other words, really is the fruit of the knowledge *of good and evil*, and we can now see through the critical lens of sexuality that our religions are as evil as they are good, and that they have always been so (and probably worse so).

To return to our allegorizing, the birth of moral awareness is the birth of sexual awareness; hence, *the moment* the couple partakes of the fruit of the knowledge of good and evil their "eyes are opened" not just to anything, *but to their genitals*. That is, they realize that they are naked. Accordingly, they feel shame for this nudity and construct crude clothes. Culture has been born and, with it, the fig leaves of prudery and denial.

On this level at least, the ancient Hebrew myth, like so many of the modern American superhero mythologies, is an adolescent myth about sexual maturation, about the anxiety and fear this process brings, and about the extraordinary new powers of cognition, emotion, and even felt divinity that commonly manifest themselves along with human sexuality. After all, very young children, even today, still live "in the garden" and feel no shame about their genitals, about running around in their innocence completely naked. They are also psychologically "immortal" to the extent that they do not worry about death; indeed, they are scarcely aware of it. They live in the garden of Eden. But once puberty arrives and the sexual characteristics (breasts, pubic hair, menstruation) begin to manifest themselves, all sorts of new emotions, thoughts, and worries are socially and hormonally activated. The adolescent now realizes that the exile has begun, that he or she is now a new being, a sexual being, and that someday he or she will die. Whereas the superhero mythologies, however, grant potential divinity to the eroticized adolescent via the fantasized superpowers, the Hebrew myth denies such a divinity to its readers. The second tree of life is mentioned only to be prohibited.

With a kind of biological half wisdom, the Hebrew myth links this same sexual maturation and exile from childhood with death itself. This, in biological fact, is true. As already noted, sexuality and death are indeed two sides of the same mortal coin. Organisms engage in procreative sexual activity *because they die*. If there were no death, there would be no need of sexual activity. Unfortunately, the Hebrew myth gets the rest very, very wrong by reversing the causality and suggesting not that we have sex because we die (which is true), but that we die because our first parents had sex (which is ridiculous). The origin point of humanity in Western monotheism, it seems, is premised on a serious sexual error, a primordial mistake or fall(acy).

But the myth gets at least one thing very, very right: human knowledge, and particularly human moral knowledge, is inextricably bound up with sexuality. I do not mean this in simply a developmental or philosophical way, as if individuals just happen to reach a new cognitive stage at about the same time they reach sexual maturity, or that sexuality is the object of much moral thought and legislation. I mean this in a concrete energetic and psychophysical way. Thought is not all about consciousness, whether single or dual. It is also about the body and its extraordinary morphing energies. Mind is always connected to matter, and matter is anything but "materialistic." It is pure energy. Hence, the attentive reader may have noticed that my earlier discussions of consciousness in the history of religions were actually discussions of consciousness *and energy*. The two, I would suggest, cannot be separated, ever.

Freud, once again, saw this more clearly than any other secular thinker. His libidinal epistemology insisted and in fact demonstrated again and again that human intellectual practices—from philosophy, ethics, and literature to art, religion, and poetry—are sublimations or "makings sublime" of basic psychophysical energies. Freud gave these energies an odd and perhaps unfortunate Latin name, *libido*, but he also insisted that his libidinal conception was more or less identical to what Plato had called *eros* and identified as the secret (homoerotic) inspiration of philosophy itself in the *Symposium* and *Phaedrus*.[9] In other words, Freud linked his libidinal epistemology to Western mystical and erotic thought. In the end, Freud may have had too weak a metaphysic to hold such a sublime conception of mystico-erotic energy, and later schools of psychoanalysis may have abandoned Freud's original energetic conceptions, but he at least saw in the beginning that consciousness and energy are bound together, and that the very highest reaches of intellectual and artistic creativity depend on the body's most "shameful" desires and powers.

This, I think, is in the end what finally separates the gnostic intellectual from the strict rationalist—a real energetic awareness that thought at its most intensely creative is often experienced as coming from elsewhere, as if it were being literally empowered by nonordinary energies or forces that temporarily overwhelm the thinker in order to bring new ideas, images, or words into the field of awareness. This is the realm, of course, of what is commonly called inspiration, yet another example of a category with clear religious roots (literally, "en-spirited" or "breathed in") that has now been secularized and rationalized but retains nevertheless many of its original religious connotations. The themes of inspiration and creativity, in other words, are fundamentally gnostic categories to the extent that they combine both rational and ecstatic dimensions and require at least two fields of consciousness to work at all.

The Romantic poets understood this. So too did Freud and Rolland. Unfortunately, however, this phenomenology of inspiration is generally neglected, if not actually ridiculed, by theorists who ally themselves with pure reason. There is a famous line in Rudolf Otto's *The Idea of the Holy* where Otto basically asks any reader who has not had an actual experience of the holy to read no further, as such an uninitiated reader, or so Otto claims, will not be able to understand what follows.[10] An experience of the holy as *mysterium tremendum*, or "mystical trembling" (note again the energetic metaphor), in other words, is finally necessary for the study or analysis of the holy. Scholars from the rationalist school have heavily criticized this line from Otto for its assumption, completely false to them, that there is something unique or special about religious experience, a sui generis nature that only actual religious experience can give access to and that, therefore, calls for the development of specific and unique methods of study. Whereas Otto confessed a certain real inspiration as a sine qua non of the field, then, his critics have denied that such a thing is possible at all.

Is Otto's position really so unreasonable, though? To invoke a purely secular analogue again (but one linked closely to our garden imaginings), what could a man or a woman who has never had a single orgasm *really* understand about human sexuality? Quite a bit really. One could know a great deal about the genetics, chemistry, anatomy, anthropology, epidemiology, and politics of sexuality, for example, and this would all be very valuable. Such an orgasm-less individual could even become a great biologist or historian of sexuality. But would any of us be willing to say that such a person really *knew* what sexuality was?

I certainly wouldn't. I would also suspect that such a person's life-long quest for understanding sexuality was rooted precisely in his or her impossible orgasms. Moreover, as far as I can tell, the sexual orgasm is about as close to a sui generis experience as anyone can imagine. If many forms of profound religious experience and human sexuality are intimately related, as the Hebrew myth suggests and as I have always argued, the implications of such a simple thought experiment are obvious enough for the discussion at hand: there most certainly is something x-traordinary about certain forms of religious and intellectual experience, and we would do well to take this into account when we construct our theories about religion. We certainly cannot allow such experiential data to determine or control, much less censor or dictate, our researches, and we would never want to make such subjective events a requirement of the field (this is where Otto erred), but none of this necessitates our ignoring or denying such important sources of insight, aesthetic appreciation, and, yes, even gnosis. One might as well argue that the orgasm is irrelevant to the study of sexuality, or that its phenomenology should not be allowed into the discussion—an exceptionally odd, not to mention patently prudish, claim.

There are serious ontological questions here, of course, questions (not answers) that call for another energetic category more open to some of the more fantastic and imaginative potentials of human creativity and sexual experience. Following both Plato and Freud, I have referred to this nonordinary energy as *the erotic*. So defined, the erotic is not simply "sexuality" (a very modern word with entirely secular connotation), nor is an orgasm exactly an orgasm here. Once again, there is a Two and a More. Mythically speaking, there is a second tree and so a second kind of forbidden fruit, a mystical erotics. Drawing on a wide comparative sweep of sources—from Plato's philosophical reflections in the *Symposium* on eros as a contemplative technique, through India's philosophy of Being as *ananda* or orgasmic "bliss,"[11] the *ch'i* of Chinese Daoist sexual yoga, and the Tantric Buddhist notion of orgasm as a form of subtle reason,[12] to Wilhelm Reich's cosmic orgone, Georges Bataille's *erotisme*, and the Lacanian and feminist *jouissance*—what I have named the erotic is an explicitly dialectical category that embraces all those advances made through the analytical categories of sexuality and gender (the fruit of the first tree of the knowledge of good and evil) but also reaches out to the nonordinary states of intense mystical rapture, religious revelation, charismatic energy, and literary and philosophical creativity (the fruit of the second tree of life). Put allegorically, the erotic designates that specific form of gnostic thought and experience that has tasted boldly of the first tree and is now reaching out for the second.

"When He Becomes Troubled, He Will Be Astonished"

Oddly but perhaps not too surprisingly, the modern study of religion has often worked very much like the primitive god of the Genesis creation myth—as a prude. That is, it has restricted itself almost entirely to the first tree in the garden, that is, to the dualisms of the rational ego and to the primarily ethical and political concerns of "good and evil." Moreover, it threatens dire professional punishments and elaborate public shamings (with footnotes no less) for any who would venture to the second tree and suggest, in print at least, that there may be more to human being than politics and power.

Still, there is a second tree in the garden, and hence a second form of human consciousness to consider. What would happen if we reached out—God or no God—and tasted the fruit of this second tree? What would happen, that is, if we began at least to think *as if* there were not one but two fields of human consciousness and energy? Once we posit the actual psychological existence of two separate but related fields of human consciousness and energy, much that is apparently paradoxical or contradictory about the history of religions as both an object of study and as a body of theory begins to make a good deal more sense.

Consider, for example, the debates between essentialism and constructivism that have defined so much of the field. Too simply put, essentialism wants to posit a general essence, nature, or common core to human religious experience, especially to certain types of religious experience that we have come to call "mystical." Constructivism, on the other hand, denies any such essence and turns instead to the minutiae of history, politics, power, sexuality, gender, and language in order to demonstrate, in significant and quite convincing detail, how religious experiences are constructed and so historically relative. Similar polarities, of course, could be easily identified in the study of sexuality as well.

The model of bimodal consciousness I am suggesting here as a working gnostic methodology would embrace *both* schools of thought as central to

any adequate theory of religion (or sexuality), since each approach addresses a different field of consciousness: whereas constructivism employs
all the tools of Enlightenment reason to analyze the socialized ego, essentialism employs comparativism, phenomenology, and a good bit of intuition (even actual mystical experience) in an attempt to imagine a larger unconscious or superconscious field (or is this universal field better framed as
the cosmic star body of DNA and the quanta light show that we all share,
that we all *are*?).

I hope it is obvious that the task of constructivism and reason is the eas-
ier and more sure-footed one here, and that we should be a good deal more
humble about any conclusion involving the second. In other words, the
fact that we choose to embrace or at least remain open to both trees in the
garden does not mean that both trees should carry equal epistemological
weight in the academy. I am thus not asking for some return to a naive
perennialism or universalism here. I am asking for a greater appreciation
of human being as complexly conscious and as creatively empowered. I
am asking for more imagination.

Or consider the controversies that have weighed down—boggled,
really—the scholarly analysis of the relationship between ethics and mysticism.[13] Too simply put again, one school asserts that mystical experiences inevitably, or at least usually, make one a better person, since the
common mystical theme of oneness and the ethical virtues of compassion, sympathy, and care appear to be ontologically related. The other
school of thought counters such a claim with the observation that oneness
is also a denial of difference, and that all vibrant ethical systems are based
on a profound sense of alterity, that is, a deep respect for the other *as other*:
there is thus no necessary relationship between mystical experience and
ethical behavior.

Central to these debates has been the evaluation of numerous charismatic figures who have both catalyzed remarkable altered states of consciousness in their disciples and engaged in some morally dubious behaviors, sexual abuse primary among them. Also central here, although it is
seldom discussed in the literature, is the subject of religious trauma, that
is, morally despicable behavior, like sexual or physical abuse, which sets
up psychological conditions (primarily the capacity to dissociate, that is,
split consciousness in Two), which in turn can result in profound and profoundly positive altered states of consciousness.

The bimodal model of consciousness I am suggesting here makes better
sense of both positions, although, in the end, it does not embrace both.
Rather, it embraces the second position (the position that there is no necessary connection between the mystical and the ethical). After all, the
phenomenon of the immoral mystic can be easily explained by pointing out
that the second, greater field of consciousness is normally accessible only
when the ego state is temporarily suspended, and that one of the "best"
ways to suspend the ego state is to traumatize, threaten, or even "kill" it

(hence all the elaborate religious symbolisms of death, annihilation, sacrifice, renunciation, crucifixion, and so on). The events surrounding a mystical state of consciousness can thus be both profound (to the extent that they grant access to a broader field of consciousness) and unethical (to the extent that they harm the socialized ego). As long as one recognizes the existence of both fields, there is no contradiction here at all.

In other words, the debate about whether mysticism is moral or not is generated primarily through an inappropriate restriction of human consciousness either to the socialized self (mysticism as the suspension of the ego is bad) or to the larger field of consciousness (mysticism as the suspension of the ego is good). Only a model that accepts *both* fields of consciousness and energy, and this without conflating or identifying the two, can adequately explain the data and do justice to our own moral sensibilities as functioning social selves and as complexly conscious beings. Once again, precisely because human consciousness is bimodal, only a bimodal psychology and logic can begin to explain the data.

Finally, this same bimodal model of consciousness, of being Two, makes very good sense of the saying from the Gospel of Thomas with which we began our return to the garden: "Let him who seeks continue seeking until he finds. When he finds, he will become troubled. When he becomes troubled, he will be astonished, and he will rule over all." Here I am particularly interested in the second and third movements of the *logos*, that is, the move from disturbance to marvel. This too, I would suggest, is precisely the seeking path of the gnostic study of religion, which begins with the socialized ego, with reductionism and constructivism, in order to demonstrate, convincingly, that virtually all of what people assume to be "transcendent" or "eternal" in religion is nothing of the sort, that "religion" rather is historical, contextual, sexual, and gendered—in a word, that it is *relative*. This indeed, to put it mildly, is troubling to any epistemology of faith.

But a gnostic methodology would proceed from this understandable and necessary disturbance to demonstrate that such a socialized self or constructed religiosity hardly exhausts the full range of human consciousness and energy, that there are indeed, exactly as Rolland wrote Freud, other ways of being religious, ways that leave the little ego far behind and venture further into the more and more complex fields of human consciousness and energy. There is a second tree in the same garden of the human body. And this, as the passage from the Gospel of Thomas puts it, is the proper realm of astonishment, or *marvel*.

As a final means of illustrating what I intend to communicate through such a gnostic hermeneutic, it is instructive to invoke a third and final thinker who uses the term in ways that merge nicely with my own, namely, Harold Bloom.[14] Such strands are most transparent in his books on American Gnosticism (*The American Religion*) and the American millenarian obsessions with angels, dreams, and resurrection motifs, *Omens of Millennium* (1996).

This last book, a self-described and remarkably confessional "Gnostic sermon," is particularly relevant here. To begin with, Bloom recognizes, and keenly so, what I have repeatedly emphasized, namely, that the gnostic element in Western religious history has been defined and persecuted as heretical.[15] Bloom speculates that this is partly because of the elitist and intellectual nature of gnosis: it is not for the many but for the few. Indeed, most are quite incapable of it. Bloom tells us that he first awoke to his own gnostic or occult self at the age of nine or ten while reading William Blake and Hart Crane: "In my instance at least, the self came to its belated birth (or second birth) by reading visionary poetry, a reading that implicitly was an act of knowing something previously unknown within me."[16] Such experiences convinced Bloom that "[t]he self's potential as power involves the self's immortality, not as duration but as the awakening to a knowledge of something in the self that cannot die, because it was never born." "It is a curious sensation," Bloom goes on, "when one realizes that she or he is not altogether the child of that person's natural parents" (16). Gnosis, then, "is not a believing that, a trusting in, or a submission. Rather, it is a mutual knowing, and a simultaneous being known, of and by God" (23). Psychologically speaking, Bloom's gnosis involves a kind of ontological separation deep within the human person: "Gnosis essentially is the act of distinguishing the *psyche*, or soul, from the deep self, an act of distinction that is also a recognition" (184). Bloom realized, in other words, exactly what I have tried to show above, that is, that the human self is both Two and More.

For Bloom, moreover, as for me again, this is no religion for the orthodox or the many, no bowing down to a King or Lord, and hence a metaphysical monarchy in disguise. Rather, in Bloom's own terms now, gnosticism is "an esoteric religion of the intellectuals" (33), a solitude without use for communal worship, and a spirituality for the assertive soul, the strong author, and the unapologetic knower: "[I]ts authors are as aggressive as they can be loving, are divided in heart, and are rich in spirit. Why should this be so? We do know, because the issue precisely *is* knowing. Gnostics, poets, people-of-letters share in the realization of knowing that they know" (21).

Bloom's fuller synopsis of such a gnosis is worth quoting at some length, both for its own literary merits and for the way it captures so powerfully and emotionally the just rage of the gnostic intellectual against the evils of faith and religion itself:

> You don't have to be Jewish to be oppressed by the enormity of the German slaughter of European Jewry, but if you have lost your four grandparents and most of your uncles, aunts, and cousins in the Holocaust, then you will be a touch more sensitive to the normative Judaic, Christian, and Muslim teachings that God is both all-powerful and benign. That gives one a God who tolerated the Holocaust, and such a God is simply intolerable, since he must be either crazy or irresponsible if his benign omnipotence was compatible with the death camps. A cosmos this obscene, a nature that contains schiz-

ophrenia, is acceptable to the monotheistic orthodox as part of "the mystery of faith." Historical Gnosticism, as far as I can surmise, was invented by the Jews of the first century of the Common Era as a protest against just such a mystery of faith which, as Emily Dickinson wrote, "bleats to understand."

Bloom goes on, then, to link this gnosis and the powers of creativity and imagination, again exactly as I have done above:

> Yet "Gnosticism" is an ambiguous term. . . . There were, so far as we can ascertain, few, perhaps no Gnostic churches or temples in the ancient world. . . . I think it is best to call it a spirituality, one that was and is a deliberate, strong revision of Judaism and Christianity, and of Islam later. There is a quality of unprecedentedness about Gnosticism, an atmosphere of originality that disconcerts the orthodox of any faith. Creativity and imagination, irrelevant and even dangerous to dogmatic religion, are essential to Gnosticism. When I encounter this quality, I recognize it instantly, and an answering, cognitive music responds in me. (23–24)

It is this same sense of "an answering, cognitive music" out of which I have written the present collection of essays. Even at the very end, I cannot adequately analyze, much less fully explain, such a gnosis. I am also well aware that in an academic milieu of cultural relativism, the epistemological disappearance of truth into power and identity politics, and the supposed death of the author, such an intellectual gnosticism and the subsequent mystical claim *to know* constitute something of an impossible challenge. Harold Bloom may claim such a gnosis at the very heart of the American academy—in his case, Yale University—but his gnosticism, like mine, remains in the end a kind of forbidden knowledge, a rage with and beyond reason against religion itself, a spirituality that is not a religion, a religion of no religion.

The Flaming Sword and the Bridal Chamber

Then the Lord God said, "Behold, the man has become like one of us, knowing good and evil; and now, lest he put forth his hand and take also of the tree of life, and eat, and live for ever"— therefore the Lord God sent him forth from the garden of Eden, to till the ground from which he was taken. He drove out the man; and at the east of the garden of Eden he placed the cherubim, and a flaming sword, which turned every way, to guard the way to the tree of life. *Genesis 3:22–24*

And so where does all of this finally leave us? Exiled from our related religious and sexual ignorances, certainly. This, though, may be part of the gnostic hermeneut's "rule over all." Such a reign, after all, implies a certain royal distance, a willingness *not* to be a part of the religious drama (which is too often a tragedy). Certainly the Hebrew myth forbids reentry into the garden of our innocence in its own judgmental and jealous way. Indeed, it stations a fierce angel with flaming sword at the gate to prevent our return.

And perhaps that is a sign of mature wisdom. We cannot, after all, go back to prepubescence, childhood, or the womb, not literally, anyway (unless, that is, we are reincarnated). In this sense at least, we are all indeed permanently exiled in this life by the inexorable progress of our own psychosexual development. But perhaps there are other ways back in, other ways to "have our eyes opened" anew. One might note, for example, that any adequate comparative perspective informed by the categories of sexuality and gender would lead us to suspect that the Hebrew tale—the angry father-god, the scapegoating of woman, that slithering snake, the phallic sword, the seed and soil symbolism—is simply one more patriarchal myth to learn from, deconstruct, and move beyond. It's just another penis posing as absolute truth.[17] We might finally tire of this tall tale.

Comparatively speaking, we might also further relativize the Hebrew myth of adolescent sexual shame by pointing out that the history of religions is filled with other sexual-spiritual orientations, other forms of embodiment and desire, other arts of repression and sublimation, and so other possibilities for new states of consciousness and energy and, with them, new theory. We could, for example, begin to take more seriously the manner in which the mythologies and mystical traditions consistently connect sexuality to the terrifying and fantastically pleasurable experiences of divinization, visionary flight, empowered literary and scriptural inspiration, magical influence, occult encounter and sexual assault, and, perhaps most commonly, immortality, a recurrent theme from Adam and Eve to Chinese Daoist sexual yoga.

Certainly this would be faithful to the gnostic texts, particularly one like the Gospel of Philip, which understands the sexual union of the bridal chamber to be a mystical sacrament that *can* return us to the garden, that reunites what Adam and Eve lost there, that is, their (and our own) unity and immortality beyond and before gender. Death and sexual difference are more or less the same thing here, and Christ came to unite—sexually *and* spiritually—that which has been separated, that is, the genders: "If the woman had not separated from the man, she would not die with the man. His separation became the beginning of death. Because of this Christ came to repair the separation which was from the beginning and again unite the two, and to give life to those who died as a result of the separation and unite them. But the woman is united to her husband in the bridal chamber. Indeed those who have united in the bridal chamber will no longer be separated."[18] Sex saves.

We cannot, of course, literally return to the Valentinian bridal chamber: too much separates us for that.[19] We can, however, draw on our now-recovered gnostic library and its hermeneutical elaborations, the history of religions, even our own secret sexual lives in order to approach the second tree of the garden in our own modern and postmodern ways, hopefully having never forgotten the bittersweet taste and hard lessons of the first.

Let us end, though, not with what we might know in the future, but with what we already know in the present, that is, with the serpent's gift of the first tree of the knowledge of good and evil. Once we accept—and I mean *really* accept—this gift, we might begin to stop fearing the serpent of our own sexualities and so cease childishly obeying the imagined voice of a petty father-god who seeks to cruelly punish us for the biological conditions of our very existence, that is, death and sexuality. We might learn to love the wise snake, listen to his many hissing whispers, and realize finally that we are not cursed to die. We have not sinned. We have not fallen. We have sex and reproduce because we die. We do not die because we have sex and reproduce. We have only grown up. We have only eaten of the tree of the knowledge of good and evil, that is, of our own sexual mortality.

And it is very good.

Introduction

1. More precisely, we might say that these were Sethian Christians whose views have come down to us in such texts as On the Origin of the World, the Hypostasis of the Archons, and, most spectacularly, the Apocryphon of John (there are three versions of this latter text in the Nag Hammadi library, making it the most popular text of that collection). The church fathers identified those Christians who favored the snake as Sethians, Barbolites, Naasenes, and Ophites. It is not clear whether these were different groups or names for the same general Christian counterculture.

2. Consider, for example, the astonishing reader of Kristen E. Kvam, Linda S. Schearing, and Valerie H. Ziegler, eds., *Eve and Adam: Jewish, Christian, and Muslim Readings on Genesis and Gender* (Bloomington: Indiana University Press, 1999).

3. Hence, Gen. 5:1–3 parallels God creating man "in the likeness of God" and Adam bearing Seth "in his own likeness." Seth, in other words, looks physically like his father, just as man looks physically like his creator.

4. David M. Carr, *The Erotic Word: Sexuality, Spirituality, and the Bible* (New York: Oxford University Press, 2003), 18.

5. Ibid., 26.

6. Steven Greenberg, *Wrestling with God and Men: Homosexuality in the Jewish Tradition* (Madison: University of Wisconsin Press, 2004), 51.

7. Quoted in David Biale, *Eros and the Jews: From Biblical Israel to Contemporary America* (Berkeley: University of California Press, 1997), 109.

8. Augustine, *The Literal Meaning of Genesis*, bk. 11, chap. 41, par. 54, in Kvam, Schearing, and Ziegler, *Eve and Adam*, 153. My thanks to Nathan Carlin for pointing this passage out to me.

9. Here I must differ with Carr's otherwise brilliant readings, which oddly look away from the immediate result of the crime (sexual shame) and the tit-for-tat sexual punishments (painful childbirth and toilsome agriculture) to argue that the serpent's gift was not sexual.

10. Apocryphon of John, CGL 126. There are actually three different variations of this passage, none of which is sex positive and all of which link this revelation to pollution and/or destruction. My rhetorical use of it, then, is just that—mine. Unless otherwise noted, all passages from the Nag Hammadi library cited in this book are taken from the standard critical edition in five volumes, James M. Robinson, ed., *The Coptic Gnostic Library: A Complete Edition of the Nag Hammadi Codices* (Leiden: E. J. Brill, 2000), abbreviated CGL. The cited page numbers refer to those of the individual translated texts, as these are separately paginated in the volumes. With rare exceptions, I have omitted the numerous Greek terms inserted into the translations.

11. Gilles Quispel, ed., *Gnosis: De derde component van de Europese cultuurtraditie* (Utrecht: HES, 1988,) 9. My thanks to Wouter Hanegraaff for both this reference and this catalytic idea. I am, of course, developing this tripartite scheme in my own way. For another use of the same tripartite scheme, see Dan Burton and David Grandy, *Magic, Mystery, and Science: The Occult in Western Civilization* (Bloomington: Indiana University Press, 2004).

12. I am fully aware that the intellectual genealogy I summarizing here is simplistic, at best, particularly in its transparent epochalism. Such thinking nevertheless carries certain general truths, and since I wish to reach an audience beyond the academy and its highly specialized debates, I prefer to err here, and throughout the present book, on the side of effective communication. These are not technical essays; they are, as advertised, public *meditations*, curiously, I must admit, with endnotes.

13. Immanuel Kant, "What Is Enlightenment?" in *The Insider/Outsider Problem in the Study of Religion: A Reader*, ed. Russell T. McCutcheon (London: Cassell, 1999), 133.

14. M. H. Abrams, *Natural Supernaturalism: Tradition and Revolution in Romantic Literature* (New York: W. W. Norton and Company, 1971).

15. Friedrich Schleiermacher, *On Religion: Speeches to Its Cultured Despisers* (New York: Harper and Row, 1954).

16. See especially Tyler T. Roberts, *Contesting Spirit: Nietzsche, Affirmation, Religion* (Princeton: Princeton University Press, 1998); and Joachim Kohler, *Zarathustra's Secret: The Interior Life of Friedrich Nietzsche*, trans. Ronald Taylor (New Haven: Yale University Press, 2002). I do not, by the way, think that Nietzsche's homosexuality is irrelevant to his philosophy. On the contrary, I think a homoerotic orientation in a heterosexual society gives one a unique "postmodern" perspective on the constructed and relative nature of social reality. The same may be true of Jesus's gospel of love and its deconstruction of orthodox purity codes, as I will explore below in chap. 1.

17. See, for example, Friedrich Nietzsche, *Twilight of the Idols*, trans. R. J. Hollingdale (New York: Penguin Books), 108–110.

18. Perhaps the classic text here is Jean-François Lyotard, *The Postmodern Condition: A Report on Knowledge*, trans. Geoff Bennington and Brian Massumi (Minneapolis: University of Minnesota Press, 1984).

19. Generally speaking, I think postmodernism has overplayed its embrace of difference and its rejection of sameness. My thought is much more dialectical here, embracing both difference and sameness. I take evolutionary psychology as emblematic here, particularly in its insistence that human behavior, including religious behavior, is a function of remarkably stable cognitive modules "programmed" by millions of years of evolutionary adaptation ("sameness") interacting with constantly changing environmental and cultural conditions ("difference"). Similarly, I do not consider something like the Freudian id to be a mere construct of early twentieth-century European culture. I am much closer to Theodore Roszak's ecopsychological framing of the category as a European expression of "the protohuman psychic core that our environment has spent millions of years moulding to fit the planetary environment" (*The Voice of the Earth: An Exploration of Ecopyschology* [Grand Rapids, Mich.: Phanes, 2001], 41). Don't we know enough now to avoid the simple and simply false dualisms of nature *or* nurture, sameness *or*

difference? Can't we begin to think in terms of a more sophisticated and accurate *both . . . and?*

20. The literature is large here. As a sample set, see John D. Caputo, *The Prayers and Tears of Jacques Derrida: Religion without Religion* (Bloomington: Indiana University Press, 1997); Harold Coward, ed., *Derrida and Indian Philosophy* (Albany, N.Y.: SUNY Press, 1990); Michael Sells, *Mystical Languages of Unsaying* (Chicago: University of Chicago Press, 1994); Elliot Wolfson, *Language, Eros, Being: Kabbalistic Hermeneutics and Poetic Imagination* (New York: Fordham University Press, 2005); and Edith Wyschogrod, *Saints and Postmodernism* (Chicago: University of Chicago Press, 1990).

21. Hence, Bulhof and ten Kate distinguish between premodern and postmodern forms of negative theology as "maximal" and "minimal echoes of an embarrassment," that is, an awareness on the part of reason that its self-made projects are "interrupted regularly by tendencies and voices that express skepticism and that point to an 'outside' the subject and to the limit of rationality" (Ilse N. Bulhof and Laurens ten Kate, eds., *Flight of the Gods: Philosophical Perspectives on Negative Theology* [Kampen, the Netherlands: Kok Agora, 2000], 4). Such echoes diverge on the subject of ontology: "We speak of a maximal echo [with respect to Neoplatonism or medieval mysticism] because the criticism or 'negation' . . . of the ontological reduction of transcendence is accompanied by a positive position: an affirmation of a Being-above-being, a Super-Being." Postmodern echoes, on the other hand, refuse any confirmation or acknowledgment of a supraessence; hence, they are minimal echoes (ibid., 12). In these terms, my present gnostic meditations can best be thought of as maximal echoes of this same embarrassment, here translated into what I will call a mystical humanism.

22. Don Cupitt, *Mysticism after Modernity* (Oxford: Blackwell, 1998).

23. For my own further thoughts on scholarship, mystical writing, and postmodernism as postcolonial theory, see my "Being John Woodroffe: Mythical Reflections on the Postcolonial Study of the Hindu Tantra," in *Anxious Subjectivities: Personal Identity, Truth, and the Study of Religion,* ed. José Ignacio Cabezón and Sheila Devaney (New York: Routledge, 2004).

24. Bulhof and ten Kate, *Flight of the Gods.*

25. There are a number of important theorists here, whose work is gratefully implied in all that follows but which I do not engage in any direct or explicitly critical fashion. My agreements and differences will, however, be obvious enough. Foremost among these authors are Timothy Fitzgerald, Daniel Gold, Bruce Lincoln, Russell T. McCutcheon, Robert Segal, Jonathan Z. Smith, Steven Wasserstrom, and Donald Wiebe. Among these, my own positions are probably closest to those of Gold, as set out in his *Aesthetics and Analysis in Writing on Religion: Modern Fascinations* (Berkeley: University of California Press, 2003).

26. The category of gnosticism, very much like that of mysticism, is a modern academic construct that serves and reflects the interests of particular academic actors (for two astute analyses of this situation, see Michael A. Williams, *Rethinking "Gnosticism": An Argument for Dismantling a Dubious Category* [Princeton: Princeton University Press, 1996]; and Karen King, *What Is Gnosticism?* [Cambridge, Mass.: Harvard University Press, Belknap Press, 2003]). As an abstract English noun, the first technical use of the expression appears in 1669 (by Henry More), although both *gnosis* and *gnostikos* ("knowledge" and "knower") are ancient.

In any case, I am not feigning objectivity or pretending some kind of ahistorical essentialism here; on the contrary, I am renouncing both from the beginning for my own "heretical" project toward self-definition, comparative reflection, and public communication. Put differently, "gnosticism" may possess all sorts of historical and categorical difficulties, as Williams and King have shown us, but it also possesses modern mythical and rhetorical resonances that are simply too effective and powerful for an author attempting to communicate with a broader public to resist (or want to resist). My own use of "gnosticism" as "mystical knowledge" with clear connections to hidden erotic themes is thus closer to the writing practices of such scholars as April DeConick (discussed in chap. 1) and Marvin Meyer (see his *The Gnostic Gospels of Jesus: The Definitive Collection of Mystical Gospels and Secret Books About Jesus of Nazareth* [New York: HarperSanFrancisco, 2005], xii–xiii). Historically speaking, my gnostic method can be traced at least as far back as the *Vernünftige Hermetik*, or "Enlightened Hermeticism," movement of the eighteenth and nineteenth centuries. This group of thinkers—most influentially represented by Ferdinand Christian Baur's *Die christliche Gnosis* (1835)—argued, in Wouter Hanegraaff's words now, "that the program of the Enlightenment should not lead to the complete annihilation of religion, but rather to the transformation of traditional religion into a new kind of gnosis" ("Gnosticism," in *Encyclopedia of Religion*, ed. Kocku von Stuckrad [Leiden: E. J. Brill, 2005]).

27. Cyril O'Regan: *The Heterodox Hegel* (Albany, N.Y.: SUNY Press, 1994); O'Regan, *Gnostic Return in Modernity* (Albany, N.Y.: SUNY Press, 2001); and O'Regan, *Gnostic Apocalypse: Jacob Boehme's Haunted Narrative* (Albany, N.Y.: SUNY Press, 2002).

28. Wouter Hanegraaff has argued that the history of Gnosticism, and particularly its modern history in the American New Age, has witnessed an increasing appreciation of embodiment. My own thoughts certainly fit into the latest stages of this incarnational pattern. See Wouter Hanegraaff, "Human Potential before Esalen: An Experiment in Anachronism," in *On the Edge of the Future: Esalen and the Evolution of American Culture*, ed. Jeffrey J. Kripal and Glenn W. Shuck (Bloomington: Indiana University Press, 2005). My positive evaluation and embrace of this incarnational-historical process are mine and do not necessarily reflect the thought of Hanegraaff.

29. Elaine Pagels, *Beyond Belief: The Secret Gospel of Thomas* (New York: Random House, 2003).

30. Meera Nanda, *Prophets Facing Backwards: Postmodern Critiques of Science and Hindu Nationalism in India* (Rutgers University Press, 2003). See also Meera Nanda, *Postmodernism and Religious Fundamentalism: A Scientific Rebuttal to Hindu Science, an Essay, a Review and an Interview* (Pondicherry: Navayana, 2003).

31. D. G. Hart does an excellent job summarizing this professional tension between the discipline's early twentieth-century churchly origins and its post-1960 academic trajectories in *The University Gets Religion: Religious Studies in American Higher Education* (Baltimore: John Hopkins University Press, 1999), 6–10. As an ironic side note, Hart's sympathetic summary of Paul V. Mankowski's conservative rants in *First Things* about the sexual preoccupations of scholars of religion, their deconstructive reading of traditional scripture and doctrine as forms of false consciousness and dangerous fiction, and their individualist calls to reimagine religion itself describe quite well, in an entirely negative and phobic mode, what I am positively calling here "gnosis" (Paul V. Mankowski, "Academic Religion: Play-

ground of the Vandals," *First Things*, vol. 23 [May 1992]; and Mankowski, "What I Was at the American Academy of Religion," *First Things*, vol. 21 [March 1992]). I am in agreement with Hart, however, that the discipline of religious studies can never free itself entirely from the religious traditions without effecting its own "self-immolation" (*The University Gets Religion*, 10).

32. I am indebted for this line of thought to Timothy Dobe.

33. Catherine Clément, *Syncope: The Philosophy of Rapture*, trans. Sally O'Driscoll and Deirdre M. Mahoney (Minneapolis: University of Minnesota Press, 1994), 19.

34. Richard M. Bucke, *Cosmic Consciousness* (New York: E. P. Dutton, 1969/1901).

35. R. C. Zaehner, *Concordant Discord: The Interdependence of Faiths, Being the Gifford Lectures on Natural Religion Delivered at St. Andrews in 1967–1968* (Oxford: Clarendon Press, 1970), 328.

36. For this story and a fuller treatment of Wolfson's thought, see Jeffrey J. Kripal, *Roads of Excess, Palaces of Wisdom: Eroticism and Reflexivity in the Study of Mysticism* (Chicago: University of Chicago Press, 2001), chap. 5.

37. Kripal, *Roads of Excess*.

38. Gerald Larson, "Polymorphic Sexuality, Homoeroticism and the Study of Religion," *Journal of the American Academy of Religion* 65, no. 3 (1997): 655–665; Jeffrey J. Kripal, "Mystical Homoeroticism, Reductionism, and the Reality of Censorship: A Response to Gerald James Larson," *Journal of the American Academy of Religion* 66, no. 3 (1998): 627–635. For a select bibliography of this controversy, see below, chap. 3, n. 22.

39. For a discussion of a few of these letters, see my "Teaching Hindu Tantrism with Freud: Psychoanalysis as Critical Theory and Mystical Technique," in *Teaching Freud in Religious Studies*, ed. Diane Jonte-Pace (New York: Oxford University Press, 2003).

40. It seems relevant to point out in this context that the ancient gnostic texts are filled with images of rape, "defilement," and sexual violence, usually committed by male spirits or divinities against female figures, and that, indeed, throughout the history of Western spiritual writing, ecstasy is often linguistically and psychologically related to having been "raped" (*raptus*) or ravished by a male divine.

41. Jordan Paper, *The Mystic Experience: A Descriptive and Comparative Analysis* (Albany, N.Y.: SUNY Press, 2004), 6.

42. C. Mackenzie Brown, response to the panel "Teaching Religion in Troubled Times: When Practitioners Meet (and Challenge) Professors," Southwest Regional Meeting of the American Academy of Religion, Dallas, March 13, 2005.

43. Paul Ricoeur, *Freud and Philosophy: An Essay on Interpretation*, trans. Denis Savage (New Haven: Yale University Press, 1970), 28–36.

44. I am indebted for this line of thought to Eugene Rogers.

Chapter One

1. I dedicate this essay to Jane Schaberg, a contemporary Mary Magdalene if ever there was one, and to Theodore Jennings, who has given us back the man Jesus loved.

2. I use the word "queer" here in the sense that it is used in contemporary queer theory, that is, as an erotic fluidity that cannot be fitted into any normative category, as an apophaticism of the sexual. Such a reading can only sit in tension

with the notion of a *canon*, a term derived from the Greek for the "guideline" or carpenter's tool that was used to measure lines, often with a plumb attached to ensure perpendicular or "straight" walls (Elaine Pagels, *Beyond Belief: The Secret Gospel of Thomas* [New York: Random House, 2003], 148).

3. As the first of these end secrets, there is one initial genealogical note to register in this context, namely, the historical likelihood that the European Gypsies, or Roma, who emigrated from India around the eleventh or twelfth century and whose ritual styles, language, and saints strongly resemble South Asian Tantric themes (e.g., their language is obviously related to Hindi, and their patron saint, Sarah-Kali, appears to be a fusion of Catholic and Tantric pieties), were also involved in the development of the cult of Mary Magdalene, particularly in southern France. They thus provide a cultural link between India, Catholicism, and many of the Gnostic-Tantric themes of the present essay. Their established if roaming presence in Europe also demolishes the common misconception that Indic ideas and practices did not enter Europe until the colonial period. According to family tradition, my paternal family descends from Czechoslovakian Roma. I have written this essay—originally unconsciously, now quite gnostically—out of this same genetico-spiritual lineage or family mythology.

4. See William E. Phipps, *Was Jesus Married? The Distortion of Sexuality in the Christian Tradition* (New York: Harper and Row, 1970); and Phipps, *The Sexuality of Jesus* (Cleveland: Pilgrim Press, 1996). Phipps's first book was marred by some rather naive heterosexual assumptions (which, I should add, were virtually universal among biblical scholars at that time), but he appears to have recognized this and begun moving beyond these in his second book.

5. Phipps, *The Sexuality of Jesus*, 8.

6. This, by the way, is the proof text for the traditional Christian prohibition against masturbation, or "onanism." Unfortunately for the traditional reading, Onan's sin has absolutely nothing to do with masturbation but involves his refusal to inseminate his dead brother's wife to produce a legitimate and clear heir for the family inheritance. So much for biblical "family values."

7. See Jane Schaberg, *The Illegitimacy of Jesus: A Feminist Theological Interpretation of the Infancy Narratives* (New York: Crossroad, 1990), 208n11, for a discussion of the relevant biblical passages for such an extreme punishment.

8. Theodore W. Jennings, Jr., *The Man Jesus Loved: Homoerotic Narratives from the New Testament* (Cleveland: Pilgrim Press, 2003), 136–137; see also 26, 88, and 101. Jennings's title appears to be a playful counter to Antti Marjanen's *The Woman Jesus Loved: Mary Magdalene in the Nag Hammadi Library and Related Documents* (Leiden: E. J. Brill, 1996).

9. Hence the later rabbinic prohibitions against committing adultery "with the foot."

10. L. William Countryman, *Dirt, Greed, and Sex: Sexual Ethics in the New Testament and Their Implications for Today* (Philadelphia: Fortress Press, 1988), 91.

11. See, for example, F. Scott Spencer's learned and playful study of this scene and the "comedic" Matthean genealogy of Jesus's "riotous foremothers" in *Dancing Girls, Loose Ladies, and Women of the Cloth: The Women in Jesus' Life* (New York: Continuum, 2004), 28–46.

12. The gnostic texts assert the same. The Gospel of Philip, for example, speaks of Jesus's sister, Mary, who always walked with his mother, Mary, and his companion,

Mary Magdalene (CGL 159). Conservative readings point out that the Greek for "brother" (*adelphos*) can also mean "cousin." Fair enough, but it is still not clear what criterion (other than the circular criterion of theological orthodoxy) should be used to determine the best reading here, and it is perfectly clear that "brother" is the more natural reading.

13. For the relevant texts and their exegesis, see Schaberg, *The Illegitimacy of Jesus*, 62–67.

14. Gospel of Philip, CGL 151.

15. I am indebted to Donald Capps for this insight. See his *Jesus: A Psychological Biography* (St. Louis: Chalice Press, 2000).

16. For extensive treatments of these cultural systems and Jesus's radical rejection and violation of their patriarchal norms, see Countryman, *Dirt, Greed, and Sex*, chaps. 8–9. This rejection, of course, was already being muted in the late pseudo-Pauline texts; it would soon be reversed under Roman influence and would remain so during two thousand years of conservative Christian history. For a study of this long reversal, see Rosemary Radford Ruether, *Christianity and the Making of the Modern Family* (Boston: Beacon Press, 2000).

17. Stevan L. Davies, *Jesus the Healer: Possession, Trance, and the Origins of Christianity* (New York: Continuum, 1995), 16; italics his.

18. See below, chap. 4, in the section "Toward a More Radical Empiricism."

19. Davies, *Jesus the Healer*, 18.

20. This raises the question of whether Jesus himself experienced some sort of abuse or trauma in his earlier life. I think this is entirely possible, but the fact remains that we lack any solid textual evidence of this. We simply do not know and probably cannot know.

21. Davies, *Jesus the Healer*, 25.

22. Ibid., 35.

23. Ibid., 86.

24. Ibid., 110.

25. Jesus hardly escapes images of male power, however, as is evident in his central metaphor of the kingdom of heaven. A kingdom, after all, implies a king and, with it, a kind of smuggled-in theological monarchy. "King," "Lord," and "God" are all interchangeable terms in biblical monotheism.

26. Elsewhere, Davies (correctly) notes that the psychological reflexitivies of ancient gnosticism, Kashmir Shaivism (a form of Indic Tantric thought), and a modern, mystically open psychoanalysis are translatable into one another. With respect to gnosticism and psychoanalysis, he writes: "If we take the metaphor of mind seriously, we can see that Gnostics took upon themselves the incredible task of psychoanalyzing God. They did this work through introspection, presuming that since each awakened human is an aspect of God, undeluded self-knowledge is equivalent to knowledge of God. The career of the divine mind, its fall into illusion and self-forgetfulness, was not something independent of human existence but quite the contrary: because each individual is or has been the Godhead failing to know itself, each individual has as a personal history the fall of God" (*The Secret Book of John: The Gnostic Gospel Annotated and Explained*, trans. Steven Davies [Woodstock, Vt.: Skylight Paths, 2005], xx).

27. Davies, *Jesus the Healer*, 117.

28. Ibid., 169.

29. Gary Taylor, *Castration: An Abbreviated History of Western Manhood* (New York: Routledge, 2000), 153.

30. Ibid., 16. Some caution is in order here from a purely medical perspective, since while it is true that castration does not prevent erection, it almost certainly reduces libido via the removal of the testosterone-generating testicles.

31. Space prevents us from pursuing such threads here, but it is worth noting that the *galli*, as castrated and often transgendered men dedicated to a goddess and known for their passive homosexual activity, may take us back to the very origins of civilization in Mesopotamia and, via Mesopotamia, link us to some of the more extreme goddess traditions of South Asia. According to Taylor, Innin/Innana/Ishtar was the goddess first associated with eunuchs. Her cultus, moreover, was centered in what was perhaps the world's first major city, Uruk in Sumer (whose earliest period dates as far back as 4500 BCE). From Sumer, her cultus appears to have spread both east and west, into India, whose history boasts a whole host of castrating goddesses and even a modern-day community similar to the ancient Roman *galli* (the *hijras*), as well as into ancient Greece and Rome. Interestingly, many of the features of Ishtar/Innana resemble those of the Tantric goddesses of South Asia: her "holy vulva" was worshipped; her sexual intercourse with her partner (Dumuzi) was celebrated and probably ritualized; she was the patron deity of prostitutes; she was a warrior goddess; she did not take on the roles of the wife or mother; and so on (see Taylor, *Castration*, 169, 177–179, 288–289).

32. Jennings, *The Man Jesus Loved*, 153.

33. For more on this idea and an analysis of castration themes in Hindu Shakta Tantra, see my "Kali in the Psychoanalytic Tradition: Or Why the Tantrika Is a Hero," in *Encountering Kali*, ed. Rachel Fell McDermott and Jeffrey J. Kripal (Berkeley: University of California Press, 2003).

34. I am indebted here to Taylor and his at once learned and wickedly humorous chapter "What Would Jesus Do?" in *Castration*. Jesus would castrate himself, of course.

35. See, for example, Will Deming, "Mark 9.42–10.12, Matthew 5.27–32, and B. Nid. 13b: A First Century Discussion of Male Sexuality," *New Testament Studies* 36, no. 1 (1990): 130–141. I find Countryman particularly balanced and convincing here (*Dirt, Greed, and Sex*, chap. 5).

36. Countryman, *Dirt, Greed, and Sex*, 96.

37. Jennings, *The Man Jesus Loved*, 67.

38. Ibid., 68.

39. For discussions of both of these writers and some of the technical literature on their erotics, see my "The Christology and Psychology of the Kiss: Re-reading Bernard of Clairvaux's *Sermones Super Cantica Canticorum*," in *Mysticism: A Variety of Psychological Perspectives*, ed. J. A. Belzen and A. Geels (Amsterdam: Rodopi, 2003).

40. Marlowe's postdeath (really postmurder) deposition accused him of claiming, "*That St. John the Evangelist was bedfellow to Christ and leaned always in his bosome, that he used him as the sinners of Sodoma*" (Arlo Karlen, *Sexuality and Homosexuality* [New York: W. W. Norton, 1971], 117; quoted in Jennings, *The Man Jesus Loved*, 81).

41. Jennings, *The Man Jesus Loved*, 82–86.

42. As Jennings points out, Groddeck considered the homosexual nature of Jesus's relationship to the Beloved to be patently obvious (Georg Walter Groddeck, *The Book of It*, trans. V. M. E. Collins [New York: Vintage Press, 1949], 263–264).

43. Morton Smith, *The Secret Gospel: The Discovery and Interpretation of the Secret Gospel according to Mark* (New York: Harper and Row, 1973). Smith's homoerotic mystical thesis was a "magical" performance of the secret (*tou mystikou euangeliou*) in the sense that it was advanced through what appears now to be an elaborate professional ruse or hoax (see Stephen Carlson, *The Gospel Hoax: Morton Smith's Invention of "Secret Mark"* [Waco: Baylor University Press, 2005]). I am persuaded by Carlson's argument and do not believe that we can continue using Secret Mark to discuss early Christianity. Oddly, however, Smith's homoerotic hoax fits in almost seamlessly with other, more convincing works of scholarship on the canonical texts. What, for example, *are* we to do with that Marcan naked fleeing youth in the garden during Jesus's arrest? Or with Jesus's male Beloved in John? More radically still, have two hundred years of historical criticism not shown us that the gospels themselves are essentially ancient hoaxes, that is, that they represent the views and agendas of the communities that produced them put in the mouth of a Jesus who probably said very little of this? How is what Smith did, then, *really* that different from, say, what the authors of John or Matthew did?

44. John Boswell, *Christianity, Social Tolerance, and Homosexuality: Gay People in Western Europe from the Beginning of the Christian Era to the Fourteenth Century* (Chicago: University of Chicago Press, 1980).

45. Montefiore suggested in a sermon preached at Cambridge's Great St. Mary's in August 1967 that Jesus was celibate because he was "not the marrying kind" and compared the repugnance this elicited in some of his hearers to "the scandal of the cross" (quoted in Jennings, *The Man Jesus Loved*, 88–89). Such sermons, I suspect, could be multiplied into the hundreds if we looked closely enough at the historical records.

46. Robert Goss, *Jesus Acted Up: A Gay and Lesbian Manifesto* (New York: HarperSanFrancisco, 1993); Goss, *Queering Christ: Beyond Jesus Acted Up* (Cleveland: The Pilgrim Press, 2002).

47. Mark Jordan, *The Silence of Sodom: Homosexuality in Modern Catholicism* (Chicago: University of Chicago Press, 2000).

48. Jennings devotes an entire chapter discussion in *The Man Jesus Loved* to this story: chap. 8, "The Centurion's 'Lad.'"

49. For a full list and study of these, see ibid.

50. Dale B. Martin, "Sex and the Single Savior," *Svensk Exegetisk Årsbok* 67 (2002): 57–58.

51. In the modern period, this was most famously argued by Anders Nygren, *Agape and Eros* (New York: Harper and Row, 1969). Similar debates can easily be found within Indology and Tantric studies with respect to the Sanskrit terms *kama* (lust), *prema* (spiritual love), and *ananda* (bliss), among others.

52. Theodore W. Jennings, Jr., *Jacob's Wound: Homoerotic Narrative in the Literature of Ancient Israel* (New York: Continuum, 2005). Jennings deals with three different kinds of same-sex complexes in the Hebrew Bible: (1) a warrior culture in which male heroes (here YHWH, Saul, and David) commonly take on younger lover pals (like Saul and David with respect to YHWH and Jonathan with respect to David); (2) a mystical or shamanistic eroticism in which "sacral power is also erotic power" and "in which the sacral power of the holy man is . . . both a product of same-sex relationship and expressed through same-sex practice" (Samuel/Saul, Elijah/Elisha, the controversial roving "sons of the prophets," and the *qedeshim* or

temple prostitutes); and (3) transgendered figures, with YHWH again "as the one who transgenders Israel and who violently accuses this male of sexual unfaithfulness, threatens and permits extreme punishment, and seeks to woo this male (dressed in metaphorical drag) back into faithful relationship" (ibid., xiii–xv). Jennings's basic point is a stunningly convincing one, namely, that the usual proof texting of a few passages in the Hebrew Bible (two or three meager passages in Leviticus and the Sodom story) to "prove" its homophobia is both a "dreary debate" and entirely beside the point, since "a focus on these well-chewed scraps has diverted attention from . . . a whole feast of homoerotic material in the Hebrew Bible" (ibid., x). In other words, what difference does it make if we can find two or three purity prohibitions against anal sex when *God himself* is consistently and countercoherently presented as the homoerotic *erastes* of Israel as *eromenos?*

53. I am relying for this crucial philological point on Jennings, *The Man Jesus Loved*, 56–58. For verbal and nominal uses of *agape* in the Septuagint version of the Song of Songs, see, for example, 1:4 and 8:6. This same language, of course, is part of a long biblical and prophetic tradition that cast God in the role of male lover or husband and Israel in the role of unfaithful or whoring wife.

54. Martin, "Sex and the Single Savior," 57.

55. I adopt and adapt the term *countercoherent* from the work of Jennings, who adopts it from Mieke Bal, *Death and Symmetry: The Politics of Coherence in the Book of Judges* (Chicago: University of Chicago Press, 1988).

56. This is not at all to suggest that every text fits or even can fit into this newly rendered whole (or any other whole). Biblical texts, like all texts, are unstable, composite, historically conditioned documents that are filled with contradictions, tensions, subtexts, countertexts, and "gaps." In the end, the puzzle metaphor fails, as the same pieces can be put together in many diifferent ways.

57. Smith, *The Secret Gospel*, 80. Because of the aforementioned hoax thesis, I am restricting my use of Smith to sources outside Secret Mark.

58. Jennings, *The Man Jesus Loved*, 165. My thanks to Jennifer Glancy for helping me with this passage and its gendered feet.

59. Ibid., 15.

60. Martin, "Sex and the Single Savior," 58.

61. Quoted in Smith, *The Secret Gospel*, 142.

62. Space prevents me from analyzing the psychosexual dimensions of the specifically sacrificial connotations of the ritual. I might only point out that homosexual desire, guilt, sacrificial symbolism, and actual death (or suicide) are intimate partners in much mystical literature. See, for example, Jim Wafer, "Vision and Passion: The Symbolism of Male Love in Islamic Mystical Literature," in *Islamic Homosexualities: Culture, History, and Literature*, ed. Stephen O. Murray and Will Roscoe (New York: New York University Press, 1997); and Kripal, "The Passion of Louis Massignon: Sublimating the Homoerotic Gaze in *The Passion of al-Hallaj* (1922)," in *Roads of Excess, Palaces of Wisdom: Eroticism and Reflexivity in the Study of Mysticism* (Chicago: University of Chicago Press, 2001). This same sacrificial homoerotic hermeneutic could be applied to the institution of the eucharist as well, if in a much more speculative vein. Also relevant here—but again well outside our present parameters—is Nancy Jay's brilliant feminist reading of sacrifice as a patriarchal strategy designed to transcend male dependence on women's reproductive powers (*Throughout Your Generations Forever: Sacrifice, Religion, and*

Paternity [Chicago: University of Chicago Press, 1992]), a ritual logic which male homosexuality can easily undergird and exaggerate.

63. In his general fashion, Smith hints at the same thesis without ever using the category of homosexuality (*The Secret Gospel*, 140).

64. Apocryphon of John, CGL 119, 145. As I will point out below, such passages are highly reminiscent of Indic Tantric systems: transculturally and transtemporally put, Eve teaches Adam the Tantra. I am not simply being suggestive here. There are places in the Apocryphon of John where I am tempted to posit actual historical diffusions from India to Egypt. For example, in one place, the text states that the Mother "became dark because her consort had not agreed with her" (ibid., 79; cf. 83), thus echoing, toward very different mythological goals, the ancient Puranic myth of the origin of Kali ("Black"), who is created when the goddess Parvati performs asceticism to win a golden skin after her husband, Shiva, has made fun of her dark blue complexion. As this dark blueness separates from her, Kali is born and Parvati becomes golden.

65. Here too we might place the early practice of the eucharistic kiss shared among Christians, again a kind of sublimated witness to the ritual's erotic origins: "For it is by a kiss that the perfect conceive and give birth. For this reason we also kiss one another. We receive conception from the grace which is in one another" (Gospel of Philip, CGL 157).

66. This is the "real" reason, I suspect, why women cannot be priests and why celibacy is required in Roman Catholicism. Allowing women or active heterosexual men to celebrate the eucharist would effectively dissolve the sublimated male homoerotic dynamics of the ritual. The latter psychosexual dynamics, I also suspect, are precisely what drives and creates both "purity" and male "sanctity" in the Catholic tradition. The Eastern Orthodox tradition, which possesses both married priests and celibate monastics but which does not allow female priests, appears to be a slightly more flexible variant of the same liturgical erotics.

67. Discussed in Jennings, *The Man Jesus Loved*, 82–86.

68. See Carlson, *The Gospel Hoax*, chap. 5, "The Modernity of Secret Mark."

69. Jennings, *The Man Jesus Loved*, 111–112.

70. Ibid., 26.

71. The same revealing gender-switch hermeneutic could easily be applied to the last supper scene. Consider, for example, what a typical heterosexual adult male would think if he were given a *woman's* body to eat and blood to drink. What would he associate with putting her body and her fluids in his mouth? He would, of course, think sex (and probably oral sex).

72. Jane Schaberg, *The Resurrection of Mary Magdalene: Legends, Apocrypha, and the Christian Testament* (New York: Continuum, 2002), 8.

73. Ibid., 83–84.

74. I find all the gnostic excitement and fundamentalist hysteria over Dan Brown's *The DaVinci Code* humorously naive and curiously misplaced, as if an effeminate figure to the right of Jesus in DaVinci's *The Last Supper* could not be an effeminate male, that is, the Beloved as gay lover.

75. Bruce Chilton, *Rabbi Jesus: An Intimate Biography* (New York: Doubleday, 2000), 145.

76. There is, not surprisingly, a good deal of debate about whether the kiss in such texts is to be read sexually or spiritually. I would suggest that it is usually, not

always, best read along both lines. I would also want to register serious reservations about the heterosexual assumptions being made in some of this debate. Marjanen, for example, in an otherwise stunning work of scholarship, reasons that, because Jesus transmitted his secret mysteries to James through a kiss and by calling him his beloved, or because Jesus and John the Baptist are said to have kissed each other in another text, "it is fully clear that kissing has no sexual connotation" (Marjanen, *The Woman Jesus Loved*, 159). What is being assumed here? What is *not* being thought?

77. Gospel of Philip, CGL 167–168.

78. Schaberg, *The Resurrection*, 152. Schaberg appears to be drawing on Marjanen's philological discussion of *koinonos* in *The Woman Jesus Loved*, 151–160.

79. Marjanen, *The Woman Jesus Loved*, 153.

80. Ibid., 154.

81. Ravi Ravindra makes a similar point in a more devotional mode in *The Gospel of John in the Light of Indian Mysticism* (Rochester, Vt.: Inner Traditions, 2005), 226.

82. The Gospel of Philip focuses much of this discussion. See, for example, Jorunn Jacobson Buckley, "A Cult Mystery in *The Gospel of Philip*," *Journal of Biblical Literature* 99 (1980): 569–581; Elaine Pagels, "Pursuing the Spiritual Eve: Imagery and Hermeneutics in the *Hypostasis of the Archons* and the *Gospel of Philip*," in *Images of the Feminine in Gnosticism*, ed. Karen King (Harrisburg, Pa.: Trinity Press International, 1988); and Robert M. Grant, "The Mystery of Marriage in the Gospel of Philip," *Vigiliae Christianae* 15 (1961).

83. This line is taken from Irenaeus's polemical tract *Against the Heresies*, as presented in *Irénée de Lyon: Contre les Hérésies*, ed. A. Rousseau and L. Doutreleau, (Paris: Les Éditions du Cerf, 1979), 2:99, and quoted by April DeConick, "The Great Mystery of Marriage: Sex and Conception in Ancient Valentinian Traditions," *Vigiliae Christianae* 57 (2003): 334.

84. April DeConick, "The True Mysteries: Sacramentalism in the Gospel of Philip," *Vigiliae Christianae* 55 (2001): 225–261.

85. DeConick, "The Great Mystery of Marriage," 342.

86. DeConick, "The True Mysteries," 250.

87. This is another clear example of how *agape* can function as a transparent sexual verb or innuendo in ancient Greek.

88. For more on this, see Stephen Benko, "The Libertine Gnostic Sect of the Phibionites according to Epiphanius," *Vigiliae Christianae* 21 (1967): 103–119.

89. Quoted in ibid., 104.

90. See especially David Gordon White, *The Alchemical Body: Siddha Traditions in Medieval India* (Chicago: University of Chicago Press, 1994); White, *Kiss of the Yogini: "Tantric Sex" in Its South Asian Contexts* (Chicago: University of Chicago Press, 2003); and Douglas Wile, *Art of the Bedchamber: The Chinese Sexual Yoga Classics Including Women's Solo Meditation Texts* (Albany, N.Y.: SUNY Press, 1992). I also want to register here two simple biological reasons to take reports about the ritual consumption of sexual fluids in the history of religions more seriously: first, such acts are entirely common in the history of human sexuality outside ritual contexts, and so we hardly need be surprised by their occasional presence in religious texts; and second, such acts provide an effective and relatively controlled access to the phenomenology of arousal and orgasm without the fear of pregnancy—oral sex is a perfect contraceptive.

91. According to later tradition, this sacramental blood is said to have first flowed from the side of Jesus on the cross along with water (John 19:34), hence the sacraments of the eucharist and baptism, the latter representing Christian birth. There are also connotations of breast milk here; indeed, the flowing blood from Jesus's side is actually and literally conflated with breast milk in medieval Christian piety and art. As a whole symbolic complex, it is difficult to resist the notion that this particular ritual *imaginaire* constitutes—exactly as Nancy Jay argued—a male attempt to overtake or subsume what are female biological prerogatives, that is, menstrual bleeding, pregnancy, birth, and breast-feeding.

92. Elaine Pagels, *The Gnostic Gospels* (New York: Vintage, 1979), xx–xxi. For more extensive discussions, see Wilhelm Halbfass, *India and Europe: An Essay in Understanding* (Albany, N.Y.: SUNY Press, 1988); J. Kennedy, "Buddhist Gnosticism, the System of Basilides," *Journal of the Royal Asiatic Society* (1902): 377–415; Edward Conze, "Buddhism and Gnosis," in *Further Buddhist Studies* (Oxford: Oxford University Press, 1975), 15–32; and, most recently and impressively, Thomas McEvilley, *The Shape of Ancient Thought: Comparative Studies in Greek and Indian Philosophies* (New York: Allworth Press, 2002).

93. I am indebted for this latter thought to Catherine Keller, "'She Talks Too Much': Magdalene Meditations" (Rockwell Lecture, Rice University, March 22, 2004).

94. Pagels, *The Gnostic Gospels*, 18.

95. Barbara Holdredge, *Veda and Torah: Transcending the Textuality of Scripture* (Albany, N.Y.: SUNY Press, 1996).

96. Such a model might also throw some comparative light on many otherwise puzzling features of the New Testament, such as passages in the Epistle of Jude, whose language, Countryman argues, "suggests that certain sectarian teachers were claiming to have sexual intercourse with [angels]," or 2 Pet., which appears to condemn early Christian sexual rites (Countryman, *Dirt, Greed, and Sex*, 134). Again, more sex with the angels.

97. Quoted in Schaberg, *The Resurrection*, 157.

98. Act of Peter, CGL 483.

99. Gospel according to Mary, CGL 469.

100. Pistis Sophia II, 72, quoted in Schaberg, *The Resurrection*, 162.

101. Donald Capps and Nathan Steven Carlin, "The Homosexual Tendencies of King James: Should This Matter to Bible Readers Today?" *Pastoral Psychology*, forthcoming.

102. Nor, by the way, are many of the gnostic systems. In the Valentinian mythology, for example, since all human beings are ontologically derived from the feminine Sophia, and since the eschatological end is to reunite with the Father, the heterosexuality of the human and angelic mystical marriages is secondary to the gendering of the final end, which feminizes *all* human beings in relation to the male Godhead. Structurally speaking, then, what we have here is what we have in medieval Kabbalah as analyzed by Elliot Wolfson, that is, an erotic mysticism that, from the human male perspective, employs heterosexual intercourse to unite with the divine Male, that is, a heterosexual homoeroticism (for a discussion of this pattern with respect to Wolfson's hermeneutic, see Kripal, *Roads of Excess*, chap. 5). I am indebted to April DeConick for pointing this out to me.

103. Jennings, *The Man Jesus Loved*, 39. I have studied this same homoerotic

pattern in the history of male mysticism in my *Roads of Excess*. Jennings's homo-erotic analyses of the gospels fit perfectly into the comparative erotics I developed there, hence my enthusiasm here for his work.

Chapter Two

1. The Thought of Norea, CGL 99.

2. See, for example, Gospel of Philip, CGL 177, discussed below in the conclusion of this chapter.

3. Apocryphon of John, CGL 88.

4. Ibid., 89.

5. Ibid., 123.

6. Ibid., 127.

7. Ibid., 129.

8. *William Blake: The Illuminated Books*, ed. Morris Eaves, Robert N. Essick, and Joseph Viscomi (Princeton: William Blake Trust and Princeton University Press, 1993), 261.

9. Ludwig Feuerbach, *The Essence of Christianity*, trans. George Eliot (Amherst, N.Y.: Prometheus Books, 1989), xxiii; henceforth cited as EC in the body of the text.

10. Frederick Engels, *Ludwig Feuerbach and the Outcome of Classical German Philosophy* (New York: International Publishers, 1941), 18. One might also cite here Marx's *Thirteen Theses on Feuerbach*.

11. Van A. Harvey, *Feuerbach and the Interpretation of Religion* (Cambridge: Cambridge University Press, 1995).

12. Ibid., 275. I am quoting Harvey for my own purposes here; he does not frame secularization as "protognostic."

13. Ibid., 5.

14. In his later works, he would abandon this category of the species as too abstract, as another unfortunate remnant of his former Hegelianism, and turn instead to the aforementioned *Sinnlichkeit*, or sensuality, that is, a kind of existentialist insistence on the physicality and particularity of individual human experience.

15. Harvey, *Feuerbach*, 27.

16. Ludwig Feuerbach, *Lectures on the Essence of Religion*, trans. Ralph Mannheim (New York: Harper and Row, 1967), 22; quoted in Harvey, *Feuerbach*, 274.

17. Harvey has some very insightful things to say about this metaphor of the movie and its relationship to the two underlying metaphors of contemporary theories of projection: *the beam* (an illusory projection of an individual psyche, as in most psychological theories or Plato's allegory of the cave) and *the grid* (a network of socially patterned information and cognitive programming that determines how thought itself proceeds within a particular society, as in contemporary sociology of knowledge and cognitive psychology) (Harvey, *Feuerbach*, 232–280). I cannot help adding here that there is a third, very modern metaphor that combines these two older ones, that is, *the hologram*. A hologram, after all, is literally a three-dimensional, information-containing illusion created by combining a beam of light and a patterned grid. Not surprisingly, modern mystical authors familiar with modern technology and science commonly claim that reality as we normally experience it is, in effect, a holographic projection of consciousness interacting

with the socially programmed human brain. Such astonishing thoughts are certainly not beyond the parameters of current scientific thinking. See, for example, Jacob D. Bekenstein, "Information in the Holographic Universe," *Scientific American* 289, no. 2 (August 2003): 56–65. The simple subtitle to this difficult essay reads: "Theoretical Results about Black Holes Suggest that the Universe Could be like a Gigantic Hologram."

18. Marilyn Chapin Massey, "Censorship and the Language of Feuerbach's *Essence of Christianity* (1841)," *Journal of Religion* 65 (1985): 173–195; John Glasse, "Why Did Feuerbach Concern Himself with Luther?" *Revue Internationale de Philosophie* 26, no. 101 (1972): 364–385. I am relying here on Harvey, *Feuerbach*, 28, 148–149.

19. Strauss is another paradigmatic example of my gnostic thesis. Inspired partly by German mystical thought, he had attempted to understand the historical Jesus as a pantheistic mystic in his pioneering *The Life of Jesus Critically Examined* (1835).

20. Feuerbach, like all thinkers, occasionally contradicts himself here, for elsewhere he states clearly that the meaning of a religious phenomenon can best be located in its origins: "[I]t is only in the origin of a thing that we can discern its true nature" (EC 118).

21. This is not to say, at all, that the study of religion cannot be aligned with specific formulations of Christian theology. Once again, what is traditionally known as negative theology or mystical theology seems particularly apt here.

22. The recent scholarly literature is particularly rich on this linking of monotheism and violence. See, for example, Jan Assmann, *Moses the Egyptian: The Memory of Egypt in Western Monotheism* (Cambridge, Mass.: Harvard University Press, 1997); Jonathan Kirsch, *God against the Gods: The History of the War between Monotheism and Polytheism* (New York: Viking Compass, 2005); and Regina M. Schwartz, *The Curse of Cain: The Violent Legacy of Monotheism* (Chicago: University of Chicago Press, 1997).

23. I find such language unfortunate, mostly because I sense that such labels function more as simplistic defense mechanisms against radical—that is, gnostic—thought than as fair descriptions of an understandable philosophical or religious position. How exactly *would* it be possible, for example, to reject the entire logic of biblical monotheism and to point out the deep structural violence of the scriptural texts without being labeled "anti-Semitic," "anti-Christian," "antireligious," or whatever?

24. The later Feuerbach would argue that the "heathen religions" are superior to Christianity to the extent that they affirm plurality, the body, nature, and the earth.

25. Harvey, *Feuerbach*, 27.

26. Or is this simply a failure to see the queerness of the Christian Trinity, that is, the structural fact that what we have here are three males in an eternal relationship of love? Such a possibility, of course, would render contemporary conservative Christian objections to "same-sex marriage" theologically unstable, to say the least. God, it appears, *is* a same-sex marriage.

27. Feuerbach expands on this same point in his 1844 essay *The Essence of Faith according to Luther*, trans. Melvin Cherno (New York: Harper and Row, 1967).

28. Apocryphon of John, CGL 18–19.

29. Elaine Pagels, *The Origin of Satan* (New York: Vintage, 1995).

30. Amy Hollywood, *Sensible Ecstasy: Mysticism, Sexual Difference, and the Demands of History* (Chicago: University of Chicago Press, 2002), 218–219.

31. Peter Berger, *The Sacred Canopy: Elements of a Sociological Theory of Religion* (Garden City, N.Y.: Anchor Books, 1969), 180. Much of my earlier work, by the way, flows from a similar dialectical reversal not of Feuerbach, but of Freud: if religious phenomena are often imbued with sexual energies and dynamics, this may mean not that the sacred can be exhaustively reduced to sex, but that sexuality can reveal the sacred, or, in my own technical terms now, that the mystical and the erotic are dialectical transformations of one another (more on this below, in "Interlude").

32. See especially Cyril O'Regan: *The Heterodox Hegel* (Albany, N.Y.: SUNY Press, 1994).

33. I do not claim to understand adequately O'Regan's corpus and certainly do not want to simplify it in any way, but it is probably fair to say that he is less enthusiastic about a gnostic modernity than I am. This is not to say that I do not have my own philosophical reservations and ethical criticisms of both the gnostic and the mystical, most of which revolve around my sense that the accomplishments of modernity and the Enlightenment (individualism, rationalism, freedom, equality, etc.) should not be surrendered to any religious or philosophical system. Hence again my ambivalent parenthetical invocation of a "(post)modernity."

34. Elliot Wolfson, *Language, Eros, Being: Kabbalistic Hermeneutics and Poetic Imagination* (New York: Fordham University Press, 2005), xiii.

35. See, for example, Apocryphon of John, CGL 19.

36. Georg Wilhelm Friedrich Hegel, *Lectures on the Philosophy of Religion*, vol. 2, *Determinate Religion*, ed. Peter C. Hodgson, trans. R. F. Brown, P. C. Hodgson, and J. M. Stewart, with the assistance of H. S. Harris (Berkeley: University of California Press, 1987), 529.

37. A full study of Feuerbach's different uses of the category of mysticism would be both fascinating and fruitful; unfortunately, a full study of these uses is well beyond the parameters of the present essay. In any case, at least three things can be said with relative certainty: (1) Feuerbach's use of the category is hardly always negative, hence his not unusual references to such things as "the profoundest, truest expression of Christian mysticism" (EC 122); (2) the modern category of mysticism, often assumed to have come into its own only in the twentieth century, is firmly in place in Germany by 1841; and (3) Feuerbach aligns the category with a number of related terms and concepts, including especially the imagination, nature and sexuality, the Orient, Jacob Boehme's theosophy, pantheism, and nihilism.

38. Feuerbach also uses a related adjective, "esoteric" (*esoterische*) (e.g., EC 89).

39. I am indebted for this line of thought to Bryan Rennie. See especially his *Reconstructing Eliade: Making Sense of Religion* (Albany, N.Y.: SUNY Press, 1996), chap. 16. Eliade's clearest statement of this model of the sacred occurs in "The Sacred in the Secular World," in *Cultural Hermeneutics* 1 (1973): 101–113.

40. "We are made of stardust—and so is all life as we know it. Every chemical element on earth except hydrogen and helium [and there is no helium in the human body] has been scattered across the Universe in great stellar explosions and recycled into new stars, planets, and parts of us" (John Gribbin with Mary Gribbin, *Stardust: Supernovae and Life, the Cosmic Connection* [New Haven: Yale University Press, 2000], back cover).

41. In truly postmodern terms, we might describe this infinitude of the species

as an infinitude of heterogeneity. My thanks to Jim Faubion for pointing this out to me.

42. Feuerbach, *The Essence of Faith according to Luther*, 106.

43. Gospel of Philip, CGL 177.

44. Feuerbach, *The Essence of Faith according to Luther*, 107.

45. Ibid. The full phrase reads, "To believe is to make God a man and man a God."

Chapter Three

1. The comparative complexities of this "Tantric" creation myth would take us far afield. For the relevant passages, see the Apocryphon of John, CGL 21 (on the invisible Spirit as "not a god"), 33 (on the Father putting "his desire in his water-light" to produce the Mother Goddess, who is the cosmic "womb of everything"), 35 (on the Mother-Father as creative Androgyne), 71 (on the creator-god's foolish claim to be the only God), 135 (on the oedipal equation of Sophia or the Mother Goddess with Adam's partner, Eve), and 159 (on human beings surpassing the creator-god in intelligence).

2. Apocryphon of John, CGL 79.

3. For example, ibid., 81, 163.

4. Gospel of Philip, CGL 175.

5. For the colonialists' own traumas, see Linda Colley, *Captives: Britain, Empire, and the World, 1600–1850* (New York: Anchor Books, 2004).

6. "Final vocabulary" is a useful term of Richard Rorty's: see *Contingency, Irony, and Solidarity* (Cambridge: Cambridge University Press, 1989).

7. Raymond Schwab, *The Oriental Renaissance: Europe's Rediscovery of India and the East, 1680–1880*, trans. Gene Patterson and Victor Reinking (New York: Columbia University Press, 1984), xxiii.

8. Ibid., xxiii.

9. Ibid., xxiii.

10. All of my own work has been motivated by what I have called a "mystical humanism," in effect a version of Schwab's integral humanism that brings together the worlds of Western critical theory and Asian mystical thought, on the one hand, and those of the Asian philosophical traditions and Western mystical thought, on the other hand.

11. The Vatican II document *Nostra Aetate* is among the most dramatic examples of this shift from the doctrine of *nulla salus extra ecclesiam* ("there is no salvation outside the church") to a more humble inclusivism. The Roman Catholic Church now acknowledges, for example, that "in Hinduism men explore the divine mystery and express it both in the limitless riches of myth and the accurately defined insights of philosophy" and that Buddhism proposes a way of life in which "men can, with confidence and trust, attain a state of perfect liberation and reach supreme illumination either through their own efforts or by the aid of divine help" (October 28, 1965, *Nostra Aetate*, or *Declaration on the Relation of the Church to Non-Christian Religions*, in *Vatican Council II: The Conciliar and Post Conciliar Documents*, ed. Austin Flannery [Collegeville, Ind.: Liturgical Press, 1992]). For a summary and analysis of this extraordinary development within Catholic theology, see Jacques Dupuis, *Toward a Christian Theology of Religious Pluralism* (Maryknoll, N.Y.: Orbis, 1997).

12. Peter van der Veer, *Religious Nationalism: Hindus and Muslims in India* (Berkeley: University of California Press, 1994); Lise McKean, *Divine Enterprise: Gurus and the Hindu Nationalist Movement* (Chicago: University of Chicago Press, 1996); Arundhati Roy, "Fascism's Firm Footprint in India," *Nation*, September 30, 2002.

13. There is a great deal of critical discussion around both the terms "Hindu" and "Hinduism." Generally speaking, this literature suggests that "Hindu" probably first occurred as a Persian geographical term for those who live beyond (that is, east of) the Indus river. As a term designating a religion, still inclusive of what were later to be differentiated as Hinduism, Buddhism, and Jainism, it may have been first deployed by the Muslim invaders of the early part of the second millennium (Brian K. Smith, *Reflection on Resemblance, Ritual and Religion* [New York: Oxford University Press, 1989], 6). As an indigenous self-description, "Hindu" was used in Sanskrit and Bengali texts as a counterterm to *Yavana* (Muslim) as early as the sixteenth century. The English term "Hindu" (or "Hindoo") was first used by British colonialists to describe the people of Hindustan, that is, the area of northwest India, and hence it did not yet carry any specific religious or sectarian meanings. The *-ism* was added around 1829 to denote the culture and religion of high-caste Brahmins and was then soon appropriated by Indian reformers to establish a national, cultural, and religious identity around ancient scriptural texts, ritual practices, and religious forms of identity. Gavin Flood is thus certainly not far off the mark when he states that "Hinduism" cannot be understood as a pure product of Western Orientalists: it also represents a development of traditional self-understandings and so "a transformation in the modern world of themes already present" (Gavin Flood, *An Introduction to Hinduism* [Cambridge: Cambridge University Press, 1996], 8).

14. Rorty, *Contingency*, xvi.

15. Bruno Latour, *War of the Worlds: What about Peace?* trans. Charlotte Bigg (Chicago: Prickly Paradigm, 2002), 29.

16. Eduardo Viveiros de Castro, "Exchanging Perspectives: The Transformation of Objects into Subjects in Amerindian Ontologies," in "Talking Peace with Gods, Symposium on the Reconciliation of Worldviews," pt. 1, ed. Jeffrey M. Perl, special issue, *Common Knowledge* 10, no. 3 (Fall 2004): 463–484.

17. Michael B. Smith, translator's note, in *The Mystic Fable*, vol. 1, *The Sixteenth and Seventeenth Centuries*, by Michel de Certeau, trans. Michael B. Smith (Chicago: University of Chicago Press, 1992), ix–x.

18. Latour, *War of the Worlds*, 40.

19. Mark J. Sedgwick, *Against the Modern World: Traditionalism and the Secret Intellectual History of the Twentieth Century* (New York: Oxford University Press, 2004).

20. See, for example, Jeffrey J. Kripal, *Esalen: America and the Religion of No Religion* (Chicago: University of Chicago Press, forthcoming).

21. I am indebted for this language to Peter Lamborn Wilson, *Scandal: Essays in Islamic Heresy* (Brooklyn: Autonomedia, 1988).

22. Jeffrey J. Kripal, *Kali's Child: The Mystical and the Erotic in the Life and Teachings of Ramakrishna* (Chicago: University of Chicago Press, 1995; 2nd ed., 1998). The critical literature around this text is very large. For my responses, see www.rice.edu/kalischild and the following texts, some of which are available on the same Web site: "Teaching Hindu Tantrism with Freud: Psychoanalysis as Critical Theory and Mystical Technique," in *Teaching Freud in Religious Studies*, ed. Diane Jonte-Pace

(New York: Oxford University Press, 2003); "The Tantric Truth of the Matter: A Forthright Response to Rajiv Malhotra," www.sulekha.com (posted September 12, 2002); "Sexuality, Textuality, and the Future of the Past: A Response to Swami Tyagananda," *Evam* 1, nos. 1-2 (2002): 191-205; "Secret Talk: Sexual Identity and the Politics of Scholarship in the Study of Hindu Tantrism," *Harvard Divinity Bulletin* 29, no. 4 (Winter 2001): 14-17; "A Garland of Talking Heads for the Goddess: Some Autobiographical and Psychoanalytic Reflections on the Western Kali," in *Is the Goddess a Feminist? The Politics of South Asian Goddesses*, ed. Alf Hiltebeitel and Kathleen Erndl (New York: New York University Press, 2000); "Pale Plausibilities," preface to the second edition of *Kali's Child* (1998); "Mystical Homoeroticism, Reductionism and the Reality of Censorship: A Reply to Gerald James Larson," *Journal of the American Academy of Religion* 66, no. 3 (1998): 627-635. Various portions of my *Roads of Excess, Palaces of Wisdom: Eroticism and Reflexivity in the Study of Mysticism* (Chicago: University of Chicago Press, 2001), particularly the autobiographical essays, can also be read as implicit reflections on the controversy.

23. See Elliot Wolfson, "Beyond Good and Evil: Hypernomianism, Transmorality, and Kabbalistic Ethics," in *Crossing Boundaries: Essays on the Ethical Status of Mysticism*, ed. G. William Barnard and Jeffrey J. Kripal (New York: Seven Bridges Press, 2002): 103-156.

24. Technically speaking, Ramakrishna was not his birth name, but it is the name by which he was known in his own adult life and in subsequent generations.

25. Mahendranath Gupta, *Srisriramakrishnakathamrita*, 31st ed., 5 vols. (Calcutta: Kathamrita Bhavana, 1987), 5:140. This five-volume text, known to Bengalis simply as the *Kathamrita*, or *Nectar Talk*, is based on diary notes that Gupta kept between 1882 and 1886. Its thirteen hundred pages constitute our best historical source for Ramakrishna's mature teachings. I will cite it henceforth as KA, followed by the volume and page number, in the body of the text, thus: KA 5:140.

26. "Gobinda" (Skt. Govinda) is a name for Krishna. See Ram Chandra Datta, *Srisriramakrishna Paramahamsadever Jivanavrittanta*, 5th ed. (Calcutta: Jogodyan, Kakurgachi, 1935), 54; henceforth cited as JV. In Datta's account, the man's name is Gobinda Das. As for his conversion to Islam, "We cannot say how far he followed its social manners and customs" (Swami Saradananda, *Srisriramakrishnalilaprasanga* [Calcutta: Udbodhan Karjalay, 1986], 2.16.9 [bk. 2, chap. 16, sec. 9]; henceforth cited as LP).

27. The first appearance of the expression in print was in a local English newspaper: "A Hindu Saint," *Indian Mirror*, March 28, 1875.

28. KA 2:22; 2:94-95; 3:40; 4:170; 5:82; 5:86; 5:92; 5:124. Shaktas can also be bigoted (KA 5:73). This attitude was shared by Ramakrishna's disciples. Saradananda, for example, describes the Vaishnavas as "fault-finders" (LP 4.3.39) and "of low-caste" (LP 4.3.32).

29. For Ramakrishna's criticism of Christianity's excessive concern with sin, see KA 1:45-46; 1:153; 5:11; 5:111; 5:173. For his criticism of the Vaishnava fixation on sin, see KA 4:166; 5:22; 5:43.

30. For a detailed study of Ramakrishna's embrace of this Tantric ontology, see Jeffrey J. Kripal, "Kali on Top of Siva: Tantra and Vedanta in Ramakrishna's Teachings and Mystical Experiences," in *Kali's Child*, chap. 3.

31. It is common these days to read in poststructuralist scholarship that the categories of "experience" or "mystical experience" are modern psychological constructions and as such reflect primarily modern anxieties about the self, about the

collapse of traditional authority, and about the need for an alternative locus of truth. There is some validity to this argument, but if we want to see, as I do, the relationship of Sri Ramakrishna and Swami Vivekananda as representing roughly the Hindu tradition's passage from a premodern worldview to a modern one, we must also admit that there is more than a little of the premodern in the modern, and that "experience" is a perfectly fine term to describe the centerpiece of Ramakrishna's traditional teachings. The constructionist case, in other words, although otherwise valuable, is also overstated and itself needs to be deconstructed as flowing from a modern relativist epistemology that is simply not shared by much of mystical literature, the Bengali *Kathamrita* included.

32. For a summary of the critical literature on the relationship between traditional Advaita Vedanta and Vivekananda's social ethics, see Kripal, "Seeing Inside and Outside the Goddess: The Mystical and the Ethical in the Teachings of Ramakrishna and Vivekananda," in Barnard and Kripal, *Crossing Boundaries*, 230–264.

33. Quoted in Shashibhusan Dasgupta, *Bharater Shakti-sadhana o Shakti Sahitya* (Calcutta: Sahitya Samsad, 1985), 264.

34. Jadunath Sinha, *The Cult of Shakti: Rama Prasada's Devotional Songs* (Calcutta: Jadunath Sinha Foundation, 1981), no. 139.

35. The expression is usually quoted in its more complete form, *yata-mata-tata-patha* ("as one's perspective, so one's path"). In the *Kathamrita*, however, Ramakrishna usually uses his shorter version, *mata-patha* (KA 2:143; 3:41; 3:144; 4:135; 5:21; 5:39; 5:161; 5:211).

36. LP 4.4.47; 4.4.50; 4.4.54.

37. "Black forms blend": Sinha, *The Cult of Shakti*, no. 170.

38. Satyacharan Mitra, *Sri Ramakrishna Paramahamsa—Jivana o Upadesha* (Calcutta: Great Indian Press, 1897), 169; henceforth cited as JU.

39. Mitra's clear preference for a Tantric reading of Ramakrishna is most likely due, among other things, to his primary oral source for the biography: a certain Damaru Mahimcandra Nakulabadhut, a "special friend of Ramakrishna" whom Mitra describes as a Tantrika. "Half this book I wrote listening to him" (JU ii).

40. The canonical biographers and even most of the later scholarship have thus more or less ignored Shakta texts like Mitra's, which will focus much of my discussion here. A recent happy exception is Rajagopal Chattapadhyaya, *Sriramakrishna: Harano Katha* [Sri Ramakrishna: Lost Conversations] (Calcutta: Sribalaram Prakashani, 2003).

41. This woman, for example, was deeply offended when Ramakrishna ate Kali's ritual offering, and she stopped coming to see him (KA 5:92).

42. "If Raja Ram Mohun Roy would not have come, we wouldn't have such a sweet Ramakrishna-*bhava*" (JU 82).

43. See also JU 88–89. For Keshab's experiments with non-Hindu religious traditions, see David Kopf, *The Brahmo Samaj and the Shaping of the Modern Indian Mind* (Princeton: Princeton University Press, 1979), chap. 9.

44. Kopf, *Brahmo Samaj*, 267, 281–286.

45. Sedgwick, *Against the Modern World*, 24. Sedgwick describes Steuco as "a Vatican librarian and Christian Platonist, author of *De perenni philosophia* [Concerning the Perennial Philosophy], 1540, dedicated to Pope Paul III" (*Against the Modern World*, 274n11).

46. Ibid., 41.

47. Ibid., 41–42.

48. I am indebted to Mark Sedgwick and especially Bryan Rennie for this line of thought. Rennie delivered an essay entitled "Mircea Eliade: A Secular Mystic in the History of Religions?" for a conference Elliot Wolfson and I codirected at New York University.

49. Friedrich Max Müller, *Râmakrishna: His Life and Sayings* (London: Longmans, 1898).

50. For this remarkable story and an in-depth analysis, see William B. Parsons, *The Enigma of the Oceanic Feeling: Revisioning the Psychoanalytic Theory of Mysticism* (New York: Oxford University Press, 1999).

51. See Kripal, *Roads of Excess*.

52. Steven M. Wasserstrom, *Religion after Religion: Gershom Scholem, Mircea Eliade, and Henry Corbin at Eranos* (Princeton: Princeton University Press, 1999).

53. Mircea Eliade, "The Secret of Dr. Honigberger," in *Two Strange Tales* (New York: Herder and Herder, 1970; reprint, Boston: Shambhala, 1986). For a fuller exposition of Eliade's Tantric mysticism, see Kripal, "'The Visitation of the Stranger': On Some Mystical Dimensions of the History of Religions," *CrossCurrents* 49, no. 3 (Fall 1999): 367–386.

54. Moshe Idel, *Kabbalah: New Perspectives* (New Haven: Yale University Press, 1988), 12. See also Joseph Dan, "Gershom Scholem: Mystiker oder Geschichtsschreiber des Mystischen?" in *Gershom Scholem Zwischen den Disziplinen*, ed. Peter Schäfer and Gary Smith (Frankfurt au Main: Suhrkamp, 1989).

55. See Scholem's speech "My Way to Kabbalah (1974)," in *On the Possibility of Jewish Mysticism in Our Time and Other Essays*, ed. Avraham Shapira, trans. Jonathan Chipman (Philadelphia: Jewish Publication Society, 1997), 20–24.

56. Quoted in David Biale, *Gershom Scholem: Kabbalah and Counter-history* (Cambridge, Mass.: Harvard University Press, 1982), 32.

57. Biale, *Gershom Scholem*, 32.

58. Discussed in Wasserstrom, *Religion after Religion*, 146.

59. See Daniel Gold, *Aesthetics and Analysis in Writing on Religion: Modern Fascinations* (Berkeley: University of California Press, 2003).

60. Wouter J. Hanegraaff, *New Age Religion and Western Culture: Esotericism in the Mirror of Secular Thought* (Albany, N.Y.: SUNY Press, 1998).

61. Leigh Eric Schmidt, "The Making of Modern 'Mysticism,'" *Journal of the American Academy of Religion* 71, no. 2 (2003): 273–302.

62. Michel de Certeau, "Mysticism," trans. Marsanne Brammer, *Diacritics* 22, no. 2 (Summer 1992): 11–25.

63. Louis Bouyer, "Mysticism: An Essay on the History of the Word," in *Understanding Mysticism*, ed. Richard Woods (Garden City, N.Y.: Image Books, 1980), 42–55.

64. I am indebted to Don Cupitt for this striking thesis. See his *Mysticism after Modernity* (Malden, Mass.: Blackwell, 1998).

65. Many scholarly and popular uses of the word *mysticism* come very close indeed. Robert K. C. Forman's notions of a "pure consciousness event" underlying all cultural expressions of the mystical, for example, is near to Ramakrishna's understanding of *brahman* as *saccidananda*, or "being-consciousness-bliss." See Forman's *The Problem of Pure Consciousness: Mysticism and Philosophy* (New York: Oxford University Press, 1990).

66. Cupitt, *Mysticism after Modernity*, 120.

67. See, for instance, David V. Erdman, *Blake: Prophet against Empire* (Princeton: Princeton University Press, 1954); and Edward Palmer Thompson, *Witness against the Beast: William Blake and the Moral Law* (New York: New Press, 1993).

68. Walter H. Capps, *Religious Studies: The Making of a Discipline* (Minneapolis, MN: Fortress, 1995), 342.

69. For an eloquent editorial mapping of this debate, see Russell McCutcheon, ed., *The Insider/Outsider Problem in the Study of Religion: A Reader* (London: Cassell, 1999).

70. For a collection of primary sources from this American story and a series of insightful introductory essays, see Thomas A. Tweed and Stephen Prothero, *Asian Religions in America: A Documentary History* (New York: Oxford University Press, 1999).

71. Allan Hunt Badiner, ed., *Zig Zag Zen: Buddhism and Psychedelics* (San Francisco: Chronicle Books, 2002). For an eloquent discussion of this cultural pattern and another story of religious hypocrisy and institutional denial, see Rick Strassman, *DMT: The Spirit Molecule* (Rochester, Vt.: Park Street Press, 2001), esp. chap. 20, "Stepping on Holy Toes."

72. An analogous expression—"the religion of no religion"—was employed by the German comparativist of religion Frederic Spiegelberg to describe and celebrate a similar mystical denial of difference and local custom. See his *The Religion of No-Religion* (Stanford, Calif.: Delkin, 1948).

73. I have written at length about this same issue and its twentieth-century history in "Debating the Mystical as the Ethical: An Indological Map," in Barnard and Kripal, *Crossing Boundaries*.

74. For a more recent study that serves to confirm this same point, see Sedgwick, *Against the Modern World*.

75. I am in agreement with Wasserstrom and others who have criticized the Eliadean tradition (scholars such as Timothy Fitzgerald, Bruce Lincoln, Russell McCutcheon, Hans Penner, J. Z. Smith, Ivan Strenski, and Donald Wiebe) for its failure to be more suspicious of its subjects of study.

76. The consistency of Meddeb's historical invocation of the mystical within Islam to answer the present ignorances and violences of Islamic fundamentalism is truly remarkable. Consider, for example, the following passages: 13, 23, 27, 39–40, 44–45, 51, 55, 59–60, 129–130 (Abdelwahab Meddeb, *The Malady of Islam* [New York: Basic Books, 2003]). He is also perfectly aware of the intimate organic, even physiological, link between sensuality and cultural creativity (see especially chap. 23).

77. Ibid., 129, 130. Ibn al-'Arabi, in other words, advanced what is in many respects the same comparative mystics that Ramakrishna would participate in six hundred years later.

78. See especially Michael Lerner, *Spirit Matters* (Charlottesville, Va.: Hampton Roads, 2000). Perhaps even more relevant is Lerner's latest book, *The Left Hand of God: Taking Back Our Country from the Religious Right* (New York: HarperSanFrancisco, 2006). Lerner's double criticism of both the "faith"-based politics of the Religious Right (for its unchecked capitalism, disregard for the poor and marginalized, and global imperialism) and the pure "reason" of secular liberalism (for its failure to engage the religious needs and natures of human beings) leads him to a mystically inclined "Left-Hand-of-God worldview" that embraces secular people, values diversity, and works toward social justice in all its forms. Such a vision of a

new or renewed left-handed spirituality often reads like a political realization of the kinds of "gnosis" I am celebrating here in a more theoretical mode.

79. William D. Davidson and Joseph V. Montville, "Foreign Policy according to Freud," *Foreign Policy* (Winter 1981–1982).

80. Gilles Quispel, ed., *Gnosis: De derde component van de Europese cultuurtraditie* (Utrecht: HES, 1988), 9. Wouter Hanegraaff proposed both this idea and the reference.

81. Paul Tillich, *The Future of Religions*, ed. Jerald Brauer (New York: Harper and Row, 1966).

82. Elaine Pagels, *Beyond Belief: The Secret Gospel of Thomas* (New York: Random House, 2003), 96, 128.

83. This colleague was D. N. Jha, harassed for his work on beef eating in ancient India, *The Myth of the Holy Cow* (London: Verso, 2002). See Emily Eakin, "Holy Cow a Myth? An Indian Finds the Kick Is Real," *New York Times*, August 17, 2002. It is common knowledge, among historians at least, that ancient Indians ate beef.

84. I would like to thank Karen Harris, Jeffrey Perl, Joseph Prabhu, and Mark Sedgwick for their critical readings, moral support, and substantive suggestions with this essay.

Interlude

1. As my third epigraph signals, the contemporary scholar whom I consider to be the master of the kinds of dialectical gnostic thinking I am proposing here is Elliot Wolfson. Beginning with historically unrelated materials (medieval Kabbalah and nineteenth-century Shakta Tantra), Wolfson and I came to identical comparative positions on the gender, ascetic, and sexual dynamics of two traditional forms of male erotic spirituality. I also consider his philosophical insights into the dialectics of kabbalistic poetics and hermeneutics to be more or less identical to what I am trying to express here in a less learned key. For a full philosophical analysis of my *logoi mystikoi*, then, I can quite reasonably say: "Read Elliot Wolfson." This does not mean, of course, that Wolfson would agree with everything I have written here, or anywhere else.

2. As will become apparent below in chap. 4, I am quite willing to imagine human potentials extending well beyond the assumed parameters of death and the egoic personality. Put simply, this *logos mystikos* neither requires nor precludes the possibility of some sort of postmortem survival, spiritual communication with departed or discarnate spirits, reincarnation, or totemic spirits, as we witness, for example, in some radical ethnographies. All of these states, however, remain for me "human." Admittedly, my categories are quivering under immense metaphysical pressure here. So be it.

3. For a fascinating expression of a similar kind of academic Platonism, see Erwin R. Goodenough, "The Mystical Value of Scholarship," *Crozer Quarterly* 22 (1945): 221–225. This is the earliest essay of which I am aware that makes a case similar to my own with respect to professional scholarship. My thanks to Steven Wasserstrom for pointing it out.

4. For the original Sufi deployment of this trope, see William C. Chittick, "The Paradox of the Veil in Sufism," in *Rending the Veil: Concealment and Secrecy in the His-*

tory of Religions, ed. Elliot R. Wolfson (New York: Seven Bridges Press, 1999), 59–85. Chittick and the Sufis, of course, are not responsible for my redeployment of the paradox of the veil here.

5. Both Jung and Eliade in turn were drawing on the fifteenth-century German cardinal and theologian Nicholas of Cusa (c. 1401–1464) and his *De docta ignorantia* (1439–1440). For a helpful discussion of this theme in Eliade's corpus, see Bryan Rennie, *Reconstructing Eliade: Making Sense of Religion* (Albany, N.Y.: SUNY Press, 1996), chap. 4.

6. The zero, or 0, is also important, particularly for mystical thought that dwells so consistently on the nothing, emptiness, and various forms of annihilation. Not surprisingly perhaps, this all-important mathematical abstraction was first invented in post-Buddhist India as a manifestation of the *shunya*, the "empty" or the "nothing."

7. Elliot R. Wolfson, *Language, Eros, Being: Kabbalistic Hermeneutics and Poetic Imagination* (New York: Fordham University Press, 2005), 261.

8. For more on Eliade's debt to Tantra, see my " 'The Visitation of the Stranger': On Some Mystical Dimensions of the History of Religions," *CrossCurrents* 49, no. 3 (Fall 1999): 367–386. Jung too found in Indian Tantra what he called "important parallels" to his depth psychology, "especially with *kundalini* yoga and the symbolism of tantric yoga" ("Yoga and the West," in *The Collected Works of C. G. Jung*, Bollingen Series, no. 20, vol. 11 [Princeton: Princeton University Press, 1989], 537).

Chapter Four

1. I dedicate this essay to three real X-Men: Jorge Ferrer, who sent me his Alex Ross comics in order to tempt me back to our shared childhood fantasies; William Parsons, who graciously sold me his *X-Men* #1 in order to help empower my creative obsessions; and Michael Murphy, whose experience of and conviction in the *siddhis*, or supernormal powers, inspired him to create, along with Richard Price, his own Westchester Academy forty-five years ago.

2. Stan Lee discusses the connotations of the term for him and the prefeminist context in his *Son of Origins of Marvel Comics* (New York: Simon and Schuster, 1975), 16.

3. My thanks to John Stroup, historian of Reformation thought, master of German theology, and academic comedian extraordinaire.

4. I am indebted to Roger Shattuck and Sissela Bok for much of my thinking here. See Sissela Bok, *Secrets: On the Ethics of Concealment and Revelation* (New York: Vintage Books, 1983/1989); and Roger Shattuck, *Forbidden Knowledge: From Prometheus to Pornography* (San Diego: Harcourt, Brace and Company, 1996).

5. Arnold van Gennep, *Rites de Passage* (Paris, 1909).

6. Victor Turner, *The Ritual Process: Structure and Anti-structure* (Chicago: University of Chicago Press, 1969).

7. The literature on the *maladie initiatique* of the traditional shaman is immense. Perhaps still the best place to start is Mircea Eliade's classic study *Shamanism: Archaic Techniques of Ecstasy* (Princeton: Princeton University Press, 1964). See especially chap. 1, "General Considerations. Recruiting Methods. Shamanism and Mystical Vocation."

8. Robert Segal has collected and commented on some of the foundational texts of this study in *In Quest of the Hero* (Princeton: Princeton University Press, 1990).

Campbell's heavily psychoanalytic discussion occurs in his *The Hero with a Thousand Faces* (Princeton: Princeton University Press, 1949).

9. *The Rough Guide to Superheroes* (New York: Penguin, 2004), 9.

10. See David D. Gilmore, *Manhood in the Making: Cultural Concepts of Masculinity* (New Haven: Yale University Press, 1990), particularly chap. 1, "The Manhood Puzzle."

11. I am drawing here on Bradford W. Wright's marvelous *Comic Book Nation: The Transformation of Youth Culture in America* (Baltimore: Johns Hopkins University Press, 2001). On this point, Wright is drawing on Jules Feiffer, a Superman fan, who suspected in print that Batman fans have "healthier egos" than Superman fans (quoted in ibid., 297, n 43).

12. Gerard Jones, *Men of Tomorrow: Geeks, Gangsters and the Birth of the Comic Book* (New York: Basic Books, 2004).

13. Art Spiegelman and Chip Kidd, *Jack Cole and Plastic Man: Forms Stretched to Their Limits!* (New York: DC Comics, 2001).

14. *The Rough Guide to Superheroes*, 268.

15. The movie changes the original comic book script, which has Peter Parker devising little web-spinning devices that he then wears around his wrists. The fact that the movie eliminates the technology and has the white webs spurting directly from Peter's body (through the manipulation of his fingers and hand, no less) certainly supports a sexual (really autoerotic) reading of the cinematic retelling.

16. *X2: X-Men United* (Twentieth-Century Fox, 2003), scene 18, "The Drake Home."

17. Quoted in *The Rough Guide to Superheroes*, 18.

18. Frederic Wertham, M.D., *Seduction of the Innocent* (New York: Rinhehart, 1954). Wertham is, if you will, the Irenaeus of the modern comic book world, who wrote a comic book equivalent to the heresiologist's *Against the Heresies*, a kind of *Against the Comics*.

19. A bit of humorous self-confession here. My first published text was in fact a letter to the editor I sent to a comic book newspaper in the early 1970s, protesting all of the eroticized comic art that appeared in its pages. I was probably eleven or twelve and obviously fighting hard against the inevitable. I was also, however, correctly seeing something. The present adult essay now corrects and expands upon that original adolescent letter, which happily I have lost (or at least claim to have lost).

20. It is important to note that Wertham's criticisms, although excessive and simplistic, were also often insightful and correct. He also, for example, convincingly demonstrated how the comics of the 1940s and 1950s were filled with racist, xenophobic, anti-Semitic, sadistic, and misogynistic tropes. He also cleverly showed how such things as the shadows of a carefully drawn shoulder muscle looked very much like a woman's pubic region. Wright does a fine job of presenting a complex, excessive, but basically well-meaning Wertham, who later deeply regretted that his name had become associated with censorship (see Wright, *Comic Book Nation*, 92-108, 157-179).

21. See Bill Boichel, "Batman: Commodity as Myth," and Andy Medhurst, "Batman, Deviance and Camp," in *The Many Lives of the Batman: Critical Approaches to a Superhero and His Media,* ed. Robert A. Pearson and William Uricchio (New York: Routledge, 1991).

22. *The Rough Guide to Superheroes*, 217.

23. *Astonishing X-Men* #2 (Marvel Comics, August 2004), 3.

24. Rudolf Otto, *The Idea of the Holy: An Inquiry into the Non-rational Factor in the Idea of the Divine and Its Relation to the Rational* (1923; reprint, London: Oxford University Press, 1969).

25. Alexander Irwin, *Saints of the Impossible: Bataille, Weil, and the Politics of the Sacred* (Minneapolis: University of Minnesota Press, 2002), xxiii, quoting Roger Caillois on Durkheim.

26. Peter Berger, *The Sacred Canopy: Elements of a Sociological Theory of Religion* (Garden City, N.Y.: Anchor Books, 1969), 3, 13.

27. Peter Berger, *Rumors of Angels* (New York: Anchor Books, 1970).

28. My thanks to my colleague Richard Smith for sharing this proverb with me.

29. Joachim Kohler, *Zarathustra's Secret: The Interior Life of Friedrich Nietzsche*, trans. Ronald Taylor (New Haven: Yale University Press, 2002).

30. I am drawing here on Charles Tart's notion of state-specific sciences. See Charles Tart, "State-Specific Sciences," *Science* 176 (1972): 1203–1210.

31. *Journey Into Mystery* #83 (Marvel Comics, August 1962).

32. Nietzsche's *Twilight of the Idols* was subtitled *or How to Philosophize with a Hammer*.

33. Numerous examples could be cited here. For a theorization of this phenomenon, see David E. Young and Jean-Guy Goulet, eds., *Being Changed by Cross-Cultural Encounters: The Anthropology of Extraordinary Experience* (Peterborough, Ont.: Broadview Press, 1994).

34. *Amazing Adult Fantasy* #14 (Marvel Comics, 1962), Stan Lee, writer, Steve Ditko, artist, Matt Webb, colorist; reprinted in *X-Men Rarities* (New York: Marvel Comics, 1995).

35. The first occurrence of this expression appears to be *X-Men* #96 (Marvel Comics, October 1975).

36. This story was originally told by Dr. Wiltse himself in *St. Louis Medical and Surgical Journal* (November 1889) and *Mid-continental Review* (February 1990). It was later retold in F. W. H. Myers' *Human Personality and Its Survival of Bodily Death* (1903), from which I take it in its most recent abridged version (Charlottesville, Va.: Hampton Roads, 2001), 171–176.

37. Herbert Thurston, S.J., *The Physical Phenomena of Mysticism*, ed. J. H. Crehan, S.J. (London: Burns Oates, 1952), 312.

38. Gardner Murphy and Robert O. Ballou, eds., *William James on Psychical Research* (New York: Viking Press, 1960).

39. Ernest Jones, M.D., *The Life and Work of Sigmund Freud*, 3 vols. (New York: Basic Books, 1957). See vol. 2, chap. 14, "Occultism."

40. Ibid., 2:381.

41. Ibid., 2:392.

42. Ibid., 2:394.

43. Stevenson's corpus is immense. The best single introduction to and summary of his work is Jim B. Tucker, *Life before Life: A Scientific Investigation of Children's Memories of Previous Lives* (New York: St. Martin's Press, 2005). Serious readers of this research, however, should consult his *Cases of the Reincarnation Type*, 4 vols. (Charlottesville: University Press of Virginia, 1983).

44. Ian Stevenson, *Reincarnation and Biology: A Contribution to the Etiology of Birthmarks and Birth Defects* (Westport, Conn.: Praeger Publishers, 1997). An abridged version of this work has also been published: *Where Reincarnation and Biology Intersect* (Westport, Conn.: Praeger, 1997). A relatively up-to-date bibliography of Stevenson's works can be found in the latter volume.

45. Quoted in Tucker, *Life before Life*, 20.

46. See especially Michael Murphy's quantum mysticism as expressed in the novel *Jacob Atabet: A Speculative Fiction* (Los Angeles: Jeremy P. Tarcher, 1977).

47. Michael Murphy, *The Future of the Body: Explorations into the Further Evolution of Human Nature* (New York: G. P. Putnam's Sons, 1992), 211–213, "Superordinary Powers in Fantasy Literature, Cartoons, Movies, and Science Fiction."

48. For a full study of Murphy's evolutionary mysticism in the context of Esalen's history, see my *Esalen: America and the Religion of No Religion* (Chicago: University of Chicago Press, forthcoming). Portions of the present essay were originally written as an (unpublished) appendix to that volume, in which I argued that what the East Coast as the New York comic industry imagined as a genre of gnostic fiction in the 1960s and 1970s the West Coast, at the same time, enacted and lived out as the human potential movement—an American mythology effectively matched by an American mysticism.

49. Jess Byron Hollenback, *Mysticism: Experience, Response, and Empowerment* (University Park, Pa.: Pennsylvania State University Press, 1996), viii.

50. Ibid., 21. Such a position "challenges the assumption that the imagination and the creations of the human imagination (e.g., religions) operate only to hinder an accurate perception of reality by creating a tissue of pleasing illusion that substitutes for an accurate knowledge of how things really are" (ibid., 22). This does not mean, of course, that the mythologies of religion are literally true, only that the empowered imagination can never work in a vacuum. This is why mystical experiences almost always confirm the local mythologies (ibid., 291).

51. Ibid., 286.

52. Ibid., 180. This is not to say clairvoyance and daydreaming are the same; it is the energetic event of empowerment that sets the two apart.

53. Ibid., 296.

54. Early anthropologists such as Andrew Lang commented on psychical phenomena, and it is not at all unusual to read of later ethnographers encountering spirits, totems, deities, and other imaginal realities in the field, or, more radically still, to find them arguing for some sort of ontological status for these presences (see, e.g., Edith Turner, "The Reality of Spirits," *ReVision* 15, no. 1 [1992]: 28–32). The Italian historian of religions Ernesto De Martino is a good example of an author who has taken the topic of shamanic and magical powers seriously (see his *Primitive Magic: The Psychic Powers of Shamans and Sorcerers* [1972; reprint, Bridport, Great Britain: Prism Press, 1988]).

55. Mircea Eliade, "Folklore as an Instrument of Knowledge," unpublished translation by Mac Linscott Ricketts. My thanks to Mac Ricketts and Bryan Rennie for sharing this with me. The essay originally appeared as "Folklorul ca instrument de cunoaştere," *Revista Fundaşmilor Regale* 4, no. 4 (April 19, 1937): 137–152.

56. Toward the end of the essay, Eliade even suggests, as if out of nowhere, the possibility of the power of invisibility. I suspect he was invoking an autobiograph-

ical event or fantasy here, as he would later explore this same superpower in one of his occult novellas, "The Secret of Dr. Honigberger,", whose central character looks a great deal like Eliade himself. See Mircea Eliade, *Two Strange Tales* (Boston: Shambalah, 1986).

57. Richard Shweder, *Thinking through Cultures: Expeditions in Cultural Psychology* (Cambridge, Mass.: Harvard University Press, 1991), 61.

58. Fred M. Frohock, *Lives of the Psychics: The Shared Worlds of Science and Mysticism* (Chicago: University of Chicago Press, 2000), 70–71.

59. I should also point out that the individualist and empowering nature of the "superpower" conflicts with most traditional religious systems, which rely on elaborate hierarchies and mechanisms of mediation that tend to suppress and distrust such an individualism. It is certainly no accident that most orthodox religions have treated the psychical and the occult with, at best, tolerant disregard and, at worst, actual persecution. There are, of course, exceptions, but one wonders if the almost absolute scholarly neglect of this material is not reproducing the traditional religious neglect. Once again, what we seem to have here is a kind of gnosis beyond both faith and reason.

60. See especially McCutcheon's "A Default of Critical Intelligence? The Scholar of Religion as Public Intellectual," in *Critics Not Caretakers: Redescribing the Public Study of Religion* (Albany, N.Y.: SUNY Press, 2001), chap. 8.

61. Wright, *Comic Book Nation*, 180.

62. Ibid., x.

63. Ibid., 287.

64. Frank Miller, *9-11*, 1:64–65; quoted in Wright, *Comic Book Nation*, 289.

65. Wright, *Comic Book Nation*, 293.

66. Shweder, *Thinking through Cultures*, 68–69.

67. Ibid., 69.

68. Ludwig Feuerbach, *The Essence of Christianity*, trans. George Eliot (Amherst, N.Y.: Prometheus Books, 1989), 23.

Conclusion

1. William B. Parsons, *The Enigma of the Oceanic Feeling: Revisioning the Psychoanalytic Study of Mysticism* (New York: Oxford University Press, 1999).

2. "But I do not aspire to anything more, for myself, other than repose and effacement, unlimited and total" (Rolland to Freud; May 3, 1931, in Parsons, *The Enigma*, 178; cf. 174); "I myself do not believe in one personal God" (Romain Rolland, *The Life of Ramakrishna*, 12th ed. [Calcutta: Advaita Ashrama, 1986], 6).

3. Rolland to Freud, December 5, 1927, in Parsons, *The Enigma*, 173–174.

4. Freud to Rolland, January 19, 1930, in Parsons, *The Enigma*, 176–177.

5. Parsons, *The Enigma*, 44–52.

6. Sigmund Freud, *New Introductory Lectures on Psycho-analysis*, in *The Standard Edition of the Complete Psychological Works of Sigmund Freud*, ed. James Strachey (London: Hogarth Press, 1975), 22:79–80.

7. David Bakan, *Sigmund Freud and the Jewish Mystical Tradition* (Boston: Beacon Press, 1958). For a later and in many ways more sophisticated return to this intuition that "Kabbalah manifests many prefigurations of Freudian doctrine," see Harold Bloom, *Kabbalah and Criticism* (New York: Continuum, 1993), 43.

8. Interestingly, this is decidedly less so with many of the minor, heterodox, or "heretical" religions, which often break from their orthodox source traditions on partly sexual or gendered grounds. There appears, in other words, to be some structural relationship between religious heterodoxy and gender experimentation and religious orthodoxy and gender oppression, respectively.

9. "In its origin, function, and relation to sexual love," wrote Freud, "the 'Eros' of the philosopher Plato coincides exactly with the love-force, the libido of psycho-analysis" (*Group Psychology and the Analysis of the Ego*, in *The Standard Edition*, 18:91). A very similar line appeared one year earlier, in his 1920 preface to the fourth edition of *Three Essays on the Theory of Sexuality* (*The Standard Edition*, 7:134).

10. Rudolf Otto, *The Idea of the Holy: An Inquiry into the Non-rational Factor in the Idea of the Divine and Its Relation to the Rational* (1923; reprint, London: Oxford University Press, 1969), 8.

11. Patrick Olivelle has convincingly argued that the Vedic origins of *ananda* lie in the ecstatic experience of orgasm and phallic pleasure in "Orgasmic Rapture and Divine Ecstasy: The Semantic History of Ananda," *Journal of Indian Philosophy* 25 (1997): 153–180.

12. "Both cognitive states and emotional states have the same basic nature, clear light, and thus are not separated off from each other in separate universes; both have luminosity as their core and exist within a continuum. . . . From this per-spective, orgasmic pleasure is a type of mind, and the state of orgasm is even uti-lized to gain realization of the clear light nature of basic mind which is often com-pared to the sky" (Jeffrey Hopkins, *Sex, Orgasm, and the Mind of Clear Light: The Sixty-four Arts of Gay Male Love* [Berkeley: North Atlantic Books, 1998], 72).

13. G. William Barnard and Jeffrey J. Kripal, eds., *Crossing Boundaries: Essays on the Ethical Status of Mysticism* (New York: Seven Bridges Press, 2002).

14. Bloom would no doubt want to distance himself from the word "mystical," which he distinguishes from the term "Gnostic" for the former's common conser-vatism: "Mysticism, though it comes in many kinds, by no means opposes itself to faith; perhaps indeed it is the most intense form of faith." "Gnosis," on the other hand, "grants you acquaintance with a God unknown to, and remote from, this world, a God in exile from a false creation that, in itself, constituted a fall" (Harold Bloom, *Omens of Millenium: The Gnosis of Angels, Dreams, and Resurrection* [New York: Riverhead Books, 1996], 183).

15. The situation is quite different in South Asia, where in many contexts some form of gnosis (*jnana, vijnana, prajna,* etc.) is often both normative and even occa-sionally orthodox.

16. Bloom, *Omens of Millennium*, 15; subsequent page references are given in the text.

17. For more on penises (and vaginas) in the history of religions, see my "Phal-lus and Vagina," in *The Encyclopedia of Religion*, 2nd ed., ed. Lindsay Jones (New York: Macmillan, 2004).

18. Gospel of Philip, CGL 183 (cf. 179).

19. For example, both the implied gender essentialism and normative heterosex-uality of the passage from the Gospel of Philip render it problematic for any con-temporary realization. I wonder, though, about the gnostic angelologies of sexual-ity, in which one is attracted not only to the physical person but to his or her abiding angel. Even if we restrict ourselves to a gender binarism, such an erotic angelology

could theoretically produce a male-in-a-male or female-in-a-male or female-in-a-female or male-in-a-female and thus any number of gender identities and sexual orientations. Do such possibilities represent an early awareness and theorization of what we today call gender and sexual orientation? It is just a thought.

The Fruit of the Tree

1. Aldous Huxley, *"The Doors of Perception" and "Heaven and Hell"* (1954; reprint, New York: Harper and Row, 1963), 20.

The Fruit of the Tree;
or, My Gnostic Library before I Have to Bury It (Again)

THERE IS A WONDERFUL SCENE in Aldous Huxley's *The Doors of Perception* in which Huxley, now tripping on mescaline, enters a library and sees that the books are all glowing "with living light," but that in some "the glory" is "more manifest than others."[1] I have never taken mescaline, but I certainly have a library, and it often seems to me that certain books glow with a similar living light, as if they were especially "mind manifesting" (*psyche-delic*).

It is those same glowing tomes I have taken off the shelf to dwell with in these four gnostic meditations. Here, then, is a very select list of this modern gnostic library, recorded for posterity before it is buried again (or I am, like that Nag Hammadi skeleton in the sand).

Collections

BINDMAN, DAVID, general ed., *William Blake: The Illuminated Books* (Princeton: William Blake Trust and Princeton University Press, 1991). Six gorgeous volumes filled with learned introductions and elaborate notes on all of Blake's illuminated works.

ROBINSON, JAMES M., ed., *The Coptic Gnostic Library: A Complete Edition of the Nag Hammadi Codices* (Leiden: E. J. Brill, 1995). The definitive critical edition of the Nag Hammadi library in five volumes, with both the original Coptic and the English translations.

Monographs and Essays

ASSMAN, JAN, *Moses the Egyptian: The Memory of Egypt in Western Monotheism* (Cambridge, Mass.: Harvard University Press, 1997). Probably the most original and provocative of the genre on the structural violence and intolerance of monotheism, or what Assman calls "the Mosaic distinction" and criticizes via the transcultural logics of ancient polytheism, Renaissance esotericism, and Freud's *Moses and Monotheism*. Should be read alongside Delaney, *Abraham on Trial*, and Schwartz, *The Curse of Cain*.

BATAILLE, GEORGES, *Erotism: Death & Sensuality* (San Francisco: City Lights, 1986). A powerful study of the analogous experiences of sexuality, death, and mystical rapture in religious texts from around the world, with a special focus on Christian materials.

BERGER, PETER, *The Sacred Canopy: Elements of a Sociological Theory of Religion* (New York: Anchor Books, 1969). Still the best introduction to the social constructionism thesis that virtually everything human beings consider to be real and objective is in sociological fact a dialectical or hermeneutical fiction made plausible through language, culture, and social interaction. Religion thus becomes a sacred canopy, "an area of meaning carved out of a vast mass of meaninglessness, a small clearing of lucidity in a formless, dark, always ominous jungle" (23). Not for the faint of heart.

BOSWELL, JOHN, *Christianity, Social Tolerance, and Homosexuality: Gay People in Western Europe from the Beginning of the Christian Era to the Fourteenth Century* (Chicago: University of Chicago Press, 1980). One of the foundational texts for the study of homosexuality and religion. Should be read before Jordan, *The Silence of Sodom*.

CALDWELL, SARAH, *O Terrifying Mother: Sexuality, Violence and Worship of the Goddess Kali* (New Delhi: Oxford University Press, 1999). A beautiful example of the kinds of gnostic methodology that I am calling for here. Caldwell intertwines her field journals, personal history of sexual abuse, and five different theoretical complexes to explore the historical, erotic, transgendered, traumatic, and mystical dimensions of the goddess Kali within a Kerala art form. Should be read alongside Kripal, *Kali's Child*.

CAMPBELL, JUNE, *Traveller in Space: In Search of Female Identity in Tibetan Buddhism* (New York: George Braziller, 1996). A Lacanian and feminist reading of Tibetan Buddhism enriched by Campbell's own firsthand (and quite negative) experience of being the Tantric consort of a high-ranking lama, this book demonstrates the deep structural gender problems with this often-idealized monastic tradition.

CARROLL, MICHAEL, *The Cult of the Virgin Mary: Psychological Origins* (Princeton: Princeton University Press, 1986). A remarkable psychoanalytic study of Marian apparitions over the past four hundred years, locating the psychological source of such visions in traumatic family contexts and oedipal dynamics. Should be read with Davies, *Jesus the Healer*.

CLÉMENT, CATHERINE, *Syncope: The Philosophy of Rapture*, translated by Sally O'Driscoll and Deirdre M. Mahoney (Minneapolis: University of Minnesota Press, 1994). A series of fascinating essays relating French feminist philosophy, psychoanalysis, and Indian mystical thought, with a special focus on Tantra. Knowing.

COUNTRYMAN, L. WILLIAM, *Dirt, Greed and Sex: Sexual Ethics in the New Testament and Their Implications for Today* (Philadelphia: Fortress Press, 1989). An early and extensive study of purity codes and their systematic transgression within the New Testament.

DASGUPTA, SHASHIBHUSAN, *Obscure Religious Cults* (1946; reprint, Calcutta: Firma KLM Private, 1969). A foundational work of scholarship on the Tantric underpinnings of Bengali culture. A mine of sparkling linguistic gems and learning hidden beneath an unfortunate title.

DAVIES, STEVAN L., *Jesus the Healer: Possession, Trance, and the Origins of Christianity* (New York: Continuum, 1995). A powerful psychoanalytic study of Jesus's healing ministry arguing, in effect, that he tended primarily to victims of physical and sexual abuse; hence the common presence of dissociation as possession in these stories and Jesus's many antifamily teachings. Should be read with Carroll, *The Cult of the Virgin Mary*.

DECONICK, APRIL, "The Great Mystery of Marriage: Sex and Conception in Ancient Valentinian Traditions," *Vigiliae Christianae* 57 (2003): 307–342.

————, "The True Mysteries: Sacramentalism in the Gospel of Philip," *Vigiliae Christianae* 55 (2001): 225–261. These two essays constitute the strongest case yet for the sexual practices behind the gnostic "bridal chamber" sacrament. All of DeConick's work is important for its refusal to shy away from the sexual and for its insistence on the experiential and mystical roots of the early Christianities.

DELANEY, CAROL, *Abraham on Trial: The Social Legacy of Biblical Myth* (Princeton: Princeton University Press, 1998). Why do the three great monotheistic religions all locate the model of faith in a father's willingness to sacrifice his first-born son? Delaney sets out to answer this question.

DIMOCK, EDWARD C., JR., *The Place of the Hidden Moon: Erotic Mysticism in the Vaisnava-Sahajiya Cult of Bengal* (Chicago: University of Chicago Press, 1966). Technical textual scholarship raised to an art form and foundational for Bengali studies in the States. Should be read after Dasgupta, *Obscure Religious Cults*.

EILBERG-SCHWARTZ, HOWARD, *God's Phallus: And Other Problems for Men and Monotheism* (Boston: Beacon, 1994). Argues, among many other points, that God's symbolic maleness in ancient Judaism and Israel's corporate femaleness sets up a homosexual dilemma for those male leaders who come to represent this "bride" or "wife" of God. Should be read before Jennings, *Jacob's Wound*.

FAURE, BERNARD, *The Red Thread: Buddhist Approaches to Sexuality* (Princeton: Princeton University Press, 1998).

————, *The Power of Denial: Buddhism, Purity, and Gender* (Princeton: Princeton University Press, 2003). These two works by Faure, the first two in a projected series, constitute the state of the art in discussions of Buddhist sexualities.

FEUERBACH, LUDWIG, *The Essence of Christianity*, trans. George Eliot (Amherst, N.Y.: Prometheus Books, 1989). Originally published in 1841 as *Das Wesen des Christentums*, this is probably the real beginning of the modern study of religion and its gnostic insistence on withdrawing or "reducing" the projections of the Adam of Light back into human being, from which they all originally emanated or were "projected." Begin here.

JAMES, WILLIAM, *William James on Psychical Research*, ed. Gardner Murphy and Robert O. Ballou (New York: Viking Press, 1960). A collection of James's essays on his psychical researches that demonstrate his honest criticisms and his final conviction in both their epistemological value and of that "extreme slowness with which the ordinary academic and critical mind acknowledges facts to exist which present themselves as wild facts, with no stall or pigeonhole, or as facts which threaten to break up the accepted system" (27–28). Should be read alongside Myers, *Human Personality and Its Survival of Bodily Death*.

JENNINGS, THEODORE W., JR., *The Man Jesus Loved: Homoerotic Narratives from the New Testament* (Cleveland: Pilgrim Press, 2003).

————, *Jacob's Wound: Homoerotic Narrative in the Literature of Ancient Israel* (New York: Continuum, 2005). Together, these two works by Jennings constitute our most sophisticated, consistent and extensive homoerotic reading of the Bible.

JONES, ERNEST, M.D., "Occultism," in *The Life and Work of Sigmund Freud*, 3 vols. (New York: Basic Books, 1957), vol. 2, chap. 14. The locus classicus for a discussion of Freud's lifelong interest in the occult and repressed conviction in psychical phenomena by a close colleague and deep skeptic. Adventurous readers might also consult George Devereux, ed., *Psychoanalysis and the Occult* (New

York: International Universities Press, 1953); and J. Eisenbud, *Psi and Psychoanalysis* (New York: Grune and Stratton, 1970).

JORDAN, MARK, *The Silence of Sodom: Homosexuality in Modern Catholicism* (Chicago: University of Chicago Press, 2000). An astonishing analysis of the simultaneously homoerotic and homophobic structures of Catholicism. Should be read after Boswell, *Christianity, Social Tolerance, and Homosexuality*, and alongside Jennings, *The Man Jesus Loved*.

KEULS, EVA C., *The Reign of the Phallus: Sexual Politics in Ancient Athens* (Berkeley: University of California Press, 1985). An impressive and entertaining display of erudition on the Greek phallus with a focused feminist lens.

KRIPAL, JEFFREY J., *Kali's Child: The Mystical and the Erotic in the Life and Teachings of Ramakrishna* (Chicago: University of Chicago Press, 1995; 2nd ed., 1998). A homoerotic reading of an influential set of Bengali texts, censored in their English translations, as a means to explore the dialectics of the erotic and the mystical. Should be read alongside Caldwell, *O Terrifying Mother*, and after Dasgupta, *Obscure Religious Cults*, Dimock, *The Place of the Hidden Moon*, and O'Flaherty, *Siva*.
————, *Roads of Excess, Palaces of Wisdom: Eroticism and Reflexity in the Study of Mysticism* (Chicago: University of Chicago Press, 2001). Argues for the epistemological relevance of mystical experience in the works and lives of scholars of religion and announces the homoerotic : heteroerotic :: orthodox : heterodox thesis.

MURRAY, STEPHEN O., and WILL ROSCOE, eds., *Islamic Homosexualities: Culture, History, and Literature* (New York: New York University Press, 1997). A sophisticated collection of essays on homosexualities in the Islamic world, with a particular focus on the Sufi or mystical traditions.

MYERS, F. W. H., *Human Personality and Its Survival of Bodily Death*, 2 vols. (London: Longmans, Green, and Company, 1903). Difficult to categorize and all too easy to dismiss without reading through its hundreds of carefully documented and analyzed real-life accounts, most of them impossible to explain with any social scientific method or materialist philosophy of mind. Should be read alongside Ian Stevenson, *Cases of the Reincarnation Type*.

OBEYESEKERE, GANANATH, *The Work of Culture: Symbolic Transformation in Psychoanalysis and Anthropology* (Chicago: University of Chicago Press, 1990). The strongest and most eloquent case of which I am aware for the cross-cultural use of psychoanalysis, always with an openness to the visionary and the gnostic. Obeyesekere sees the symbolic forms of culture as complex products of the unconscious interacting with the social and historical fields. Should be read alongside Shweder, *Thinking Through Cultures*.

O'FLAHERTY, WENDY DONIGER, *Siva: The Erotic Ascetic* (London: Oxford University Press, 1973). Still one of our most sophisticated studies of the dialectics of eroticism and asceticism in a particular mythology.

OLIVELLE, PATRICK, "Orgasmic Rapture and Divine Ecstasy: The Semantic History of Ananda," *Journal of Indian Philosophy* 25 (1997): 153–180. Demonstrates convincingly that the earliest meanings of *ananda*, or "bliss," referred to the orgasmic pleasure of the penis as mystical organ.

PAGELS, ELAINE, *The Origin of Satan* (New York: Random House, 1995). An eloquent historical-critical argument that the origin of Satan lies in the projections of early gospel and Christian writers, who used the figure to attack their Jewish and later Roman enemies. "Satan," in other words, is the religious or cultural other writ large.

PARSONS, WILLIAM B., *The Enigma of the Oceanic Feeling: Revisioning the Psychoanalytic Theory of Mysticism* (New York: Oxford University Press, 1999). The foundational text for anyone attempting a gnostic rereading of Freud.

ROGERS, EUGUENE F., JR., *Sexuality and the Christian Body: Their Way into the Triune God* (London: Blackwell, 1999). A positive theology of sexuality, with a special homoerotic focus on the Trinity, the graced body, the motif of incarnation, and same-sex marriages.

SCHABERG, JANE, *The Illegitimacy of Jesus: A Feminist Theological Interpretation of the Infancy Narratives* (New York: Crossroad, 1990). A sensitive and beautifully written study of the virgin birth motif as a scriptural "spin" on an earlier story of illegitimacy, seduction, or sexual violence.

———, *The Resurrection of Mary Magdalene: Legends, Apocrypha, and the Christian Testament* (New York: Continuum, 2002). Another powerful and poetic book from Schaberg, this one on Jesus's intimate companion and "first apostle," Mary Magdalene.

SCHWARTZ, REGINA M., *The Curse of Cain: The Violent Legacy of Monotheism* (Chicago: University of Chicago Press, 1997). Argues, from a literary perspective, that the biblical narratives of ancient Jewish monotheism are inherently violent and exclusionary.

SHWEDER, RICHARD, *Thinking Through Cultures: Expeditions in Cultural Psychology* (Cambridge: Harvard University Press, 1991). Anthropology become art form. A stunning collection of essays on the dialectics of psyche and culture, the inseparability of rationality and cultural relativity, and the rebirth of polytheism as the ontological ground of any viable model of human potentiality. Clearly informed by Shweder's fieldwork in Assam, India. My favorite chapters are the first and the last: "Post-Nietzschean Anthropology: The Idea of Multiple Objective Worlds" and "How to Look at Medusa without Turning to Stone: On Gananath Obeyeskere." Should be read alongside Obeyesekere, *The Work of Culture*.

STEINBERG, LEO, *The Sexuality of Christ in Renaissance Art and in Modern Oblivion* (Chicago: University of Chicago Press, 1983). Basing his thesis on more than a thousand paintings and sculptures, Steinberg argues that Christ's penis was a major focus of Renaissance art and, as such, functioned as a means to affirm the full incarnation of God in humanity. Lots of pictures for the doubting.

STEVENSON, IAN, *Cases of the Reincarnation Type*, 4 vols. (Charlottesville: University Press of Virginia, 1983). Like Myers's *Human Personality and Its Survival of Bodily Death*, impossible to read without a serious questioning of both materialism and reductionism. Like Myers again, completely ignored by contemporary scholarship. Readers ready for more metaphysical traumas might also consult Stevenson's massive *Reincarnation and Biology: A Contribution to the Etiology of Birthmarks and Birth Defects* (Westport, Conn.: Praeger Publications, 1997). Good luck.

STRASSMAN, RICK, *DMT: The Spirit Molecule* (Rochester, Vt.: Park Street Press, 2001). My personal favorite of that genre of modern mystical literature still unprocessed in the study of religion, that involving the psychopharmacology of ecstatic and visionary experience. Drawing on data from a five-year clinical research program at the University of New Mexico, Strassman argues that out-of-body experiences occur when the pineal gland naturally releases DMT, that these events are often connected to "sexual transcendence" and/or traumatic

situations (like near-death), and that the modern phenomenon of the alien abduction can be brought on by accidental releases of DMT (many of his subjects
reported terrifying encounters with seemingly objective alien presences). Rejecting both traditional faith and purely rational approaches, Strassman argues
within a gnostic methodology that the pineal gland "facilitates the soul's movement in and out of the body and is an integral part of the birth and death experiences" (from the back cover).

THURSTON, HERBERT, S.J., *The Physical Phenomenon of Mysticism*, edited by J. H.
Crehan, S.J. (London: Burns Oates, 1952). A truly remarkable volume on some of
the physical transfigurations and "superpowers" (from levitation and incor-
ruptibility to telepathy and stigmata phenomena) both richly documented and
powerfully doubted in Roman Catholic hagiographic and canonization literature. Thurston's openness to both psychiatric and traditional mystical models
of sanctity render his dual approach fundamentally "gnostic." Virtually un-
touched and almost completely ignored by scholars of religion. Anomalous in
the best sense.

WHITE, DAVID GORDON, *The Alchemical Body: Siddha Traditions in Medieval India*
(Chicago: University of Chicago Press, 1994).

———, *Kiss of the Yogini: "Tantric Sex" in Its South Asian Contexts* (Chicago: University of Chicago Press, 2003). These two works by White constitute the state of
the art of Indic Tantric studies in the United States, with a special focus on the
alchemy of sexuality and the ritual use of sexual fluids. Beautifully and often
humorously written.

WILE, DOUGLAS, *Art of the Bedchamber: The Chinese Sexual Yoga Classics Including
Women's Solo Meditation Texts* (Albany, N.Y.: SUNY Press, 1992). An erudite study
of Chinese Taoist sexual yoga that is particularly adept at relating these symbolisms and rituals to modern critical theory and Western cultural assumptions.

WILSON, PETER LAMBORN, *Scandal: Essays in Islamic Heresy* (Brooklyn: Autonomedia, 1988). A series of anomalous essays inspired by the imaginal scholarship
of Henry Corbin that together compose what Wilson presents as a long poem
on the Unity of Being beyond the Law. Both the author's gnostic methodology,
which combines the "inside" of experiential practice and the "outside" of scholarly hermeneutics, and his central thesis that scandal constitutes a "hidden
mode of discourse between civilizations" and an especially creative means of
cultural transfer resonate deeply with the serpent's gift offered here.

WOLFSON, ELLIOT R., *Through a Speculum That Shines: Vision and Imagination in
Medieval Jewish Mysticism* (Princeton: Princeton University Press,1994).

———, *Language, Eros, Being: Kabbalistic Hermeneutics and Poetic Imagination* (New
York: Fordham University Press, 2005).

———. *Venturing Beyond: The Law and Ethics in Jewish Mysticism* (New York: Oxford
University Press, 2006). A sparkling trilogy from one of this generation's most
gifted and learned scholars of religion. Wolfson's simultaneous insights into
the visionary, hermeneutical, poetic, and homoerotic complexities of medieval
Jewish mysticism and his astonishing grasp of modern and postmodern critical theory—from feminist philosophy, psychoanalysis, and poetics to the history of religions and Continental philosophy—render his texts unsurpassed,
and probably unsurpassable, examples of what I have called our (post)modern
gnosis.

INDEX

MY SINCERE THANKS to my graduate student Hae Young Seong for writing this index, which somehow managed to begin with the AAR and end with the Zohar, thus coincidentally reproducing my thesis in an indexical (and rhyming) form.